LOCAL GOVERNMENT
IMMUNITY TO LAWSUITS
IN NORTH CAROLINA

TREY ALLEN

The School of Government at the University of North Carolina at Chapel Hill works to improve the lives of North Carolinians by engaging in practical scholarship that helps public officials and citizens understand and improve state and local government. Established in 1931 as the Institute of Government, the School provides educational, advisory, and research services for state and local governments. The School of Government is also home to a nationally ranked Master of Public Administration program, the North Carolina Judicial College, and specialized centers focused on community and economic development, information technology, and environmental finance.

As the largest university-based local government training, advisory, and research organization in the United States, the School of Government offers up to 200 courses, webinars, and specialized conferences for more than 12,000 public officials each year. In addition, faculty members annually publish approximately 50 books, manuals, reports, articles, bulletins, and other print and online content related to state and local government. The School also produces the *Daily Bulletin Online* each day the General Assembly is in session, reporting on activities for members of the legislature and others who need to follow the course of legislation.

Operating support for the School of Government's programs and activities comes from many sources, including state appropriations, local government membership dues, private contributions, publication sales, course fees, and service contracts.

Visit sog.unc.edu or call 919.966.5381 for more information on the School's courses, publications, programs, and services.

Michael R. Smith, DEAN
Thomas H. Thornburg, SENIOR ASSOCIATE DEAN
Jen Willis, ASSOCIATE DEAN FOR DEVELOPMENT
Michael Vollmer, ASSOCIATE DEAN FOR ADMINISTRATION

FACULTY

Whitney Afonso
Trey Allen
Gregory S. Allison
David N. Ammons
Ann M. Anderson
Maureen Berner
Mark F. Botts
Anita R. Brown-Graham
Peg Carlson
Leisha DeHart-Davis
Shea Riggsbee Denning
Sara DePasquale
James C. Drennan
Richard D. Ducker
Jacquelyn Greene

Norma Houston
Cheryl Daniels Howell
Jeffrey A. Hughes
Willow S. Jacobson
Robert P. Joyce
Diane M. Juffras
Dona G. Lewandowski
Adam Lovelady
James M. Markham
Christopher B. McLaughlin
Kara A. Millonzi
Jill D. Moore
Jonathan Q. Morgan
Ricardo S. Morse
C. Tyler Mulligan

Kimberly L. Nelson
David W. Owens
William C. Rivenbark
Dale J. Roenigk
John Rubin
Jessica Smith
Meredith Smith
Carl W. Stenberg III
John B. Stephens
Charles Szypszak
Shannon H. Tufts
Aimee N. Wall
Jeffrey B. Welty
Richard B. Whisnant

Printed in the United States of America

22 21 20 19 18   1 2 3 4 5

ISBN 978-1-56011-929-6

Contents

Chapter 3

The Governmental/Proprietary Distinction in Practice   31

Acknowledgments

Several of my colleagues at the School of Government were kind enough to review all or portions of the manuscript of this book. I am grateful to Bob Joyce, Fradya Bluestein, Kara Millonzi, and Norma Houston for their many helpful suggestions, most of which I had the good sense to accept. I am likewise indebted to Rebecca Badgett for checking the accuracy of the more than 600 footnotes that accompany the text. Sincere thanks are also due to Melissa Twomey, Dan Soileau, and other members of the School's publications team who helped transform the manuscript into a finished product. Any remaining errors are solely my responsibility.

Finally, I thank my wife, Teryn Allen, for her love and support. *tu supergressa es universas.*

Chapter 1

Governmental Immunity Overview

Public and private employers commonly face lawsuits over injuries allegedly inflicted through the on-the-job carelessness or deliberate misconduct of their personnel. Unlike private employers, however, cities, counties, school districts, and other units of local government in North Carolina enjoy liability protection in the form of *governmental immunity*.[1] The judicial decisions on governmental immunity constitute a large and, in many respects, confusing body of case law. This book surveys that case law, highlighting its major problems and attempting, where feasible, to resolve apparent inconsistencies. It begins with an outline of the immunity's main features, including the immunity's origin. Although the primary concern throughout is the immunity of cities and counties, the book also considers the immunity of other units at various points.

---

1. Under the legal doctrine of *respondeat superior*—Latin for "Let the master answer"—employers are liable for torts committed by their employees, but only if the employees acted within the scope of their employment. CHARLES E. DAYE & MARK W. MORRIS, NORTH CAROLINA LAW OF TORTS § 23.20, at 554 (3d ed. 2012). Many cases have recognized that *respondeat superior* principles apply to tort claims against local government units. *E.g.*, Rogers v. Town of Black Mountain, 224 N.C. 119, 121–22 (1944) (applying doctrine of *respondeat superior* to wrongful death claim against defendant town). Accordingly, the negligence or deliberate wrongdoing of a local government employee does not expose a unit to tort liability when the employee's conduct falls outside the scope of the employee's duties. *See id.* at 122 (town was not liable for death of 15-year-old boy who fell from a town truck negligently driven by a town employee acting outside the scope of employment); DAYE & MORRIS, *supra*, § 19.40[2][c][v], at 465 ("In order for the plaintiff to recover against a city, the injury must have arisen from a tort committed by a city employee within the scope of employment."). It follows that, if a court finds that a unit's employee acted outside the scope of employment in causing the plaintiff's injury, there is no need to reach the issue of governmental immunity because no legal basis exists for imposing liability on the unit. This last principle is sometimes muddled in the case law. *See* Childs v. Johnson, 155 N.C. App. 381, 389 (2002) (county was not entitled to governmental immunity inasmuch as its emergency medical services director was not acting within the scope of employment when the county vehicle he was driving collided with plaintiffs' automobile).

1.1 "Governmental Immunity" Defined

In North Carolina, governmental immunity is a legal doctrine that bars negligence and other tort claims against local government units when (1) the claims arise from the performance of governmental functions, not proprietary functions (these terms are discussed more fully in Section 1.4, *infra*), and (2) the units have not waived their immunity.

1.2 Relationship to Sovereign Immunity

The doctrine of sovereign immunity protects the state from liability for tort claims premised on the negligence or intentional wrongdoing of its officers, employees, or agents, except to the extent that the state has waived this immunity by statute.[2] Governmental immunity is that portion of the state's sovereign immunity that extends to local governments. It is not as robust as sovereign immunity, which can apply to claims against the state regardless of whether they stem from governmental or proprietary activities. Although some appellate decisions refer to "sovereign immunity" when discussing the immunity of local governments to lawsuits, the North Carolina Supreme Court has said that "governmental immunity" is the more accurate term.[3]

---

2. Great Am. Ins. Co. v. Gold, 254 N.C. 168, 173 (1961) ("The State is immune from suit unless and until it has expressly consented to be sued. It is for the General Assembly to determine when and under what circumstances the State may be sued."); Prudential Ins. Co. of Am. v. N.C. Unemployment Comp. Comm'n, 217 N.C. 495, 499 (1940) ("Except in a limited class of cases the State is immune against any suit unless and until it has expressly consented to such action.").

The North Carolina General Assembly has enacted several limited waivers of the state's sovereign immunity, the most important being the Tort Claims Act (TCA), which exposes the state to liability for injuries caused by the negligence of its officers, employees, or agents acting within the scope of their duties under circumstances that would expose the state to liability if it were a private individual. Chapter 143, Section 291(a) of the North Carolina General Statutes (hereinafter G.S.). The TCA does not waive the state's immunity to tort claims arising from intentional misconduct. Moreover, the TCA places a $1,000,000 cap on what the state may be required to pay for harm to an individual resulting from a single incident. G.S. 143-299.2. For the most part, actions brought under the TCA must be litigated in the North Carolina Industrial Commission, not in superior or district court. Guthrie v. N.C. Ports Auth., 307 N.C. 522, 536 (1983). The state may be brought into a tort action in superior or district court as a third party or third-party defendant pursuant to Rule 14(e) of the North Carolina Rules of Civil Procedure.

3. Irving v. Charlotte-Mecklenburg Bd. of Educ., 368 N.C. 609, 611 (2016) ("Here '[defendant] is a county agency. As such, the immunity it possesses is more precisely identified as governmental immunity, while sovereign immunity applies to the State and its agencies.'"); Craig v. New Hanover Cty. Bd. of Educ., 363 N.C. 334, 335 n.3 (2009) ("The [New Hanover County] Board [of Education] is a county agency. As such,

1.3 Common Law Origin

Sovereign immunity is a common law doctrine, that is, a judicial creation.[4] It originated in England and appears to have been based on the concept that, as a matter of law, "the king can do no wrong."[5] It was thought that the king's status as sovereign prevented the bringing of lawsuits against the king in his own courts.[6]

In North Carolina, the state takes the place of the king for purposes of sovereign immunity.[7] Like sovereign immunity, governmental immunity is a creature of the common law.[8] The judiciary may therefore modify or even abolish it.[9] Moreover, since legislative enactments generally trump the

---

the immunity it possesses is more precisely identified as governmental immunity, while sovereign immunity applies to the State and its agencies.").

For a case that uses the term *sovereign immunity* in reference to local governments, see *Bullard v. Wake County*, 221 N.C. App. 522, 525 (2012) ("Under North Carolina law, counties are entitled to sovereign immunity unless the county waives immunity or otherwise consents to be sued."). There are quite a few cases in which the terms *sovereign immunity* and *governmental immunity* are treated as interchangeable. *E.g.,* Lucas v. Swain Cty. Bd. of Educ., 154 N.C. App. 357, 361 (2002) ("'As a general rule, the doctrine of governmental, or sovereign immunity bars actions against, *inter alia,* the state, its counties, and its public officials sued in their official capacity.'").

4. Corum v. Univ. of N.C., 330 N.C. 761, 785 (1992).

5. OSBORNE M. REYNOLDS, JR., LOCAL GOVERNMENT LAW § 26.1, at 686 (4th ed. 2015). *See also* Steelman v. City of New Bern, 279 N.C. 589, 592 (1971) ("In feudal England the monarchy was sovereign and could not be liable for damage to its subjects. This was based on the theory that "the king could do no wrong.").

6. REYNOLDS, *supra* note 5, § 26.1, at 686. *See also* W. PAGE KEETON ET AL., PROSSER AND KEETON ON THE LAW OF TORTS § 131, at 1033 (5th ed. 1984) ("Though the modern state gradually replaced the individual sovereign, the idea [that the king can do no wrong] was carried over, partly on the ground that it seemed illogical to enforce a claim against the very authority that created the claim in the first place.").

7. *See Corum,* 330 N.C. at 785 (linking the state's sovereign immunity to "the feudal concept that the king could do no wrong"). *See also* REYNOLDS, *supra* note 5, § 26.1, at 686 ("[R]ather mystifyingly, [the concept that the king can do no wrong] became the basis of the American doctrine of immunity of the state and federal government.").

8. It seems that governmental immunity was first applied to bar tort claims against a local government in the English case of *Russell v. Men of Devon*, 100 Eng. Rep. 359 (1788). Governmental immunity was not initially part of the common law of North Carolina. *Corum,* 330 N.C. at 785; *Steelman,* 279 N.C. at 592. As a newly independent state, North Carolina adopted the common law of England as it stood in 1776. *Corum,* 330 N.C. at 785; *Steelman,* 279 N.C. at 592. The *Russell* case was not part of the English common law at that time. The North Carolina Supreme Court did not recognize governmental immunity as a valid defense until *Moffitt v. City of Asheville*, 103 N.C. 237 (1885).

9. *See Steelman,* 279 N.C. at 594 (acknowledging that the North Carolina Supreme Court made governmental immunity part of the state's law but declining plaintiff's request that the court abolish the doctrine). *See also* KEETON ET AL., *supra* note 6,

common law, the North Carolina General Assembly may narrow the immunity's scope or eliminate the immunity altogether.[10]

1.4 Governmental Functions vs. Proprietary Functions

Because governmental immunity covers governmental functions but not proprietary functions, many of the cases focus on distinguishing between the two categories. The classic formulation is that governmental functions are discretionary, political, legislative, or public in nature and performed for the public good, while proprietary functions are chiefly commercial or undertaken for the private advantage of the compact community.[11]

Some local government activities are readily identifiable as governmental (law enforcement) or proprietary (operation of public arena to generate revenue).[12] Yet judges have struggled in many cases to apply the classic formulation to specific activities. The result has been "irreconcilable splits of authority" and a "tradition of confusion" as to "what functions are governmental and what functions are proprietary."[13] In an effort to provide lower courts with a more workable test, the North Carolina Supreme Court in 2012 restated in *Estate of Williams v. Pasquotank County Parks & Recreation Department* the criteria to be used in classifying undertakings as either governmental or proprietary.[14] Chapter 2 looks closely at the *Williams* test, while Chapter 3 catalogues many of the governmental/proprietary distinctions made by the appellate courts since governmental immunity became part of the state's common law.

1.5 Waiver of Governmental Immunity

As Sections 1.1 and 1.4, *supra*, make clear, local governments step out from under the umbrella of governmental immunity anytime they undertake proprietary functions. Assorted statutes authorize cities, counties, and certain

---

§ 3, at 18 ("From a very early point in the history of the common law . . . it was assumed that a court could and should occasionally overrule a precedent.").

10. *See Steelman*, 279 N.C at 595 ("[A]ny further modification or the repeal of the doctrine of sovereign immunity should come from the General Assembly . . . ."). *See also* KEETON ET AL., *supra* note 6, § 3, at 19 ("In tort law as in other fields, courts are obliged, with exceptions founded in constitutional law, to follow statutory mandates.").

11. Millar v. Town of Wilson, 222 N.C. 340, 341 (1942).

12. Young v. Woodall, 119 N.C. App. 132, 135 (1995) (law enforcement is a governmental function), *rev'd on other grounds*, 343 N.C. 459 (1996); Aaser v. City of Charlotte, 265 N.C. 494, 497 (1965) (operation of public area to generate revenue is a proprietary function).

13. Koontz v. City of Winston-Salem, 280 N.C. 513, 528 (1972).

14. 366 N.C. 195 (2012).

other units to waive their immunity for governmental functions by purchasing liability insurance, though any such waiver is restricted to the extent of coverage.[15] Additionally, by entering into valid contracts, units implicitly agree to be sued for alleged breaches of those contracts. Chapter 4 explores the mechanisms of waiver in more detail.

1.6 Covered Entities

Governmental immunity applies to cities, counties, and public school districts when they carry out governmental functions. It can also protect special purpose local governments such as sanitary districts, rural fire protection districts, housing authorities, water and sewer authorities, and mental health area authorities when they act governmentally rather than proprietarily. The courts have recognized, for instance, that governmental immunity can bar tort claims against mental health area authorities and city housing authorities.[16]

Incorporated nonprofit fire departments have successfully asserted governmental immunity in some circumstances. Governmental immunity shielded an incorporated fire department from liability for an automobile pileup allegedly caused by one of its employees.[17] Major factors in the outcome were that the department had contracted to provide emergency medical services for the county and that the employee was responding to an emergency call at the time of the accident.

1.7 Claims against Individuals

When a plaintiff sues a local government officer or employee in the person's official capacity, the plaintiff is really suing the unit.[18] For this reason, governmental immunity can be a defense to the plaintiff's tort claims.[19] Under current case law, governmental immunity is not a defense to tort claims

---

15. G.S. 115C-42 (local school boards); 122-152 (area authorities); 153A-435 (counties); 160A-485 (cities).

16. Evans v. Hous. Auth. of City of Raleigh, 359 N.C. 50, 55 (2004) (housing authority); Warren v. Guilford Cty., 129 N.C. App. 836, 838–89 (1998) (area authority).

17. Pruett v. Bingham, 238 N.C. App. 78, 85 (2014).

18. *E.g.*, Meyer v. Walls, 347 N.C. 97, 110 (1997) ("A suit against a defendant in his individual capacity means that the plaintiff seeks recovery from the defendant directly; a suit against a defendant in his official capacity means that the plaintiff seeks recovery from the entity of which the public servant defendant is an agent.").

19. *E.g.*, Mullis v. Sechrest, 347 N.C. 548, 555 (1998) (teacher sued in his official capacity was entitled to governmental immunity to the same extent as local school board).

alleged against officers or employees sued in their individual capacities.[20] Public official immunity, a derivative form of governmental immunity, can shield public officers such as police officers and building inspectors from personal liability for conduct within the scope of their duties, except when they act maliciously or corruptly.[21] On the other hand, public employees who do not qualify as "public officials"—teachers and emergency medical technicians are examples—remain personally liable for their negligence or intentional wrongdoing, except when a statutory immunity applies.[22] For instance, G.S. 166A-19.60(a) provides liability protection to city and county emergency management workers who injure others or damage property while undertaking emergency management activities, "except in cases of willful misconduct, gross negligence, or bad faith."

20. *E.g.*, Wright v. Gaston Cty., 205 N.C. App. 600, 602 (2010) ("Plaintiffs' complaint also alleges claims against the 911 operators in their individual capacities, for which governmental immunity is not applicable.").

21. "The doctrine of public official immunity is a derivative form of governmental immunity. Public official immunity precludes suits against public officials in their individual capacities and protects them from liability [a]s long as a public officer lawfully exercises the judgment and discretion with which he is invested by virtue of his office, keeps within the scope of his official authority, and acts without malice or corruption." Hart v. Brienza, ___ N.C. App. ___, ___, 784 S.E.2d 211, 215 (2016) (internal quotation marks omitted) (citations omitted).

22. *E.g.*, Murray v. Cty. of Person, 191 N.C. App. 575, 579 (2008) ("It is well established that [p]ublic officers are shielded from liability unless their actions are corrupt or malicious[;] however, public employees can be held personally liable for mere negligence.").

Much of the case law on public official immunity is occupied with distinguishing between public officers and public employees. In deciding whether an individual qualifies as public officer for purposes of public official immunity, the courts examine whether (1) the individual's position originates in state law, (2) the person's duties require the use of discretion, and (3) the individual exercises a portion of the state's sovereign power. Isenhour v. Hutto, 350 N.C. 601, 610 (1999). For lists of positions that the courts have classified as either eligible or ineligible for public official immunity, see the appendices in Trey Allen, *Do Intentional Tort Claims Always Defeat Public Official Immunity?*, LOCAL GOV'T L. BULL. No. 139 (UNC School of Government, Sept. 2016), https://www.sog.unc.edu/sites/www.sog.unc.edu/files/reports/2016-09-21%20 20160844%20LGLB%20139%20TORTs.pdf.

One example of a statutory immunity that can protect public employees from personal liability is G.S. 115C-390.3, which exempts school personnel from civil liability for using reasonable force in conformity with state law, as when necessary to correct students or to quell a disturbance threatening injury to others.

1.8 Covered Claims

Governmental immunity is primarily a defense to tort claims.[23] The kinds of tort claims against which local governments have successfully asserted the immunity include the following:

- *assault*, the intentional placing of a person in reasonable apprehension of imminent harmful or offensive contact;[24]
- *battery*, the intentional harmful or offensive contact with the person of another without the person's consent;[25]
- *false imprisonment*, the intentional and illegal restraint of another individual against his or her will;[26]
- *false arrest*, a form of false imprisonment that occurs when an unlawful arrest takes place;[27]
- *malicious prosecution*, which happens when a civil or criminal proceeding instituted against the plaintiff with malice and without probable cause terminates in the plaintiff's favor;[28]
- *negligence*, the failure to exercise reasonable care in the performance of a legal duty owed to another under the circumstances, such as a driver's duty to his or her passengers and other motorists not to exceed the speed limit;[29]
- *negligent infliction of emotional distress*, causing another severe and foreseeable emotional distress through negligent behavior;[30]
- *trespass to land*, "any unauthorized entry onto land in the actual or constructive possession of the plaintiff;"[31] and
- *wrongful discharge*, the firing of an employee in violation of public policy.[32]

---

23. The term *tort* is notoriously difficult to define. *See* KEETON ET AL., *supra* note 6, § 1, at 1 ("Even though tort law is now recognized as a proper subject, a really satisfactory definition of a tort is yet to be found."). One tentative definition is that a tort is conduct—other than a breach of contract—that causes harm for which the injured party may be entitled to recover money damages in a lawsuit. 1 DAN B. DOBBS ET AL., THE LAW OF TORTS § 1, at 1 (2d ed. 2011).

24. DAYE & MORRIS, *supra* note 1, § 2.20, at 5.

25. *Id.* § 3.20, at 18.

26. *Id.* § 4.20, at 29.

27. *Id.* § 4.50, at 41.

28. *Id.* § 9.40, at 99.

29. Moore v. Moore, 268 N.C. 110, 112 (1966) ("Negligence is the failure to exercise proper care in the performance of a legal duty which the defendant owed the plaintiff under the circumstances surrounding them."); Norfleet v. Hall, 204 N.C. 573, 577 (1933) ("The speed at which the defendant was driving his automobile was unlawful [because it violated a statute prohibiting the operation of automobiles on a state highway at more than 45 miles per hour], and therefore constituted negligence.").

30. Fox-Kirk v. Hannon, 142 N.C. App. 267, 273 (2001).

31. DAYE & MORRIS, *supra* note 1, § 6.20, at 58.

32. *Id.* § 12.20, at 136.

Governmental immunity can also apply to certain contract-related equitable claims, like those sounding in unjust enrichment and quasi contract. Chapter 7 examines the relationship between governmental immunity and equitable claims of that sort.

1.8.1 Claims Not Covered

There are several types of claims to which governmental immunity is not a defense.

- *Constitutional claims.* Governmental immunity will not defeat allegations that a unit has infringed upon rights guaranteed by the Constitution of the United States or the North Carolina Constitution.[33] A local school board could not invoke the immunity, for instance, to block a student from pursuing allegations that the board had violated the state constitution by negligently failing to protect him from sexual assault by another student.[34] Chapter 8 analyzes the relationship between governmental immunity and state constitutional claims in greater depth.
- *Statutory claims.* Governmental immunity usually will not stop plaintiffs from pursuing alleged violations of federal or state statutes. The immunity is not a defense, for example, to allegations that a city or county has discriminated against an employee based on race, color, religion, sex, or national origin in violation of Title VII of the Civil Rights Act.[35]
- *Some tort claims.* There are some tort claims to which governmental immunity does not apply, even if the activity that injured the plaintiff qualifies as governmental and the unit has not waived immunity through the purchase of liability insurance. Chapter 9 reviews the most prominent of these exceptions.

---

33. *See* Corum v. Univ. of N.C., 330 N.C. 761, 772 (1992) ("[U]nder the federal cases interpreting [42 U.S.C. § 1983], sovereign immunity alleged under state law is not a permissible defense to section 1983 actions."); *see id.* at 785–86 ("The doctrine of sovereign immunity cannot stand as a barrier to North Carolina citizens who seek to remedy violation of their rights guaranteed by the [North Carolina Constitution's] Declaration of Rights . . . [W]hen there is a clash between these constitutional rights and sovereign immunity, the constitutional rights must prevail.").

34. Craig v. New Hanover Cty. Bd. of Educ., 363 N.C. 334, 340 (2009) ("[I]n *Corum* . . . this Court did clearly establish the principle that sovereign immunity could not operate to bar direct constitutional claims.").

35. Paquette v. Cty. of Durham, 155 N.C. App. 415, 419 (2002). *See also* Craig v. Asheville City Bd. of Educ., 142 N.C. App. 518, 521 (2001) (governmental immunity was no defense to a teacher's statutory claim that defendant school board violated G.S. 115C-325(m)(2) in not renewing the teacher's employment).

- *Declaratory judgment actions.* "[T]he Declaratory Judgment Act [DJA] does not act as a general waiver of the State's sovereign immunity."[36] Presumably, the same may be said about the DJA and the governmental immunity of local governments.[37] It is clear, however, that governmental immunity will not defeat a declaratory judgment action in at least two circumstances.
  - **Action on a contract.** By entering into a valid contract, the state waives its immunity to "causes of action on contract."[38] Such causes of action embrace not only breach of contract claims but also declaratory relief actions "seeking to ascertain the rights and obligations owed under an alleged contract."[39] This rule should be understood to apply to units of local government, inasmuch as they waive governmental immunity by entering into contract.[40]
  - **Action alleging act in excess of authority.** Sovereign immunity does not bar a declaratory relief action against the state when the plaintiff seeks a declaration that a state agency has exceeded its statutory authority and unlawfully invaded or threatened to invade the plaintiff's personal or property rights.[41] This same principle has been applied to declaratory relief actions against local governments.[42]

1.9 Criticisms of Governmental Immunity

The doctrine of governmental immunity has attracted significant criticism. Many of the critiques are longstanding and acknowledged in the case law.[43]

---

36. Atl. Coast Conference v. Univ. of Md., 230 N.C. App. 429, 442 (2013).

37. *See* Petroleum Traders Corp. v. State, 190 N.C. App. 542, 546–47 (2008) (discussing sovereign immunity and governmental immunity in similar terms and rejecting the argument that the DJA waived state's sovereign immunity as to plaintiff's claims).

38. *Atl. Coast Conference,* 230 N.C. App. at 442 (internal quotation marks omitted) (citations omitted).

39. *Id.*

40. Data Gen. Corp. v. Cty. of Durham, 143 N.C. App. 97, 102–03 (2001).

41. T & A Amusements, LLC v. McCrory, ___ N.C. App. ___, ___, 796 S.E.2d 376, 380 (2017).

42. *See, e.g.,* Phillips v. Orange Cty. Health Dep't, 237 N.C. App. 249, 256–57 (2014) (governmental immunity did not prohibit plaintiff from seeking a declaration that defendant lacked statutory authority to inspect plaintiff's spray irrigation wastewater system).

43. *See, e.g.,* Koontz v. City of Winston-Salem, 280 N.C. 513, 529–30 (1972) ("[W]e recognize merit in the modern tendency to restrict rather than to extend the application of governmental immunity. This trend is based, *inter alia,* on the large expansion of municipal activities, the availability of liability insurance, and the plain injustice of denying relief to an individual injured by the wrongdoing of a municipality.

- *The doctrine produces serious injustices.* When a plaintiff's injuries stem from a governmental function, governmental immunity can bar the plaintiff from pursuing a tort claim against the local government unit, regardless of the validity of the plaintiff's claim. The upshot is that many individuals harmed by the negligence or deliberate wrongdoing of local government officers or employees find themselves without any effective legal recourse.
  - **The rules on waiver make further injustices possible.** Suppose that County A has purchased liability insurance for a particular governmental function but County B has not. If County A's employees negligently injure someone while carrying out the activity, County A's immunity waiver will allow the injured party to pursue a negligence claim against County A for damages within the coverage limits. On the other hand, if substantially the same thing happens in County B, the injured party cannot proceed with a negligence lawsuit against County B because the latter has not waived its immunity from claims arising from the activity.

    Now suppose that both County A and County B have purchased liability insurance for the same governmental function but that County B's policy limits are dramatically lower than County A's. While both counties have waived immunity, persons harmed by the covered activity in County A may have a better chance of obtaining adequate compensation than those injured by the same undertaking in County B. In short, under the present law of governmental immunity, a plaintiff's capacity to obtain relief from a unit for harms inflicted by the unit's officers or employees depends not just on the nature of the harmful activity, but also on the extent of the unit's liability coverage, both factors that have nothing to do with the rightness of the plaintiff's claim.
- *The availability of liability insurance renders the doctrine obsolete.* According to this view, governmental immunity is unnecessary because modern liability insurance enables local governments to minimize the threat to their fiscal health that lawsuits against them might otherwise pose.
- *The doctrine seems inappropriate given the large expansion of local government activities.* Today, city and county operations encompass a wide range of services and activities, many of which private actors can perform. Examples include art galleries and museums, auditoriums and coliseums, community appearance programs, drug abuse

---

A corollary to the tendency of modern authorities to restrict rather than to extend the application of governmental immunity is the rule that in cases of doubtful liability application of the rule should be resolved against the municipality.")

programs, hospitals, recreation programs, rescue squads, and trash collection services.[44] For the most part, units perform these functions voluntarily: state law permits but does not mandate the undertakings. With cities and counties opting to assume so many roles not unique to government, it can be argued that they should face tort liability on the same terms as private entities.

In light of the criticisms of governmental immunity, the North Carolina Supreme Court has endorsed the modern tendency to restrict rather than expand the reach of governmental immunity.[45] It is not obvious that this endorsement has had a major impact. Only a handful of appellate cases cite it as a reason for classifying a disputed activity as proprietary rather than governmental.[46]

1.10 Justifications for Governmental Immunity

The state supreme court has repeatedly expressed doubt about the ongoing soundness of governmental immunity.[47] Its continued adherence to the doctrine can be attributed to two factors.

- *Deference to the legislative branch.* As noted in Section 1.5, *supra,* the General Assembly has enacted statutes allowing cities, counties, and other units to waive governmental immunity through the purchase of liability insurance. The court has looked upon this

---

44. David M. Lawrence, *An Overview of Local Government, in* County and Municipal Government in North Carolina 6 (Frayda S. Bluestein ed., 2d ed. 2014).

45. *Koontz*, 280 N.C. at 529–30.

46. Sides v. Cabarrus Mem'l Hosp., Inc., 287 N.C. 14, 25–26 (1975) (operation of county hospital is a proprietary function); Childs v. Johnson 155 N.C. App. 381, 386–88 (2002) (emergency medical services director's detour to bank was not a governmental activity); (Pulliam v. City of Greensboro, 103 N.C. App. 748, 754 (1991) (city was not immune from tort liability in the operation of its sewer system); Waters v. Biesecker, 60 N.C. App. 253, 255 (1983) (operation of an ABC store is a proprietary function).

Some cases actually cite the endorsement but go on to hold that the activity in dispute is governmental. *E.g.*, McIver v. Smith, 134 N.C. App. 583, 589 (1999) ("We acknowledge that the modern tendency is to restrict rather than expand the application of governmental immunity . . . However, we are of the opinion that the operation of government-operated ambulance services is clearly a government function that should have immunity.").

47. Steelman v. City of New Bern, 279 N.C. 589, 595 (1971) ("It may well be that the logic of the doctrine of sovereign immunity is unsound and that the reasons which led to its adoption are not as forceful today as they were when it was adopted."). *See also Williams*, 366 N.C. at 198–99 (same); Town of Sandy Creek v. E. Coast Contracting, Inc., 226 N.C. App. 576, 580 (2013) (same); Jones v. Kearns, 120 N.C. App. 301, 311 (1995) (same); Vaughn v. Durham Cty., 34 N.C. App. 416, 421 (1977) (same).

legislative action as tantamount to recognition of the doctrine as state policy.[48] The idea seems to be that, if the General Assembly had disapproved of governmental immunity, it would not have left the doctrine fundamentally intact. Given the legislature's acceptance of governmental immunity, the court has left it to the General Assembly to decide whether the doctrine should be further restricted or eliminated.[49]

- *Taxpayer protection.* Governmental immunity does not just protect local government units; it also shields the taxpayers who fund them.[50] Without the immunity, units would face unlimited liability for tort claims arising from their performance of governmental functions. Although they could mitigate this risk by purchasing liability insurance, units would still be on the hook for any claims excluded by their policies and for any damages awards outside the policy limits. They might have to divert tax dollars from important public services to pay civil judgments. In extreme cases, civil judgments might bankrupt units, an outcome neither fair to innocent taxpayers nor in keeping with good public policy.[51]

1.11 Other Liability Defenses

Governmental immunity should not be confused with related defenses that can play decisive roles in lawsuits against units or their officers or employees.

- *Qualified immunity to federal claims.* Qualified immunity can protect local government officers and employees from personal liability for

---

48. *E.g.*, Estate of Williams v. Pasquotank Cty. Parks & Recreation Dep't, 366 N.C. 195, 199 (2012) (quoting Smith v. State, 289 N.C. 303, 312 (1976)) ("[A]lbeit the doctrine [of governmental immunity] was 'judge-made,' the General Assembly . . . recognized it as the public policy of the State by enacting legislation which permitted municipalities and other governmental bodies to purchase liability insurance and thereby waive their immunity to the extent of the amount of insurance so obtained.").

49. *Steelman*, 279 N.C. at 595 ("[W]e feel that any further modification or the repeal of the doctrine of sovereign immunity should come from the General Assembly, not this Court.").

50. *See* State *ex rel.* Hayes v. Billings, 240 N.C. 78, 80 (1954) (governmental immunity "shields a county and its innocent taxpayers from liability for the negligence of its officers in the exercise of governmental . . . functions"); Gentry v. Town of Hot Springs, 227 N.C. 665, 666 (1947) (governmental immunity "shields a municipality and its innocent taxpayers from liability for the negligent acts of its officers, done in the exercise of a purely governmental function").

51. *See* REYNOLDS, *supra* note 5, § 26.1, at 688 ("Fears of insolvency, and the belief that tax money raised for public use should not be diverted to compensate for the torts of government agents, have no doubt been considerably responsible for [governmental immunity's] longevity.").

violations of an individual's rights under federal law. The immunity covers personnel engaged in the performance of discretionary functions "insofar as their conduct does not violate clearly established statutory or constitutional rights of which a reasonable person would have known."[52]

- *Public official immunity.* Section 1.7, *supra*, briefly discusses this immunity, which shields public officers, but not mere public employees, from tort liability so long as they act within the scope of their duties and without malice or corruption.

- *Legislative immunity.* Local officials, including county commissioners and city council members, enjoy absolute immunity from personal liability for civil claims arising from their performance of legitimate legislative functions.[53] The adoption of zoning ordinances is one example of a covered legislative activity.[54] Legislative immunity does not extend to mere administrative actions, such as votes on whether to hire or fire particular employees.[55]

- *Quasi-judicial immunity.* Local officials, including county commissioners and city council members, enjoy absolute immunity from personal liability for civil claims arising from their exercise of judicial functions.[56] Quasi-judicial proceedings on special use permits and variances fit into this category.[57]

- *Public duty doctrine.* Generally, under the public duty doctrine, cities and counties may not face liability for the negligent failure of their law enforcement agencies to prevent harm to specific individuals

---

52. Pearson v. Callahan, 555 U.S. 223, 231 (2009) (internal quotation marks omitted) (citations omitted). "To defeat a qualified immunity defense, a plaintiff must show (1) that the official violated a statutory or constitutional right, and (2) that the right was 'clearly established' at the time of the challenged conduct." Crouse v. Town of Moncks Corner, 848 F.3d 576, 583 (4th Cir. 2017) (internal quotation marks omitted) (citations omitted).

53. Scott v. Greenville Cty., 716 F.2d 1409, 1422 (4th Cir. 1983); Northfield Dev. Co., Inc. v. City of Burlington, 136 N.C. App. 272, 281 (2000); Vereen v. Holden, 121 N.C. App. 779, 782 (1996).

Legislative immunity comprises a testimonial privilege. Accordingly, a mayor and members of a city council could not be compelled to testify about their personal motives for certain zoning decisions. Novak v. City of High Point, 159 N.C. App. 229 (2003) (unpublished) (not paginated on Westlaw).

54. *Northfield Dev. Co.*, 136 N.C. App. at 282.

55. *Vereen*, 121 N.C. App. at 783. When the budget adopted by a board eliminates an employee's position, the action is legislative, not administrative, in nature. Bogan v. Scott-Harris, 523 U.S. 44, 54 (1998).

56. *Northfield Dev. Co.*, 136 N.C. App. at 281–82. Quasi-judicial immunity, too, encompasses a testimonial privilege. *Novak*, 159 N.C. App. 229.

57. *Northfield Dev. Co.*, 136 N.C. App. at 281–82.

by third parties.[58] The doctrine applies regardless of whether a unit has purchased liability insurance that covers a plaintiff's negligence claim. It is not a defense when a law enforcement agency has actually promised to protect a person or when the agency has created a special relationship in which protection is expected, as in the case of a police informant.[59]

1.12 Statutory Immunity Defenses

The General Assembly may expand or contract the tort immunity of local governments through legislation. It has exercised this power in, for example, the Emergency Management Act (EMA), which exempts cities and counties from liability for any deaths, personal injuries, or property damage resulting from their performance of emergency management functions.[60] This statutory immunity appears broader than governmental immunity in that the EMA does not authorize a unit to waive the EMA's protections through the purchase of liability insurance. Appendix C sets out the pertinent provisions of the EMA and other legislation that address the liability of units for various undertakings.

---

58. Lovelace v. City of Shelby, 351 N.C. 458, 460–61 (2000). The public duty doctrine is not a barrier to lawsuits for injuries directly inflicted by law enforcement officers as opposed to third parties. In such cases, the city or county will want to rely on governmental immunity as a defense unless it has waived immunity through the purchase of liability insurance. Additionally, the public duty doctrine is not a defense to a claim that an agency failed to comply with a mandatory ministerial requirement, such as the statutory duty to report suspected child abuse. Smith v. Jackson Cty. Bd. of Educ., 168 N.C. App. 452, 461–62 (2005).

59. Multiple Claimants v. N.C. Dep't of Health & Human Servs., Div. of Facility Servs., Jails & Detention Servs., 361 N.C. 372, 374 (2007).

60. G.S. 166A-19.60(a).

Chapter 2

Distinguishing Between Governmental and Proprietary Functions

The distinction between governmental and proprietary functions is a critical feature of governmental immunity because of the judiciary's decision to restrict the immunity to claims arising from governmental functions. This chapter reviews the origin of the distinction in immunity cases, the other uses to which the courts have sometimes put the distinction, the rationale for limiting governmental immunity to governmental functions, and the problems the courts have experienced in applying the governmental/proprietary distinction to particular activities. The chapter then turns to *Estate of Williams v. Pasquotank County Parks & Recreation Department*,[61] the 2012 case in which the North Carolina Supreme Court reformulated the criteria for classifying specific undertakings as either governmental or proprietary. The chapter examines each part of the *Williams* test and considers the potential impact of *Williams* on classifications made in earlier cases.[62]

2.1 Origin of Governmental/Proprietary Distinction

The North Carolina Supreme Court first held that cities are immune to tort claims arising from governmental but not proprietary functions in *Moffitt v. City of Asheville*,[63] an 1889 case. Prior to *Moffitt*, the default rule seems

---

61. 366 N.C. 195 (2012).

62. This chapter incorporates material from Trey Allen, *The Impact of* Williams v. Pasquotank County *on Local Government Liability, Part I: Public Parks and Government Office Buildings*, Loc. Gov't L. Bull. No. 137 (May 2015), https://www.sog.unc.edu/sites/www.sog.unc.edu/files/reports/lglb137.pdf.

63. 103 N.C. 237 (1889). *See* Daye & Morris, *supra* note 1, § 19.40[2][c][i], at 449 n.335 (the rule that cities are immune to tort claims stemming from governmental functions "was applied in North Carolina in 1889 by *Moffit* [sic] *v. City of Asheville*"); Joseph S. Ferrell, *Civil Liability of North Carolina Cities and Towns for Personal Injury and Property Damage Arising from the Construction, Maintenance, and Repair of Public Streets*, 7 Wake Forest L. Rev. 143, 144 (1971) (the court "adopted the doctrine of governmental immunity" in *Moffitt*).

It can be argued that the state supreme court endorsed governmental immunity for city governmental functions five years before *Moffitt* in *Bunch v. Town of Edenton*, 90 N.C. 431, 433 (1884) ("An action does not lie against a municipal corporation for

to have been that cities were liable for the negligence of their officers and employees, regardless of whether the particular activity that injured a plaintiff qualified as governmental.[64]

In *Moffitt* the defendant city argued that the trial court had incorrectly instructed the jury on the circumstances under which it could find the city liable for injuries the plaintiff had allegedly sustained during an overnight stay in the city jail. On the way to ruling in the city's favor, the North Carolina Supreme Court distinguished between a town's "corporate and governmental powers."[65] It explained that cities rely on their corporate powers when they manage property "for their own profit" or exercise powers "assumed voluntarily for their own advantage[.]"[66] The court identified the cleaning of sewers and grading of streets as examples of activities in the "corporate powers" category. When engaged in such undertakings, the court said, cities "are impliedly liable for damage caused by the negligence of officers or agents subject to their control."[67]

The court further explained that a city exercises governmental powers when it makes use of its "judicial, discretionary, or legislative authority" or discharges a duty "imposed solely for the [public's] benefit[.]"[68] For examples of activities in the "governmental powers" category, the court pointed to cases from other jurisdictions holding that cities were not liable for assault and similar claims arising from the efforts of police officers to enforce city ordinances or effect valid arrests. When a city's officers undertake endeavors of this kind, the supreme court opined, the city is not liable for their negligence "unless some statute (expressly or by necessary implication) subjects the [city] to pecuniary responsibility."[69]

---

damages . . . for the manner in which, in good faith, it exercises discretionary powers of a public or legislative character . . .").

64. *See, e.g.,* Manuel v. Bd. of Comm'rs of Cumberland Cty., 98 N.C. 9, 12 (1887) ("Cities and towns . . . are, in many respects, held responsible as such corporations for damages occasioned by the neglect of their agents."); Meares v. Comm'rs of Town of Wilmington, 31 N.C. 73, 86 (1848) ("[A] corporation, whether private or municipal, . . . in any and all of these cases, is liable for any damage resulting from a want of ordinary skill and caution in doing the work . . . ."). *See also* Ferrell, *supra* note 63, at 143–44 ("The general law of negligence continued to be the test of municipal tort liability until 1889, when Justice Avery, writing for the court in *Moffitt v. City of Asheville*, discovered the very New York cases which Justice Pearson had previously considered and rejected in *Meares*.")

65. *Moffitt*, 103 N.C. at 260. The terms "governmental function," "proprietary function," and "governmental immunity" do not appear in *Moffitt*. The present nomenclature of governmental immunity developed over succeeding decades.

66. *Id.* at 254.

67. *Id.*

68. *Id.* at 255.

69. *Id.*

In the nearly 130 years that have elapsed since *Moffitt*, the initial distinction between corporate powers and governmental powers has developed into the current jurisprudence on governmental and proprietary functions. The number of undertakings classified as governmental, on the one hand, or proprietary, on the other, has grown significantly over the decades as plaintiffs have pursued tort claims against local governments in varied contexts. Chapter 3 catalogues many classifications made by the courts.

2.1.1 Other Uses of Governmental/Proprietary Distinction

Although the governmental/proprietary distinction plays a major role in the law of governmental immunity, state law puts the distinction to other uses.[70]

- *Statutes of Limitation.* The courts invoke the governmental/proprietary distinction when they must decide whether a statute of limitation or repose prevents the state or a local government unit from pursuing a claim of its own in a lawsuit. If a civil claim by the state or unit involves a governmental function, the relevant statute of limitation or repose will not bar the claim, unless the statute expressly includes the state. The court of appeals thus held that a one-year statute of limitation did not bar the City of Greensboro from suing an individual over unpaid parking tickets because "the collection of fines and fees to enforce [a city's] parking regulations . . . is a governmental function."[71]
- *Constitutional Funding Restraints.* The courts have employed the term "governmental function" to assert that an activity satisfies the requirement in Article V, Subsection 2(1) of the state constitution that public funds be spent for public purposes only.[72] In one case, the court upheld the constitutionality of a statute authorizing the expenditure of public funds on economic development programs because "[e]conomic development has long been recognized as a proper governmental function."[73]

---

70. In addition to the uses discussed here, the North Carolina Supreme Court has on one occasion employed the governmental/proprietary distinction to resolve a zoning dispute. McKinney v. City of High Point, 237 N.C. 66 (1953).

71. City of Greensboro v. Morse, 197 N.C. App. 624, 627 (2009).

72. "The power of taxation shall be exercised in a just and equitable manner, for public purposes only, and shall never be surrendered, suspended, or contracted away." N.C. CONST. art. V, § 2(1). "[T]his provision requires that all public funds, no matter what their source, be expended for the benefit of the citizens of a unit generally and not solely for the benefit of particular persons or interests." KARA A. MILLONZI, *The Public Purpose Requirement, in* INTRODUCTION TO LOCAL GOVERNMENT FINANCE 4 (Kara A. Millonzi ed., 4th ed. 2018).

73. Maready v. Winston-Salem, 342 N.C. 708, 723 (1996). Similarly, the court held that a city could take on debt to finance the construction and operation of water and power plants because such activities were "necessary to fully protect the lives and

The same endeavor may be classified as governmental for one purpose but not for another. If this were not so, neither the state nor local governments could spend public funds on any of the many undertakings that have been deemed proprietary functions in governmental immunity cases. The constitutional ban on the expenditure of public funds for non-public purposes would outlaw such expenditures.

2.2 Rationale for the Distinction in Immunity Cases

Why has the North Carolina Supreme Court held that governmental functions warrant immunity but proprietary functions do not? The distinction "grows out of the dual character of municipal corporations."[74] Every city "has a two-fold existence—one as a governmental agency, the other as a private corporation."[75] In other words, cities perform some functions for the public good on behalf of the state and some primarily for the benefit of their respective compact communities. To the degree that cities act in place of the state "in promoting or protecting the health, safety, security, or general welfare of [their] citizens," the court has deemed it appropriate to grant them the state's immunity from tort liability.[76] On the other hand, to the extent that cities act like corporations by engaging in commercial undertakings for the benefit of their compact communities, the court has been inclined to let them face tort liability on roughly the same basis as private corporations.[77]

2.3 A Different Rule for Counties?

The state supreme court initially declined to apply *Moffitt*'s distinction between governmental powers and corporate powers to tort claims against counties. It continued to hold, as it had in pre-*Moffitt* cases, that counties were liable in tort only when a statute provided for such liability.[78] In other words,

---

comfort and property of [the town's] inhabitants" and to preserve "the peace and order of the community." Fawcett v. Town of Mt. Airy, 134 N.C. 125, 129 (1903). *See also* Rhodes v. City of Asheville, 230 N.C. 134, 137 (1949) ("Since this Court handed down . . . *Fawcett v. Mt. Airy* . . . the construction, maintenance, and operation of a water and light plant by a municipality, has been held to be a necessary governmental expense.").

74. DAYE & MORRIS, *supra* note 1, § 19.40[2][c][ii], at 451.

75. Britt v. City of Wilmington, 236 N.C. 446, 450 (1952).

76. *Id.*

77. See Section 4.3, *infra*, for more on the liability of local government units for harms arising from proprietary functions.

78. *See, e.g.,* Bell v. Comm'rs of Johnston Cty., 127 N.C. 85, 90–91 (1900) ("[C]ounties, being a branch of the State government, can be sued only in such cases and for such causes as are authorized by statute"); Prichard v. Comm'rs of Morganton, 126 N.C. 908, 912 (1900) ("Counties . . . are not liable for damages, in the absence of statutory provisions giving a right of action against them."); Manuel v. Bd. of Comm'rs of Cumberland Cty., 98 N.C. 9, 11 (1887) ("Generally, a county is not liable for damages

counties possessed the same immunity to tort claims as the state. The apparent rationale for treating counties and cities differently in tort cases was that cities exercised their corporate powers chiefly for the advantage of their own residents—much as private corporations exist to benefit their shareholders—while counties operated as extensions of state government.[79]

Subsequently, the supreme court began to apply the governmental/proprietary distinction to tort claims against counties.[80] This shift in the law appears to have resulted from the increasing tendency of counties, starting about the middle of the twentieth century, to undertake functions traditionally associated with cities, such as garbage collection.[81] Today it is clear that cities, counties, public school systems, and other local government units operate largely outside the protection of governmental immunity when they undertake proprietary functions.[82]

---

sustained by individuals by reason of the neglect of its officers or agents, and there is no statute of this State creating such liability."); White v. Comm'rs of Chowan, 90 N.C. 437, 439 (1884) ("[Counties] may be sued only in such cases and for such causes as may be provided for and allowed by the statute.").

79. *White*, 90 N.C. at 438, 440 (The primary purpose of counties is "to effectuate the political organization and civil administration of the state" at the local level, but cities use their corporate powers "not so much to aid in the administration of the government of the state as for local advantage and convenience."). *See also Bell*, 127 N.C. at 90–91 (describing counties as "a branch of the state government," unlike cities, which are "municipal corporations"); *Manuel*, 98 N.C. at 10, 12 (counties are "mere instrumentalities" of the state, whereas cities "are incorporated largely and mainly for the benefit of the corporators"); LAWRENCE, *supra* note 44, at 5 ("Originally, counties were established to serve state purposes, that is, to carry out government on behalf of the state. . . . Cities, by contrast, were created to adopt regulations and provide services more appropriate to built-up or urban areas.").

80. For an early example of this shift in the court's approach to county liability, see *Rhodes v. City of Asheville*, 230 N.C. 134, 141 (1949) ("But when it undertakes, with legislative sanction, to perform an activity which is proprietary or corporate in character, such a county may be liable in tort to the same extent as a city or town would be if engaged in the same activity.").

81. *See* LAWRENCE, *supra* note 44, at 5:

> Around the middle of the twentieth century, citizens living outside cities began to request some of the governmental services characteristic of cities but not of counties. They wanted community water or sewer systems, organized fire protection, and recreational spaces or programs. They wanted to be able to dispose of their trash in some way other than dumping or burning. And they wanted the protection of zoning. The General Assembly's response, over time, was to empower counties to engage in these city-like activities.

82. *See, e.g.*, Viking Utils. Corp., Inc. v. Onslow Water & Sewer Auth., 232 N.C. App. 684, 686–89 (2014) (explaining how the governmental/proprietary distinction should be applied to claims against a county water and sewer authority); Willett v. Chatham Cty. Bd. of Educ., 176 N.C. App. 268, 270–72 (2006) (applying the governmental/proprietary distinction to claims against a local board of education); Robinson v. Nash Cty., 43 N.C. App. 33, 35 (1979) ("It is well established in this State that counties or

2.4 "Governmental Function" and "Proprietary Function" Defined

By making the immunity of a local government unit dependent on whether the activity that damaged the plaintiff was governmental or proprietary, the state supreme court created the need for standards to distinguish the two kinds of functions. In one oft-cited formulation, the court described governmental functions as undertakings that are "discretionary, political, legislative, or public in nature and performed for the public good in behalf of the State"; it described proprietary functions as activities that are "commercial or chiefly for the private advantage of the compact community." [83] In a later case, the court declared that it had consistently acknowledged "one guiding principle" for determining whether an activity is governmental or proprietary: "If the undertaking . . . is one in which only a governmental agency could engage, it is governmental in nature. It is proprietary and 'private' when any corporation, individual, or group of individuals could do the same thing." [84]

These standards had serious shortcomings, as discussed in more detail below. In practice, the court tended to regard as governmental functions those activities traditionally performed by local governments and ordinarily not engaged in by private corporations. [85] Undertakings classified by the court as proprietary functions usually involved some kind of monetary charge that generated revenue—though not necessarily a profit—for units of local government. [86] The court did not invariably classify fee-based activities as proprietary functions, however. [87]

---

municipal corporations have no governmental immunity for activities that are 'proprietary' in nature.").

83. Millar v. Town of Wilson, 222 N.C. 340, 341 (1942).

84. Evans v. Hous. Auth. of City of Raleigh, 359 N.C. 50, 54 (2004) (quoting Britt v. City of Wilmington, 236 N.C. 446, 451 (1952)).

85. Sides v. Cabarrus Mem'l Hosp., Inc., 287 N.C. 14, 23 (1975) ("[I]t appears that all of the activities held to be governmental functions by this Court are those historically performed by the government, and which are not ordinarily engaged in by private corporations."). The court identified the following examples of undertakings traditionally performed by local governments but not by private corporations: erecting and maintaining a county jail, installing and maintaining traffic signals, operating a police car, erecting and maintaining a police and fire alarm system, and supplying water for extinguishing fires. *Id.*

86. *Id.* at 22–23. The court noted that it had previously ruled that cities act proprietarily when they impose charges for the use of a landfill, admission to a public park, the supply of drinking water, or the distribution of electricity. *Id.*

87. *See, e.g.,* James v. City of Charlotte, 183 N.C. 630, 631–33 (1922) (city was not liable for injuries caused by a speeding city garbage truck, even though it charged a fee to cover the cost of garbage removal).

2.5 Problems in Classifying Undertakings as "Governmental" or "Proprietary"

In some cases, the judiciary has had little trouble classifying the specific activities under consideration as governmental or proprietary. The state supreme court, for example, had no trouble summarily classifying a county's operation of a public library as a governmental function and a city's maintenance of a golf course as a proprietary function.[88] Yet in other instances the courts have found it quite difficult to categorize particular undertakings as governmental or proprietary.[89] Indeed, as the supreme court itself admitted, this difficulty has "resulted in irreconcilable splits of authority" and created a "tradition of confusion" as to "what functions are governmental and what functions are proprietary."[90] Thus, although the judiciary generally views the maintenance of public roads and highways as a governmental function, longstanding precedents allow cities to be held liable if they fail to maintain their streets and sidewalks in a reasonably safe condition.[91] The supreme court has described this significant wrinkle in the case law as an "'illogical' exception" to foundational principles of governmental immunity.[92]

The confused state of the case law set the stage for the court's 2012 attempt in *Estate of Williams v. Pasquotank County Parks & Recreation Department*[93] to formulate a more straightforward and systematic method for making governmental/proprietary determinations.

---

88. Lowe v. City of Gastonia, 211 N.C. 564, 566 (1937) ("Defendant's contention . . . that it is not liable to the plaintiff . . . because it owned and maintained the golf course in the exercise of a governmental function, cannot be sustained."); Seibold v. Kinston-Lenoir Cty. Pub. Library, 264 N.C. 360, 361 (1965) ("The operation of a public library meets the test of 'governmental function' . . . .").

89. *See* Millar v. Town of Wilson, 222 N.C. 340, 342 (1942) ("The line between municipal operations that are proprietary and, therefore, a proper subject of suits in tort and those that are governmental and, therefore, immune from suits is sometimes difficult to draw.").

90. Koontz v. City of Winston-Salem, 280 N.C. 513, 528 (1972). The court conceded that it had contributed to the confusion by adopting "apparently divergent views" on whether an otherwise governmental function becomes proprietary when a local government uses it to generate income. *Id.*

91. *E.g., Millar*, 222 N.C. at 342 ("While the maintenance of public roads and highways is generally recognized as a governmental function, exception is made in respect to streets and sidewalks of a municipality . . . the maintenance of [city] streets and sidewalks is classed as a ministerial or proprietary function.").

92. *Id.* Another example of inconsistency is found in the law concerning city liability for sewer systems. Under current case law, a city's *construction* of a sewer system is a governmental function, even if the system will be fee-based, but the *operation* of a fee-based sewer system is proprietary. See Section 3.4.2, *infra*, for more information.

93. 366 N.C. 195, 201 (2012).

2.6 The *Williams* Test

In *Williams,* the estate of Erik Williams filed suit against Pasquotank County and its parks and recreation department alleging that the county's negligence had led to Mr. Williams's drowning in the Swimming Hole, an area rented to private parties in Fun Junktion, a county park open to the public. The county argued that governmental immunity barred the estate's claims because Chapter 160A, Section 351 of the North Carolina General Statutes (hereinafter G.S.) "asserts that 'the operation of public parks is a proper governmental function.'"[94] Both the trial court and the North Carolina Court of Appeals ruled that governmental immunity did not protect the county.[95] The county appealed to the North Carolina Supreme Court.

2.6.1 Overview of the *Williams* Test

The state supreme court vacated the decision of the court of appeals. It rejected the lower court's identification of the most important factor in governmental/proprietary determinations: whether a nongovernmental actor could perform the activity that led to the plaintiff's injury. The supreme court stated that henceforth judicial efforts to classify particular undertakings as governmental or proprietary for immunity purposes must be guided by a three-part inquiry:

1. whether, and to what degree, the legislature has designated the specific activity that caused the plaintiff's injury as governmental or proprietary;
2. whether the activity is one that only a governmental entity could undertake; and
3. whether additional factors reveal the undertaking to be either governmental or proprietary. In particular, a court must examine whether the activity is one traditionally undertaken by local governments, whether the defendant local government charged a substantial fee as part of the activity, and whether any such fee generated a profit.

---

94. *Id.* at 201. The statute reads:

> The lack of adequate recreational programs and facilities is a menace to the morals, happiness, and welfare of the people of this State. Making available recreational opportunities for citizens of all ages is a subject of general interest and concern, and a function requiring appropriate action by both State and local government. The General Assembly therefore declares that the public good and the general welfare of the citizens of this State require adequate recreation programs, that *the creation, establishment, and operation of parks and recreation programs is a proper governmental function,* and that it is the policy of North Carolina to forever encourage, foster, and provide these facilities and programs for all its citizens.

G.S. 160A-351 (emphasis added).

95. *Williams,* 211 N.C. App. 627, 632, *vacated and remanded,* 366 N.C. 195 (2012).

The high court explained that when the legislature has designated a particular activity as governmental or proprietary, the judiciary will usually defer to its determination, making consideration of the remaining two prongs unnecessary. Similarly, when an activity is one that only the government can undertake, it is *ipso facto* a governmental function, and the third part of the *Williams* test will not be in play.[96] When the third prong is applied, the additional factors listed therein suggest that a nontraditional—or even a traditional—local government undertaking will likely be categorized as proprietary if it produces significant revenue.

The *Williams* test can be represented graphically as follows:

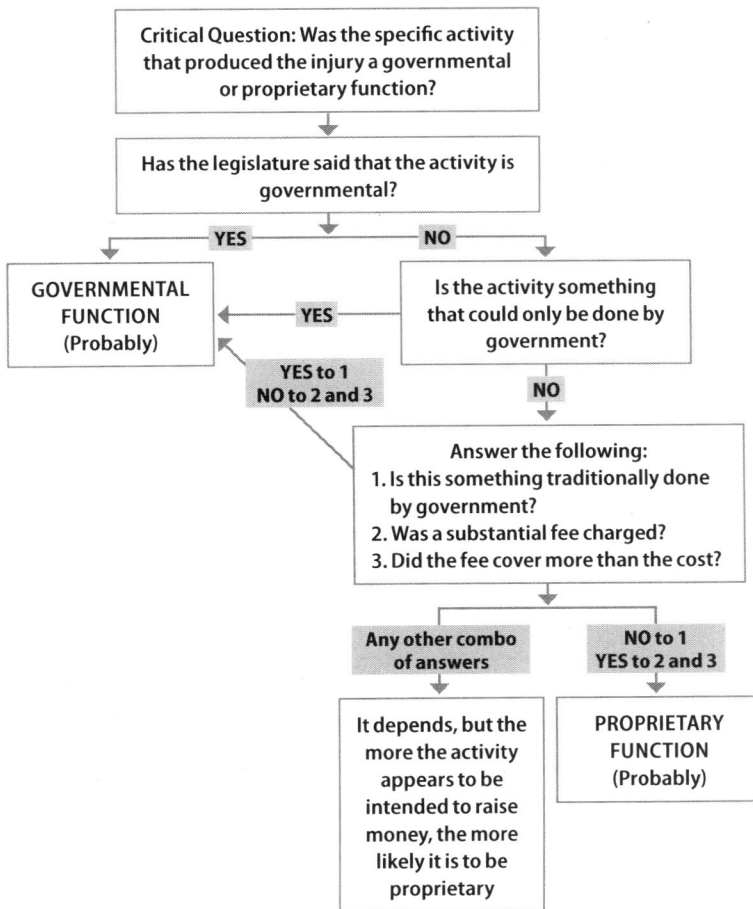

```
┌──────────────────────────────────┐
│ Critical Question: Was the specific activity │
│ that produced the injury a governmental │
│ or proprietary function? │
└──────────────────────────────────┘
               │
┌──────────────────────────────────┐
│ Has the legislature said that the activity is │
│ governmental? │
└──────────────────────────────────┘
        YES              NO
┌────────────────┐      ┌─────────────────────────┐
│ GOVERNMENTAL   │ ◄─YES─│ Is the activity something │
│ FUNCTION       │      │ that could only be done by │
│ (Probably)     │      │ government? │
└────────────────┘      └─────────────────────────┘
        ▲                        NO
   YES to 1                       │
   NO to 2 and 3       ┌──────────────────────────────────┐
                       │ Answer the following: │
                       │ 1. Is this something traditionally done │
                       │    by government? │
                       │ 2. Was a substantial fee charged? │
                       │ 3. Did the fee cover more than the cost? │
                       └──────────────────────────────────┘
                              │
                  Any other combo        NO to 1
                  of answers             YES to 2 and 3
              ┌─────────────────┐    ┌──────────────┐
              │ It depends, but the │  │ PROPRIETARY  │
              │ more the activity │    │ FUNCTION │
              │ appears to be     │    │ (Probably) │
              │ intended to raise │    └──────────────┘
              │ money, the more   │
              │ likely it is to be │
              │ proprietary       │
              └─────────────────┘
```

---

96. 366 N.C. at 202 ("When the legislature has not directly resolved whether a specific activity is governmental or proprietary in nature, other factors are relevant. We have repeatedly held that if the undertaking is one in which *only* a governmental agency could engage, it is perforce governmental in nature.").

However coherent the *Williams* test seems on the surface, a closer look at each of its components provides reason to believe that it will prove significantly easier to articulate than to apply in practice.

2.6.2 The *Williams* Test's First Prong: Statutory Designations of Activities as Governmental or Proprietary

There is more than one way for the General Assembly to designate an activity as governmental or proprietary. The most obvious method is for the legislature to include the term "governmental" or "proprietary" in the statutory provision authorizing the activity, as it did in G.S. 160A-351, the statute at issue in *Williams*. The state supreme court has also treated statutes that *require* local government units to undertake specific activities as legislative declarations that those compulsory activities are governmental functions. Thus, for example, in *Bynum v. Wilson County*, the court held that G.S. 153A-169 classifies the maintenance of at least some county buildings as a governmental function.[97] Although the statute omits the term "governmental," it mandates that boards of county commissioners "supervise the maintenance, repair, and use of all county property."

Statements of legislative intent can influence a court's classification of an activity as governmental or proprietary, even when they neither use the term "governmental function" nor require action on the part of local governments. In one case, the supreme court turned to the statement of purpose in the Housing Authorities Law (HAL) for "useful direction" as it analyzed whether cities act governmentally by exercising their discretionary power under the HAL to provide affordable housing to tenants of low and moderate incomes.[98] According to the statement, the legislature enacted the HAL with a view toward addressing "unsanitary or unsafe dwelling accommodations . . . in urban and rural areas throughout the State . . . that . . . cannot be remedied by the ordinary operation of public enterprise[.]"[99] The court characterized the statement as a "statutory indication that the provision of low and moderate income housing is a governmental function."[100] Pointing to similar language in the Urban Redevelopment Law and the Municipal Service District Act of 1973, the North Carolina Supreme Court in the post-*Williams* case of *Meinck v. City of Gastonia* spotted "statutory indications" that urban redevelopment projects can be governmental undertakings.[101]

---

97. 367 N.C. 355, 360 (2014).

98. Evans v. Hous. Auth. of City of Raleigh, 359 N.C. 50, 55 (2004).

99. *Id.* (quoting G.S. 157-2(a)).

100. *Id.*

101. Meinck v. City of Gastonia, No. 130PA17, 2018 WL 5310160, at *9 (N.C. Oct. 26, 2018) (comparing provisions in the HAL with similar provisions in G.S. 160A-501, -502, and -536).

2.6.2.1 Legislative Designations Not Always Determinative

The first prong of the *Williams* test is unlikely to resolve many cases. In the first place, very few statutes expressly designate local government functions as governmental, and none classify any as proprietary. Furthermore, even when the legislature has classified an activity as governmental, the matter is not necessarily closed. Prior cases demonstrate that judicial deference to such legislative declarations is not absolute. In *Rhodes v. City of Asheville*, the defendant local governments were sued for the wrongful death of a man who had been fatally shot by a security guard at the Asheville-Henderson Airport.[102] The units argued that governmental immunity barred the wrongful death claims. In particular, they asserted that they could not be liable for the man's death because G.S. 63-50 describes the construction, maintenance, and operation of municipal airports as "governmental and municipal functions exercised for a public purpose and matters of public necessity."[103]

The supreme court ruled that G.S. 63-50 did not bar the wrongful death claims against the defendants, offering three reasons for its holding.

- Classification of an activity as a governmental function does not necessarily mean that governmental immunity applies. For example, the supreme court had long held that a city may be liable for injuries resulting from its failure to keep its streets in a reasonably safe condition, even though the maintenance of city streets is undoubtedly a governmental function.
- Appellate courts in other states had overwhelmingly viewed the operation of municipal airports as a proprietary function that may result in tort liability for local governments.
- The General Assembly did not enact G.S. 63-50 with governmental immunity in mind. Rather, "the intent of the Legislature [was] to declare that the acquisition, construction, and maintenance of an airport . . . was a governmental function in the sense that it was a public purpose."[104] In other words, the statute expresses the legislature's view that public funds may be spent on municipal airports.

Significantly, although it rejected the defendants' immunity argument, the court remarked that the General Assembly has the power to exempt the operation of airports from tort liability, even though the undertaking is proprietary in nature. It explained that, if the legislature wished to take such action, it had to expressly confer immunity on airport-related activities. The court repeated this point in rejecting the defendants' petition for rehearing, with a sharp reminder that the judiciary, not the legislature, enjoys the last

---

102. 230 N.C. 134, 135 (1949).
103. *Id.* at 136.
104. *Id.* at 140.

word on whether an undertaking is governmental or proprietary.[105] It reaffirmed this stance in a later case, when it remarked that, notwithstanding G.S. 63-50, an airport authority functions in a proprietary capacity when setting airport landing and rental fees.[106]

2.6.2.2 Degree of Specificity Required

The *Williams* opinion suggests that, even when a statute expressly labels an undertaking as governmental, the designation will not control an immunity determination if the breadth of the statutory text leaves the court unsure about whether the General Assembly intended to capture the precise act or omission alleged to have produced the plaintiff's injury. While describing G.S. 160A-351 as "clearly relevant" to the question of whether the activity that led to Erik Williams's death was governmental or proprietary, the supreme court declined to decide whether the statute ultimately resolved the matter.[107] Instead, it remanded the case with instructions for the trial court to consider the effect, if any, of G.S. 160A-351 on the county's immunity defense.[108] The supreme court noted that, although G.S. 160A-351 generally describes park operations as a governmental function, the statute does not cover every "nuanced action" that could take place in a public park or recreational facility.[109] The precise issue for the trial court was whether, taking the statute into account, "the specific operation of the Swimming Hole component of Fun Junktion, in this case and under these circumstances, [was] a governmental function."[110] Thus, the supreme court left open the possibility that, due to its broad wording, G.S. 160A-351 might not control the outcome of the trial court's immunity ruling.

2.6.2.3 Treatment of Legislative Designations in Governmental/Proprietary Determinations

Read together, *Williams* and *Rhodes* appear to support the following statements about the role of statutes that classify activities as governmental functions in governmental immunity determinations.

- When a statute classifies the specific undertaking that led to a plaintiff's injury as a governmental function, it can be important for

---

105. *Rhodes*, 230 N.C. 759, 759 (1949) ("Unquestionably the Legislature intended to declare that the operation of the Asheville-Hendersonville Airport should be deemed and held to be in furtherance of a governmental function. But the mere legislative declaration to that effect did not make it so, for that is a judicial and not a legislative question.").

106. Piedmont Aviation v. Raleigh-Durham Airport Auth., 288 N.C. 98, 102–03 (1975).

107. Estate of Williams v. Pasquotank Cty. Parks & Recreation Dep't, 366 N.C. 195, 201 (2012) (emphasis omitted).

108. The lawsuit was settled on remand.

109. *Williams*, 366. N.C. at 202.

110. *Id.* at 201.

a court to identify the reason for the classification. If the purpose of the designation is to assert that public funds may be spent on the activity, the statute may have little bearing on whether governmental immunity bars the plaintiff's tort claims. The presence of the words "public purpose" in the statute is a signal that the General Assembly was more worried about constitutional restraints on public funds than about tort claims against local governments.

- When a statute classifies the specific activity that resulted in a plaintiff's injury as a governmental function, and the court does not think that the classification was made for reasons unrelated to liability, the court should usually defer to the legislature's pronouncement. Even in such circumstances, though, it is not always a given that governmental immunity will cover the activity. As remarked in *Rhodes*, governmental immunity does not bar tort claims arising from a city's failure to keep its streets reasonably safe, even though cities are statutorily required to maintain their streets in a reasonably safe condition.[111]

- It may be appropriate for a court to reject the General Assembly's designation of a specific activity as governmental when the courts of other states have overwhelmingly classified the undertaking as proprietary for liability purposes.

- If a statute broadly defines a governmental function, a court may have to apply the second and third parts of the *Williams* test in order to properly characterize the precise conduct that led to a plaintiff's injury. The breadth of the language used in G.S. 160A-351, for instance, may make the statute a minor factor in most tort cases arising from the operation of public parks.[112]

- Even when the case law defines an activity as proprietary, the legislature has the power to exempt the undertaking from tort liability. An unambiguous declaration of the legislature's intent is required to create an exemption for a proprietary undertaking.

2.6.3 The *Williams* Test's Second Prong: Activities Only Governments Can Undertake

Like the first prong, the second prong of the *Williams* test may not help the lower courts identify particular functions as governmental or proprietary in very many cases. The state supreme court acknowledged that the usefulness of the second prong is limited in a changing world where the private sector now performs many services once thought to belong exclusively to the public

---

111. Rhodes v. City of Asheville, 230 N.C. 134, 138 (1949) (citing G.S. 160-54, a forerunner of G.S. 160A-296).

112. The implications of *Williams* for city and county liability for injuries at public parks is considered at length in Chapter 6.

sector. "[I]t is increasingly difficult," the court explained, "to identify services that can only be rendered by a governmental entity."[113]

One post-*Williams* case identifies an activity that, according to the court of appeals, only a county can perform. In *Fuller v. Wake County*, the court held that a county acts governmentally in deciding how to go about making emergency medical services (EMS) available to its residents.[114] State law requires counties to ensure that EMS are provided to their residents, and the court reasoned that it takes a county to fulfill this statutory obligation.[115] Although private entities can furnish EMS, they are not subject to the mandate.

2.6.4 The *Williams* Test's Third Prong: Other Factors

Given the limitations of the first two prongs in the *Williams* inquiry, it seems probable that judges will ordinarily have to resort to the third prong when they attempt to categorize activities as governmental or proprietary. The additional factors that make up the third step focus primarily on revenue, which, as noted in Section 2.6.1, *supra*, strongly indicates that an activity runs a high risk of being deemed proprietary if it yields substantial income for a unit of local government. The court's opinion in *Williams* cautions against over-reliance on the third prong's additional factors, however. Why? According to the court, "distinctions between proprietary and governmental functions are fluid and courts must be advertent to changes in practice."[116] The implication seems to be that changing circumstances could make factors other than those listed in *Williams* pertinent to future governmental/proprietary determinations.

2.6.5 The Potential Impact of *Williams* on Precedent

If, as *Williams* says, "distinctions between proprietary and governmental functions are fluid and courts must be advertent to changes in practice,"[117] then *Williams* may call into question the ongoing soundness of prior cases that classify particular activities as governmental or proprietary. Even when confronting an activity designated as governmental or proprietary by a pre-*Williams* decision, a lower court should apply the *Williams* test to the facts of the case. It may be that, at least in a few instances, the application of this test will lead to a different classification, especially if the relevant precedent employs criteria inconsistent with the factors set out in *Williams*. Given the

---

113. Estate of Williams v. Pasquotank Cty. Parks & Recreation Dep't, 366 N.C. 195, 202 (2012).

114. ___ N.C. App. ___, ___, 802 S.E.2d 106, 112–13 (2017).

115. While it is up to the county to make EMS available, it may satisfy this obligation by contracting for EMS, as explained in Section 3.2.2.2, *infra*.

116. *Williams*, 366 N.C. at 203.

117. *Id.*

cloud of uncertainty that *Williams* has hung over prior classifications, the decision may not represent quite the positive break from the "tradition of confusion" in governmental immunity cases that the state supreme court hoped to achieve.

Chapter 3

The Governmental/Proprietary Distinction in Practice

One takeaway from Chapter 2 is that the judiciary has the last word on whether a particular activity counts as governmental or proprietary for immunity purposes (though the General Assembly can exempt local governments from liability even for proprietary functions). In the nearly 130 years since the North Carolina Supreme Court adopted the governmental/proprietary distinction in *Moffitt v. City of Asheville*,[118] the state's appellate courts have classified a large number of undertakings as either governmental or proprietary in response to assertions of governmental immunity.

Without claiming to be comprehensive, this chapter reviews specific undertakings that have been categorized as either governmental or proprietary functions.[119] The reader should keep the following points in mind, however.

- The overwhelming majority of classifications described in this chapter occurred prior to *Estate of Williams v. Pasquotank County Parks & Recreation Department*.[120] As noted in Section 2.6.5, *supra*, *Williams* seems to leave open the possibility that the application of its criteria to undertakings previously deemed governmental or proprietary could yield different outcomes in future cases. A pre-*Williams* case classifying a particular activity as governmental, for example, might not dictate the result in a later case involving the same kind of activity, if practices surrounding the two undertakings differ materially.
- Some activities comprise both governmental phases and proprietary phases. The mere fact that one aspect of an endeavor has been

---

118. 103 N.C. 237 (1889).

119. Many of the cases referenced in this chapter are cited in § 19.40 of Daye & Morris, *supra* note 1; in Chapter 3 of Anita R. Brown-Graham, A Practical Guide to the Liability of North Carolina Cities and Counties (1999); or in *Understanding Sovereign and Governmental Immunity: Tips and Techniques for Theories of Liability*, a paper prepared by Carlos E. Mahoney for a continuing legal education program offered by North Carolina Advocates for Justice. The author gratefully acknowledges that these sources provided useful starting points for his own research.

120. 366 N.C. 195 (2012).

categorized as proprietary does not mean that other aspects cannot be governmental or vice-versa.[121]

- As explained more fully in Chapter 4, the classification of an undertaking as a governmental function does not relieve a local government unit from liability if the unit has purchased liability insurance applicable to the plaintiff's claim(s). Many of the cases referred to in this chapter that were decided in favor of a local government would have been resolved in the plaintiff's favor had the unit purchased such insurance.
- In some of the cases cited below, the plaintiffs asserted constitutional claims in addition to tort claims. As noted in Chapter 1, governmental immunity is not a defense to allegations that a local government unit has violated a person's rights under the United States Constitution or the North Carolina Constitution. One should not assume each time a unit is said to have prevailed over a plaintiff's tort claims on immunity grounds that the court's ruling ended the lawsuit against the unit.

3.1 Local Governing Board Actions (Governmental and Proprietary)

3.1.1 Failure to Adopt or Enforce Ordinances (Governmental)

An array of state laws authorize city councils and boards of county commissioners to adopt and enforce ordinances regulating or prohibiting conditions detrimental to the health, safety, or welfare of their citizens.[122] The North Carolina Supreme Court long ago declared that no tort liability attaches to a local governing board's non-exercise of its discretionary power to adopt or enforce ordinances.[123] In one case, the supreme court ruled that a town

---

121. Sides v. Cabarrus Mem'l Hosp., Inc., 287 N.C. 14, 21 (1975) ("[A]lthough an activity may be classified in general as a governmental function, liability in tort may exist as to certain of its phases; and conversely, although classified in general as proprietary, certain phases may be considered exempt from liability.").

122. *E.g.*, Chapter 153A, Section 121 of the North Carolina General Statutes (hereinafter G.S.) (county general ordinance-making power); G.S. 153A-123 (county ordinance enforcement); 153A-126 (county begging ordinances); 153A-133 (county noise ordinance); 160A-174 (city general ordinance-making authority); 160A-175 (city ordinance enforcement); 160A-179 (city begging ordinances); 160A-184 (city noise ordinances).

For an analysis of the general regulatory and enforcement powers of cities and counties, see TREY ALLEN, *General Ordinance Authority, in* COUNTY AND MUNICIPAL GOVERNMENT IN NORTH CAROLINA 77–91 (Frayda S. Bluestein ed., 2d ed. 2014).

123. Hill v. Bd. of Aldermen of the City of Charlotte, 72 N.C. 55, 56–57 (1875).
The courts . . . have held almost with unanimity that a [city] is not civilly liable for the failure to pass ordinances, even though they

was not liable for failing to adopt and enforce nuisance ordinance provisions against a property owner whose hog pens drained onto the plaintiff's property, thereby impairing the health of the plaintiff's wife and infant child.[124] In another case, the court determined that the local governing board's temporary suspension—from December 25 through January 1—of an ordinance prohibiting the exploding of fireworks did not render the city liable for damage to the plaintiff's building caused by fireworks set off during the suspension period.[125]

At least one case—the hog pens case—cites the doctrine of governmental immunity to justify the judiciary's unwillingness to impose liability on local government units for the non-exercise of legislative powers.[126] An alternative explanation exists in the form of the discretionary immunity doctrine, under which "the courts will not review decisions left by law to the discretion of a local legislative body."[127] Were a court to entertain a tort claim based on a board's failure to adopt or enforce an ordinance, it would "arrogate to itself the legislative power" of the local governing board, "and it cannot be supposed possible that any court will be guilty of such a usurpation."[128]

3.1.2 Granting Franchises (Governmental)

In granting a franchise to a public utility, a local governing board performs a governmental function.[129] Accordingly, a city governing board's franchise grant to a natural gas company did not expose the city to liability for the death of a man killed by an explosion allegedly caused by the company's negligence.[130]

---

would, if passed, preserve the public health or otherwise promote the public good. . . . It is equally well settled that if the [city] has enacted ordinances . . . it is not civilly liable for any omission to enforce them or to see that they are properly observed within the corporate limits.

Hull v. Town of Roxboro, 142 N.C. 453, 455–56 (1906) ("[A city] is exempt from liability for any injury resulting from a failure to exercise its governmental powers, or for their improper or negligent exercise, but it is amenable to an action for any injury caused by its neglect to perform its ministerial functions, or by an improper or unskilful [sic] performance of them.").

124. *Hull*, 142 N.C. at 461. *See also* Harrington v. Town of Greenville, 159 N.C. 632, 635 (1912) (town that ignored the plaintiff's requests that it condemn and remove certain rotten buildings was not liable for the destruction of the plaintiff's property in a fire that originated among those same buildings).

125. *Hill*, 72 N.C. at 57.

126. *Hull*, 142 N.C. at 455–56.

127. ANTHONY J. BAKER, *Civil Liability of the Local Government and Its Officials and Employees, in* COUNTY AND MUNICIPAL GOVERNMENT IN NORTH CAROLINA 104 (Frayda S. Bluestein ed., 2d ed. 2014).

128. *Hill*, 72 N.C. at 57.

129. Denning v. Goldsboro Gas Co., 246 N.C. 541, 543 (1957).

130. *Id.*

3.1.3 Setting Public Enterprise Rates (Proprietary)

Section 3.4, *infra*, discusses public enterprises such as city water and sewer services in more detail. In exercising its statutory authority to set rates and charges for its public enterprises, a city or county governing board acts in a proprietary role.[131] Nonetheless, because the legislature has committed the setting of these rates and charges to the discretion of local governments, ordinarily the courts will not invalidate them absent a showing of arbitrary or discriminatory action.[132]

3.1.4 Imposing Invalid Impact Fees (Governmental but Liability Anyway)

Governmental immunity will not bar a lawsuit for the recovery of impact fees unlawfully imposed by a local governing board. The North Carolina Court of Appeals reached this conclusion on the way to holding that developers and homebuilders were entitled to a refund of impact fees imposed by a board of county commissioners on new residential construction inside the defendant county.[133] Although the purpose of the fees was laudable—to generate funds for needed school construction—the board had exceeded its authority under the relevant statutes.

The court appeared to accept that the board had acted governmentally in adopting the impact fee.[134] Its opinion suggests that a finding of immunity would not have been appropriate because the imposition of the fee invaded constitutionally protected interests.[135]

---

131. Pulliam v. City of Greensboro, 103 N.C. App. 748, 753 (1991); Town of Hope Springs v. Bissette, 53 N.C. App. 210, 212 (1981). *See also* Piedmont Aviation, Inc. v. Raleigh-Durham Airport Auth., 288 N.C. 98, 102 (1975) ("[I]n determining the fee it will charge for the privilege of landing an aircraft upon its runway and the rent it will charge for the use of its properties, the [Raleigh-Durham Airport] Authority is acting as the proprietor of the property, not as a regulatory agency.").

The basic authority of local governments to establish and revise rates and charges for their public enterprises is found in G.S. 160A-314(a) (cities) and 153A-277(a) (counties).

132. *Bissette*, 53 N.C. App. at 212–13.

133. Durham Land Owners Ass'n v. Cty. of Durham, 177 N.C. App. 629, 640–41 (2006).

134. *See id.* at 641 (it was "not the case" that the board acted in a proprietary capacity).

135. *See id.* at 640 (measures such as the impact fee "invade or threaten to invade personal or property rights of a citizen in disregard of the law").

3.2 Law Enforcement and Emergency Services (Governmental)

3.2.1 Law Enforcement (Governmental)

Most local enforcement of the state's criminal laws is done by city police departments and county sheriffs' offices.[136] Not surprisingly, given the obviously governmental nature of law enforcement, the courts have held that law enforcement officials discharge governmental functions when they act within the scope of their duties.[137]

Although governmental immunity often shields units of local government from tort claims arising from law enforcement activities, a unit may not escape liability if the officer's conduct violated the plaintiff's constitutional rights and reflected the unit's policy or custom. Moreover, the offending officer may face personal liability in tort if the officer acted maliciously, corruptly, or outside the scope of his or her duties. The officer may also be held personally liable for constitutional violations unless the defense of qualified immunity applies.[138]

3.2.1.1 Arrest (Governmental)

Police officers act in a governmental capacity when they effect arrests. So long as a city has not waived governmental immunity through the purchase of liability insurance, it is not liable in tort for an arresting officer's unlawful conduct, even if the officer's actions rise to the level of assault, battery, false imprisonment or arrest, or malicious prosecution.[139] Moreover, a plaintiff

---

136. *See generally* ROBERT L. FARB, *Law Enforcement, in* COUNTY AND MUNICIPAL GOVERNMENT IN NORTH CAROLINA 495–502 (Frayda S. Bluestein ed., 2d ed. 2014) (describing state and local law enforcement agencies and the territorial and subject matter jurisdiction of city police officers, sheriffs and deputy sheriffs, and county police officers).

137. *See, e.g.,* Galligan v. Town of Chapel Hill, 276 N.C. 172, 175 (1970) ("A police officer in the performance of duties is engaged in a governmental function."); Croom v. Town of Burgaw, 259 N.C. 60, 61 (1963) (per curiam) ("A municipality is not liable in tort for the wrongful acts of its police officers committed in connection with the performance of their duties as such officers."); Greene v. Barrick, 198 N.C. App. 647, 651 (2009) (quoting Coleman v. Cooper, 89 N.C. App. 188, 192 (1988) ("Ordinarily a municipality providing police services is engaged in a governmental function for which there is no liability."); Young v. Woodall, 119 N.C. App. 132, 135 (1995) ("It is well established that law enforcement is a governmental function."), *rev'd on other grounds*, 343 N.C. 459 (1996); Jones v. Kearns, 120 N.C. App. 301, 305 (1995) ("It is well established that law enforcement is a governmental function."); Messick v. Catawba Cty., 110 N.C. App. 707, 714 (1993) ("Police services are ordinarily considered governmental functions, the performance of which does not subject a municipality to liability.").

138. See Section 1.11, *supra*, for a brief explanation of qualified immunity.

139. *E.g.,* Scales v. City of Winston-Salem, 189 N.C. 469, 471 (1925) ("The nonliability of a municipal corporation for injury caused by negligence in the exercise of its

cannot overcome this immunity with allegations that the city negligently hired or retained the officer despite notice of the officer's unsuitability. In one case, the plaintiff filed suit against a city over his "brutal" arrest at the hands of a police officer "notorious for his cruelty and want of judgment in making arrests."[140] The court held that the city was exempt from liability for any tort claims arising from the arrest, including any claim that the city officials had appointed or retained the officer "with knowledge of his unfitness."[141] Similarly, in another case, governmental immunity defeated the plaintiff's arrest-related tort claims against a town, despite the plaintiff's allegation that a reasonable background investigation by the town would have revealed the offending officer to be "a person of bad character and reputation and who had a criminal record."[142]

3.2.1.2 Pursuit of Convicted or Suspected Lawbreakers (Governmental with Statutory Limitation)

Police officers perform a governmental function when they pursue convicted or suspected lawbreakers.[143] Thus, under general principles of governmental immunity, cities and counties are not liable for bodily injuries or property damage caused by such pursuits.

The liability picture is clouded by G.S. 20-145, which exempts automobiles under police direction from posted speed limits during pursuits of convicted or suspected lawbreakers, provided the vehicles are "operated with due regard for safety." The statute's final sentence declares that G.S. 20-145 "shall not . . . protect the driver of any such vehicle from the consequence of a reckless disregard of the safety of others." As construed by the courts, the statute imposes personal liability on police officers who, in the pursuit of convicted

governmental functions may be illustrated by cases in which it is held that a city is not liable for a policeman's assault with excessive force[.]"); Fullwood v. Barnes, ___ N.C. App. ___, ___, 792 S.E.2d 545, 550 (2016) (governmental immunity barred plaintiff's claims of assault and battery, false arrest/false imprisonment, and malicious prosecution against defendant police officer in his official capacity); Schlossberg v. Goins, 141 N.C. App. 436, 444–45 (2000) (except to degree it had waived immunity by purchasing liability insurance or participating in governmental risk pool, city was immune to plaintiff's claims of battery, false imprisonment/false arrest, and malicious prosecution arising from plaintiff's arrest on an obstruction of justice charge that was later dismissed).

140. McIlhenney v. City of Wilmington, 127 N.C. 146, 149 (1900).

141. *Id*. at 152.

142. *Croom*, 259 N.C. at 61.

143. Young v. Woodall, 119 N.C. App. 132 (1995), *rev'd on other grounds*, 343 N.C. 359 (1996).

or suspected lawbreakers, injure other motorists or pedestrians by driving in a grossly negligent manner.[144]

Although G.S. 20-145 plainly contemplates liability for police officers who violate its provisions, the statute does not expressly address whether local government units are liable under its provisions for harms caused by gross negligence on the part of officers in police pursuits. The court of appeals has described claims brought pursuant to G.S. 20-145 "as falling outside the general rule of governmental immunity."[145] The implication is that governmental immunity does not shield a unit of local government from tort claims arising from an officer's violation of the statute's gross negligence standard.

3.2.1.3 Non-Emergency Operation of Police Automobiles (Governmental)

The operation of local government vehicles for law enforcement purposes constitutes a governmental function, even if the automobile is not responding to an emergency call. A police officer performs a governmental function, for example, by transporting an individual whom the officer has taken into custody pursuant to an arrest warrant.[146] Likewise, the operation of police automobiles for maintenance reasons is a governmental function. Governmental immunity therefore preserved a city from liability when a city employee, who had been working on a patrol car's radio, ran over a woman while returning the patrol car to the police garage.[147] Although the employee was not a police officer, he was performing duties "incident to the police power of the city—a purely governmental function."[148]

3.2.1.4 Operation of Aircraft for Law Enforcement Purposes (Governmental)

The employment of aircraft in law enforcement activities qualifies as a governmental function. Thus, governmental immunity barred negligence and other tort claims arising from the death of a deputy sheriff who was killed in a helicopter crash during a drug eradication flight, except to the extent that immunity was waived under the sheriff's surety bond.[149] Waiver of governmental immunity by surety bond is taken up in Section 4.4.9, *infra*.

---

144. *Young*, 343 N.C. at 462. The court of appeals has also ruled that G.S. 20-145 applies to an officer who drives recklessly in response to another officer's call for help in apprehending a convicted or suspected lawbreaker. Jones v. City of Durham, 168 N.C. App. 433, 439 (2005), *rev'd in part on other grounds*, 361 N.C. 144 (2006).

145. Truhan v. Walston, 235 N.C. App. 406, 421 (2014).

146. Clayton v. Branson, 153 N.C. App. 488, 493 (2002).

147. Lewis v. Hunter, 212 N.C. 504, 509 (1937).

148. *Id. See also* Dobrowolska v. Wall, 138 N.C. App. 1 (2000) (police officer carried out a governmental function when he drove to work on a Monday morning in a city van that he had driven home the preceding Friday following a trip to the repair shop).

149. Greene v. Barrick, 198 N.C. App. 647, 652 (2009).

3.2.1.5 Crowd Control (Governmental)

Law enforcement officers perform a governmental function when they take steps to control and disperse a large and unruly crowd.[150] Thus, governmental immunity barred a negligence claim against a city for injuries the plaintiff allegedly sustained when a police horse stepped on the plaintiff's foot as the officer riding the horse assisted with restoring order at a city-sponsored fair.[151] In response to the plaintiff's argument that the fair constituted a proprietary function, the court explained that the applicability of governmental immunity turned on "the mission or purpose of the municipal employee [who inflicted] the injury and whether the employee was acting in her official capacity at the time of the alleged negligence."[152]

3.2.1.6 Jails and Holding Cells (Governmental)

Almost every county in North Carolina has a jail, though some counties have joined together to establish district jails.[153] State law allows cities to run lockups for the temporary detention of individuals pending their transfer to county or district jails.[154]

The erection, operation, and maintenance of local jails qualify as governmental functions.[155] Accordingly, a county was not liable for the death of a mentally disturbed detainee who, upon being allowed to roam around the county jail, fell from an open space at the end of the upstairs hallway onto a concrete portion of the jail's first floor.[156] The lawsuit alleged that the county was liable for negligently maintaining the open space without guardrails or other safety features designed to prevent people from falling.

Some relatively old cases note the possibility that cities may be liable for jail-related tort claims based on facts that would not lead to liability for counties.[157] It may well be that they apply to the city lockups authorized under

---

150. Jones v. Kearns, 120 N.C. App. 301 (1995).

151. *Id.* at 305.

152. *Id.* at 304. This approach seems consistent with *Estate of Williams v. Pasquotank County Parks & Recreation Department*, 366 N.C. 195, 202 (2012), which emphasizes that the precise activity that led to the plaintiff's injury is the one to be analyzed.

153. JAMES M. MARKHAM, *The County Jail, in* COUNTY AND MUNICIPAL GOVERNMENT IN NORTH CAROLINA 719–20 (Frayda S. Bluestein ed., 2d ed. 2014).

154. G.S. 160A-287.

155. *E.g.,* State *ex rel.* Hayes v. Billings, 240 N.C. 78, 80 (1954) ("A county acts in a purely governmental capacity in erecting and maintaining a jail, and is therefore not liable to a person imprisoned or locked up therein for injuries sustained by reason of its improper construction or negligent maintenance."); Kephart v. Pendergraph, 131 N.C. App. 559, 563 (1998) (citations omitted) ("The provision of police services . . . and the erection and operation of prisons and jails . . . have previously been determined to constitute governmental functions.").

156. *Hayes*, 240 N.C. at 80–81.

157. *Id.* (recognizing that "a municipality is liable for injuries proximately caused by its negligent construction or maintenance of a prison or lockup" but declining to

current state law. These cases hold that governmental immunity will not bar claims against a city for injuries caused by its failure to construct a city jail properly or to furnish the jail so "as to afford to prisoners reasonable comfort and protection from suffering and injury to health."[158] This exception to general immunity principles appears to be quite narrow, however. So long as a city jail is properly constructed and reasonably supplied, governmental immunity will shield a city from tort liability if, for example, a detainee is harmed by an officer's negligent failure to provide the detainee with resources the city has made available.[159]

It is worth noting that the continued soundness of the special immunity rule for city jails is open to question. For one thing, there is no longer, if there ever was, any logical reason to treat cities and counties differently when it comes to liability for injuries stemming from the construction, maintenance, or operation of jails. Additionally, in formulating the exception, the state supreme court relied on a provision of the North Carolina Constitution of 1868 that does not appear in the present state constitution.[160]

3.2.1.7 County Non-Liability for Sheriffs and Deputy Sheriffs

Counties are not directly liable in tort for the negligence or intentional wrongdoing of sheriffs or sheriffs' deputies.[161] They do not exercise enough control over sheriffs or deputies for the doctrine of *respondeat superior* to apply.[162]

---

extend that principle to counties); Manuel v. Bd. of Comm'rs of Cumberland Cty., 98 N.C. 9, 12 (1887) (same).

158. Parks v. Town of Princeton, 217 N.C. 361, 365 (1940). *See also* Coley v. City of Statesville, 121 N.C. 301, 316 (1897) ("The [city] is liable only for failure to properly construct the prison, or to so furnish it as to afford reasonable comfort and protection from suffering and injuries to health."); Nichols v. Town of Fountain, 165 N.C. 166, 168 (1914) ("[I]n respect to jails and 'lock ups' the municipality is held only to the duty of properly constructing and furnishing the prison, and in exercising ordinary care in providing the usual necessaries for the prisoners.").

159. Shields v. Town of Durham, 116 N.C. 394, 407–08 (1895).

160. Article XI, Section 6 of the 1868 constitution mandated the enactment of legislation requiring that the "structure and superintendence" of prisons and jails "secure the health and comfort of prisons." For cases citing the provision in support of the city jail exception, see *Moffitt v. City of Asheville*, 103 N.C. 237, 256 (1885), and *Parks*, 217 N.C. at 364.

161. However, there is authority for the proposition that a county may face liability under 42 U.S.C. § 1983 when a sheriff's law enforcement practices violate an individual's federal constitutional rights. The basis for imposing liability on the county in that scenario is the sheriff's status as the county's "ultimate policymaker for . . . matters of law enforcement." Wilcoxson v. Buncombe Cty., 129 F. Supp. 3d 308, 317 (W.D.N.C. 2014). *But see* Parker v. Bladen Cty., 583 F. Supp. 2d 736, 739–40 (E.D.N.C. 2008) (county is not liable under 42 U.S.C. § 1983 for constitutional violations arising from "personnel decisions or other law enforcement policies over which the [sheriff] maintains exclusive authority").

162. See note 1, *supra*, for a discussion of *respondeat superior*.

In other words, counties are not liable for the actions of sheriffs and their deputies because, for purposes of tort law, neither sheriffs nor their deputies count as county employees. Sheriffs enjoy "substantial independence" from county government.[163] They are "directly elected, hold office for four-year terms, and are not employed by the Board of County Commissioners."[164] Moreover, state law invests each sheriff with "'the exclusive right to hire, discharge, and supervise the employees in his office.'"[165] Inasmuch as sheriffs have exclusive control over the employees in their offices, "[a] deputy is an employee of the sheriff, not the county."[166]

Sheriffs may face official capacity claims for their own torts and those of their deputies when the claims against them arise from the performance of official duties.[167] Although law enforcement activities constitute governmental functions, the sheriff's official bond waives governmental immunity to the extent of the bond, as explained more fully in Section 4.4.9, *infra*.[168]

3.2.2 Emergency Services (Governmental)

3.2.2.1 Fire Services (Governmental)

State law authorizes cities and counties to provide fire protection services.[169] Their options for providing such services include establishing their own fire departments or contracting with nonprofit incorporated fire departments or fire departments in other jurisdictions.[170]

---

163. *Parker*, 583 F. Supp. 2d at 739.

164. *Id.*

165. G.S. 153A-103(1).

166. Clark v. Burke Cty., 117 N.C. App. 85, 89 (1994). *See also* Peele v. Provident Mut. Life Ins. Co., 90 N.C. App. 447, 449 (1988) ("It is clear to the Court that plaintiff [deputy sheriff] was an employee of the sheriff and not Watauga County and its Board of Commissioners.").

167. Young v. Bailey, 368 N.C. 665, 671 (2016) ("Deputies . . . serve as the alter egos of their sheriff and, if liability results from the acts of a deputy, the sheriff is held responsible.").

168. Additionally, sheriffs can be personally liable in tort if they act maliciously, corruptly, or outside the scope of their duties. Slade v. Vernon, 110 N.C. App. 422, 428 (1993), *implied overruling on other grounds recognized in* Boyd v. Robeson Cty., 169 N.C. App. 460 (2005).

169. Sanitary districts (regional units of local government created by the state's Commission for Public Health) are also authorized to provide fire protection services). KARA A. MILLONZI, *Fire Services, in* COUNTY AND MUNICIPAL GOVERNMENT IN NORTH CAROLINA 504–08 (Frayda S. Bluestein ed., 2d ed. 2014). *See also* G.S. 153A-233 ("[c]ounty may establish, organize, equip, support, and maintain a fire department"); 160A-291 (same for cities).

170. MILLONZI, *supra* note 169, at 504. *See also* G.S. 153A-233 (county "may contract for fire-fighting or prevention services with . . . other units of local government or . . . one or more incorporated volunteer fire departments").

"The organization and operation of a fire department is a governmental, not a private or proprietary function."[171] In line with this principle, governmental immunity can block both personal injury and property damage claims premised on a city or county fire department's negligence in responding to a fire.[172] In one case, the plaintiff sued a firefighter in his official capacity for bodily injuries and property damage the plaintiff allegedly sustained when a city firetruck driven by the firefighter collided with the plaintiff's automobile at an intersection. The court ruled that governmental immunity defeated the plaintiff's negligence lawsuit because, at the time of the collision, the firefighter "was responding to a fire alarm at a high rise housing complex for the elderly."[173]

The supplying of water to fight fires also constitutes a governmental function, even when the city or county employs the same system to sell water for private consumption.[174] A city was thus not liable for failing to provide the water pressure necessary to extinguish the fire that ultimately consumed the plaintiff's home.[175]

---

171. Great Am. Ins. Co. v. Comm'r of Revenue, 257 N.C. 367, 370 (1962). The court first acknowledged the governmental nature of establishing and regulating city fire departments in *Peterson v. City of Wilmington*, 130 N.C. 76 (1902).

172. *See* Harrington v. Town of Greenville, 159 N.C. 632, 636 (1912) (town not liable for fire damage partly attributable to its failure to provide adequate water pressure and equipment necessary to suppress the fire); *Peterson*, 130 N.C. at 78 (city not liable for injuries a firefighter suffered in a fall resulting from the collapse of a hose-reel).

Cities that enter into agreements to provide fire protection outside their corporate limits also have statutory liability protections. Pursuant to G.S. 160A-293(b), no such city may be held liable "for failure or delay in answering calls for fire protection outside the corporate limits" or "for the acts or omissions of its officers or employees in rendering fire protection services outside its corporate limits." The court of appeals has interpreted this statutory language quite strictly. *See* Davis v. Messer, 119 N.C. App. 44, 53–54 (1995) (although plaintiffs lived outside the fire district, G.S. 160A-293 did not shield town from liability for the fire chief's order, issued within the corporate limits, directing firefighters to return to the fire station when they were within sight of plaintiffs' burning residence), *overruling on other grounds recognized in* Willis v. Town of Beaufort, 143 N.C. App. 106 (2001).

173. Taylor v. Ashburn, 112 N.C. App. 604, 605 (1993).

174. Howland v. City of Asheville, 174 N.C. 749, 752 (1917). *See also* Mabe v. City of Winston-Salem, 190 N.C. 486, 488 (1925) ("A city may not be sued for loss sustained by fire, where the wrongful act charged was neglect in cutting off water from a hydrant, but for which the fire might have been extinguished, or in failing to keep a reservoir in repair, whereby the supply of water became inadequate, or because the pipes were not sufficient or out of order, or because the officers and members of the fire department were negligent in the performance of their duties.").

175. *Howland*, 174 N.C. at 752. It is possible, though, that a similar case would turn out differently if the plaintiff could establish that the city charged customers for water used to fight fires. *See id.* ("[The plaintiff] was . . . served just as were other citizens of the same community, there being no extra charge made . . . for the use of water at fires, if such a payment would make any difference, which we do not decide, as it is

When a local government unit contracts with an incorporated nonprofit fire department to provide fire protection services, the department enjoys limited statutory immunity from tort claims. The scope of immunity depends on whether a department falls under G.S. 58-82-5, which limits the liability of rural fire departments, or G.S. 69-25.8, which restricts the exposure of fire protection districts.

- G.S. 58-82-5 shields a rural fire department from liability for bodily injuries or property damage allegedly resulting from the department's negligence related to (1) the suppression of a reported fire or (2) the direction of traffic or enforcement of traffic laws or ordinances at the scene of or in connection with a fire, accident, or other hazard.[176] Unlike governmental immunity, G.S. 58-82-5 does not protect rural fire departments from liability for the gross negligence, wanton conduct, or intentional wrongdoing of their firefighters.[177]
- G.S. 69-25.8 affords fire protection districts the same immunity from suit that county and city fire departments receive. Consequently, the purchase of liability insurance by a fire protection district waives tort immunity to the extent of coverage.[178] (Waiver by insurance is discussed in Chapter 4.)

---

not necessary to do so."). *See also* Peerless Indem. Ins. Co. v. City of Greensboro, No. 1:13CV1104, 2015 WL 2151898, at *6 (M.D.N.C. May 7, 2015) (unpublished) (applying the *Williams* test (see Section 2.6, *supra*) and holding that the city's allegedly negligent failure to provide water to the fire suppression line leading to sprinklers in the plaintiffs' building concerned a governmental function, in part because the city did not meter or charge for water used from the fire suppression line), *aff'd*, 628 F. App'x 202 (4th Cir. 2016) (per curiam).

176. The liability protection afforded to rural fire departments by G.S. 58-82-5 can cover negligent acts or omissions away from the scene of a fire. In *Spruill v. Lake Phelps Volunteer Fire Department*, 351 N.C. 318, 321–22 (2000), the plaintiff sued two rural fire departments over bodily injuries and property damage allegedly sustained when his car hit a sheet of ice on a rural paved road and skidded into a ditch bank. The plaintiff contended that the ice had formed from water spilled by firefighters as they filled the tanks on their fire trucks while preparing to respond to a fire approximately one-half mile away. In ruling that the departments were not liable for the plaintiff's damages, the state supreme court interpreted G.S. 58-82-5 to encompass any negligence claim against a rural fire department related to the suppression of a reported fire, regardless of whether the claim concerns acts or omissions at the scene of the fire. *Spruill*, 351 N.C. at 324. In that same opinion, the court explained that the immunity afforded to individual firefighters under G.S. 58-82-5 is more limited. The statute protects them from personal liability for negligence at the scene of a fire only. *Id.* at 322.

177. *Spruill*, 351 N.C. at 318.

178. Luhmann v. Hoenig, 358 N.C. 529, 533–34 (2004).

The courts have wrestled with how to determine whether G.S. 58-82-5 or G.S. 69-25.8 applies to a particular department. For purposes of G.S. 58-82-5, the term "rural fire department" means

> a bona fide fire department incorporated as a nonprofit corporation which under schedules filed with or approved by the Commissioner of Insurance, is classified as not less than Class "9" in accordance with rating methods, schedules, classifications, underwriting rules, bylaws, or regulations effective or applied with respect to the establishment of rates or premiums used or charged pursuant to Article 36 or Article 40 of . . . Chapter [58 of the General Statutes] and which operates fire apparatus of the value of five thousand dollars ($5,000) or more.[179]

The case law indicates, however, that a court must look to G.S. 69-25.8 when analyzing the potential liability of a rural fire department, if the department has entered into a contract with a county to provide fire protection services within a fire service district in exchange for compensation generated by an ad valorem tax levied on property located within the district.[180]

3.2.2.2 Emergency Medical Services (Governmental)

State law mandates that counties make emergency medical services (EMS) available to their citizens.[181] A county may satisfy this obligation in any of several ways, including by operating its own ambulance service, by franchising the service, or by contracting with an incorporated fire department to provide EMS.[182]

The operation of a county ambulance service constitutes a governmental function, so a plaintiff injured when a county ambulance responding to a 911 call collided with his automobile lacked a valid negligence claim against the county.[183] The fact that the county charged a user fee to defray the cost of its ambulance service did not transform the endeavor into a proprietary function.[184]

---

179. G.S. 58-82-5(a).

180. *Luhmann*, 358 N.C. at 533; Pruett v. Bingham, 238 N.C. App. 78, 82–84 (2014).

181. G.S. 143-517.

182. G.S. 153A-250; 153A-309(a). Although cities are not required to provide their residents with emergency medical services, they have the option of doing so. G.S. 153A-250.

183. McIver v. Smith, 134 N.C. App. 583, 588–90 (1999).

184. *Id.* at 587. Notwithstanding revenue from the fee, the county operated the ambulance service at a loss of nearly two million dollars per year during a ten-year period. *Id.* It is unclear whether the court would have reached a different result had the county profited from the service.

Governmental immunity also extends to discretionary decisions a county makes regarding the provision of emergency medical services. Thus, the former treasurer of a nonprofit EMS provider franchised by the county could not proceed with his lawsuit alleging that the county had fabricated embezzlement charges against him as a pretext for seizing control of the nonprofit. The complaint's allegations concerned the county's "statutory obligations to ensure its citizens [received] EMS and to regulate EMS within its jurisdiction, both of which are governmental functions[.]"[185]

When a county contracts with an incorporated fire department to provide EMS, governmental immunity extends to the department's provision of services pursuant to the contract.[186] Accordingly, an incorporated fire department was not liable for an automobile pileup allegedly caused by negligence on the part of a department employee in responding to an emergency call.[187]

3.2.2.3 911 Call Center (Governmental)

A county performs a governmental function by operating a 911 call center for the health and welfare of its citizens, "regardless of the fee charged in order to defray operating costs."[188] In the primary case on point, the court ruled that governmental immunity prevented the mother and grandmother of a deceased child from pursuing wrongful death and related tort claims against the county over the alleged negligence of 911 operators in responding to reports that the child had stopped breathing, was possibly running a fever, and may have had a seizure.[189]

3.2.2.4 Police and Fire Alarm System (Governmental)

The erection and maintenance of police and fire alarm systems are governmental functions.[190] Accordingly, the court indicated in one case that the defendant city likely could avoid tort liability for the death of an employee who fell from a telephone poll while attempting to remove a wire that was part of the city's police and fire alarm system.[191]

---

185. Fuller v. Wake Cty., ___ N.C. App. ___, ___, 802 S.E.2d 106, 115 (2017).
186. Pruett v. Bingham, 238 N.C. App. 78, 85 (2014).
187. *Id.*
188. Wright v. Gaston Cty., 205 N.C. App. 600, 606 (2010).
189. *Id.* at 608.
190. Cathey v. City of Charlotte, 197 N.C. 309, 312 (1929).
191. *Id.* at 313.

3.3 Land Use Regulation and Affordable Housing (Governmental)

3.3.1 Code Enforcement (Governmental)

"In North Carolina all cities and counties are required by state law to adopt and enforce the North Carolina State Building Code."[192] Many city and county inspection departments also enforce local minimum housing codes, zoning codes, and nuisance codes.

Appellate court decisions uniformly treat code enforcement by local government inspectors as a governmental function to which governmental immunity attaches.[193] In one case, property owners discovered major structural defects in their new house following the county inspection department's issuance of a certificate of occupancy declaring that all known building code violations had been corrected. The owners sued the county alleging negligent inspection and misrepresentation by building inspectors, but the court of appeals held that governmental immunity barred their claims.[194] In another case, the owners of mobile homes demolished by a city for minimum housing code violations sued the city alleging tort claims for conversion, trespass to chattels, and trespass.[195] The court of appeals affirmed the trial court's order rejecting the claims on governmental immunity grounds.[196]

In yet another case, the county operated an Appearance and Code Enforcement (ACE) Program under which it removed junk items such as dilapidated mobile homes, junked automobiles, and abandoned structures from citizens' properties upon request and free of charge. After county employees mistakenly demolished barns on the plaintiffs' properties, the plaintiffs filed suit against the county alleging negligence, unjust enrichment, and conversion. Observing that the goal of the ACE Program was to "improve the [county's] appearance . . . , protect and maintain property values and eliminate any potential public health and/or environmental nuisances[,]"

---

192. David W. Owens, Land Use Law in North Carolina 55 (2d ed. 2011) (citing G.S. 153A-351 and 160A-411).

193. The state supreme court has expressly described zoning ordinance enforcement as a governmental activity. City of Raleigh v. Fisher, 232 N.C. 629, 635 (1950) ("In enacting and enforcing zoning regulations, a municipality acts as a governmental agency and exercises the police power of the State.").

194. Bullard v. Wake Cty., 221 N.C. App. 522, 535, *discretionary review denied*, 336 N.C. 409 (2012).

195. "In general, chattels are any specie of tangible property, distinguished from real property or land because chattels are movable property and land is not." Daye & Morris, *supra* note 1, § 7.20, at 73–74. The law in North Carolina treats mobile homes as personal property rather than as improvements to real property. Patterson v. City of Gastonia, 220 N.C. App. 233, 248 (2012).

196. *Patterson*, 220 N.C. App. at 248.

the court categorized the county's conduct of the program as a governmental function for immunity purposes.[197]

3.3.2 Public Housing for Low/Moderate-Income Tenants (Governmental)

The state's Housing Authorities Law (HAL) authorizes cities with populations greater than five hundred and counties to form housing authorities for the purpose of making housing available to tenants of low and moderate incomes.[198] In providing such housing, a housing authority performs a governmental function.[199] Although the authority may charge rent to low- and moderate-income tenants, doing so does not transform its activities into a proprietary endeavor.[200] In reaching this conclusion, the North Carolina Supreme Court noted that the HAL requires housing authorities to keep rentals for low- and moderate-income tenants "within the financial reach of such persons."[201] The court further observed that, when federal subsidies were excluded from the calculation, the defendant housing authority had operated at a loss.

3.3.3 Urban Development/Downtown Revitalization (Governmental)

Urban blight is a significant problem in many of North Carolina's cities. The Urban Redevelopment Law (URL) authorizes cities to undertake redevelopment projects in blighted areas. The Municipal Service District Act of 1973 (MSDA) likewise allows cities to establish service districts that carry out downtown revitalization projects.[202]

In a case decided after *Estate of Williams v. Pasquotank County Parks & Recreation Department*,[203] the North Carolina Supreme Court ruled that a city had acted governmentally in leasing a building to a nonprofit arts group

---

197. Estate of Hewett v. Cty. of Brunswick, 199 N.C. App. 564, 571 (2009).

198. C. TYLER MULLIGAN, *Community Development and Affordable Housing, in* COUNTY AND MUNICIPAL GOVERNMENT IN NORTH CAROLINA 471 (Frayda S. Bluestein ed., 2d ed. 2014). The Housing Authorities Law is contained in Article I of Chapter 157 of the General Statutes.

199. Evans v. Hous. Auth. of City of Raleigh, 359 N.C. 50, 55 (2004). In an older case involving a housing project not created or operated under the HAL, the state supreme court held that the defendant city's management of the project constituted a proprietary activity, largely because the project generated "substantial financial returns" for the city. Carter v. City of Greensboro, 249 N.C. 328, 333 (1959).

200. *Evans*, 359 N.C. at 55.

201. *Id.* (quoting G.S. 157-29(b)(2)). The HAL also prohibits a housing authority from constructing or operating housing projects so as to provide revenue for other city activities. G.S. 157-29(a).

202. *See generally* G.S. 160A-500, -526 (Urban Redevelopment Law); 160A-535, -544 (Municipal Service District Act of 1973).

203. 366 N.C. 195 (2012).

as part of a downtown redevelopment and revitalization initiative.[204] The plaintiff brought the lawsuit seeking damages for injuries allegedly sustained in a fall down unsafe steps located at the building's rear exit.

The court described certain provisions in the URL and MSDA as "statutory indications that an urban redevelopment project undertaken in accordance with these statutes and for the purpose of 'promot[ing] the health, safety, and welfare of the inhabitants' of the State of North Carolina is a governmental function[.]"[205] Nonetheless, because neither law expressly exempts all redevelopment and downtown revitalization projects from suit, the court examined the particular facts of the case in light of the additional factors that *Williams* identifies as relevant to governmental/proprietary determinations. It classified the lease as governmental in nature based on evidence that (1) the lease was a valid urban redevelopment or revitalization activity, (2) the city had not sought to make a profit, and (3) the fees charged by the city were not substantial and did not cover the city's operating costs.

The court stressed that its ruling "should not be construed as holding that every urban redevelopment activity is a governmental function or even that every lease of historic property to a nonprofit arts group for the purpose of promoting the arts is a governmental function."[206] It left open the possibility of different outcomes in cases where redevelopment projects are "more commercial in nature or less geared towards remedying blighted areas and promoting the public interest[.]"[207]

---

204. Meinck v. City of Gastonia, No. 130PA17, 2018 WL 5310160 (N.C. Oct. 26, 2018). The lease agreement obliged the city to maintain the building's exterior and required the nonprofit to use the building solely for an art gallery, artists' studios, and a gift shop. The agreement guaranteed the city 90 percent of all rents paid by subtenants and 15 percent of the gross receipts on all sales or commissions occurring on the property. *Id.*, at *1–2.

205. *Id.*, at *9. The court pointed specifically to the URL's declaration that (1) the acquisition and re-planning of blighted areas amounts to a public use for which public money may be spent and (2) the social and economic problems caused by blight cannot be remedied by private enterprise alone. *Id.* (citing G.S. 160A-501). The court also noted that both the URL and the MSDA assert that downtown revitalization is in the public interest. *Id.* (citing G.S. 160A-502, -536).

206. *Id.*, at *11.

207. *Id.*

3.4 Public Enterprises (Mix of Governmental and Proprietary)

As used in this section, the term *public enterprise* refers to a local government activity of a commercial nature that the private sector could undertake.[208] In the early 1970s, as part of its rewriting and recodification of the primary statutes governing cities and counties, the General Assembly enacted new laws on city and county public enterprises.[209] Although water and sewer utilities are the most common public enterprises, cities and counties also have authority to provide water supply and distribution systems, sewage collection and treatment systems, solid waste collection and disposal systems, airports, public transportation, off-street parking, and stormwater management programs and drainage systems.[210] Cities may also operate public enterprises for electric power generation and distribution, cable television, and gas production and distribution.[211]

"The majority of public enterprises are funded with user charges and are self-supporting (or predominately self-supporting)."[212] The fact that so many public enterprises charge for services that the private sector could furnish likely accounts for the judiciary's tendency to regard public enterprises as proprietary functions in governmental immunity cases.[213] As the discussion below makes clear, however, certain aspects of some public enterprises remain governmental under current case law.

3.4.1 Water Supply and Distribution (Proprietary with Exception)

There is some confusion in the case law over whether the *construction* of a water system that a unit will use to sell water constitutes a governmental function.[214] Unquestionably, though, in the *operation* of such a system, a unit

---

208. Kara A. Millonzi, *Public Enterprises, in* County and Municipal Government in North Carolina 527 (Frayda S. Bluestein ed., 2d ed. 2014).

209. S.L. 1973, Ch. 822, § 1; S.L. 1971, Ch. 698, § 1.

210. G.S. 153A-274, -275; 160A-311, -312.

211. G.S. 160A-311, -312.

212. Millonzi, *supra* note 201, at 527.

213. *See* Pulliam v. City of Greensboro, 103 N.C. App. 748, 753–54 (1991) (city's operation of a sewer system should be viewed as a proprietary function based on (1) "accepted practice in North Carolina for cities and counties to compete with private enterprises," (2) precedents holding that cities act proprietarily in setting rates for public enterprise services, and (3) the "modern tendency to restrict the application of governmental immunity").

214. In *McKinney v. City of High Point*, 237 N.C. 66, 75 (1953), the court held that the city carried out a governmental function in locating and erecting a water tank "for the purposes of public health, sanitation, fire protection and selling water for gain to its inhabitants and businesses within the city." Several years later, in *Bowling v. City of Oxford*, 267 N.C. 552 (1966), the court held that a city may be liable for damage proximately caused by its negligent construction or maintenance of a dam used to supply

acts "in its proprietary or corporate capacity and is liable for injury or damage resulting from such operation to the same extent and upon the same basis as a privately owned water company would be."[215]

A city's water system includes any dam the city uses to create a reservoir for that system. Consequently, plaintiffs could hold a city liable for damage done to their farm by a torrent of water that escaped from a broken city dam, but only if negligence by the city in the dam's construction or maintenance proximately caused the dam's collapse.[216]

Of course, the absence of governmental immunity as a defense does not relieve plaintiffs of their obligation to prove the elements of negligence claims, including foreseeability. In one case, for example, water flowing from a broken water main formed ice on the street in front of the plaintiff's house.[217] The plaintiff slipped on the ice, fracturing her right leg. Evidence in the plaintiff's negligence lawsuit against the city indicated that unexpected bad weather the night before the plaintiff's fall had frozen the water and concealed the ice under a thin layer of snow. Although a supervisor from the city's water department had observed the leak one day before the plaintiff's fall, the department did not repair the water main until three days later because the leak was not a big one. In ruling that the plaintiff had failed to show negligence, the court explained that, "[s]o long as the flow of water continued as it . . . was [when the superintendent visited the plaintiff's street], it could not be reasonably foreseen that [the flow] would cause injury to a person using the street in the normal manner."[218]

In a more recent case, the plaintiffs alleged that an employee of the defendant town had negligently restored the water at a residence on property they had recently purchased.[219] The plaintiffs further alleged that the prior owner's real estate agent had made the request to reconnect the water without their knowledge and consent and that the town employee had received no answer upon knocking at the door of the residence. Thanks to an open bathroom spigot, the bathtub overflowed, flooding the house for several days and doing

---

water for the city's fee-based water system. The court also said that the same rules apply to the construction or maintenance of the mains and pipes by which the city distributes water. *Id.* at 557–58.

215. Mosseller v. City of Asheville, 267 N.C. 104, 107 (1966), *citing* Faw v. N. Wilkesboro, 253 N.C. 406 (1960); Candler v. Asheville, 247 N.C. 398 (1958); Woodie v. N. Wilkesboro, 159 N.C. 353 (1912). *See also* Fussell v. N.C. Farm Bureau Mut. Ins. Co., Inc., 364 N.C. 222, 225 (2010) ("We have long held that a municipal corporation selling water for private consumption is acting in a proprietary capacity and can be held liable for negligence just like a privately owned water company.").

216. *Bowling*, 267 N.C. at 558.

217. *Mosseller*, 267 N.C. at 105–06.

218. *Id.* at 110.

219. *Fussell*, 364 N.C. at 223–24.

substantial damage. In holding that the plaintiffs had successfully asserted a negligence claim against the town, the state supreme court remarked that the employee's alleged conduct "creat[ed] a reasonably foreseeable risk of flooding and resulting damage to the property[.]"[220]

Although a city's operation of a fee-based water system qualifies as a proprietary function in most respects, the case law recognizes at least one important exception. The supplying of water to fight fires constitutes a governmental function, even when the city uses the same system to sell water for private consumption.[221] Thus, a city was not liable for its allegedly negligent failure to provide the water pressure necessary to extinguish the fire that ultimately consumed the plaintiff's home.[222] The court emphasized that the city did not charge customers for the water used to fight fires.[223]

3.4.2 Sewage Collection and Treatment (Governmental and Proprietary Phases)

In *McCombs v. City of Asheville*, the plaintiff brought a wrongful death claim against the defendant city for the death of a six-year-old boy who, according to the complaint, was killed when a ditch dug by city workers for a new sewer line collapsed on him.[224] In upholding the trial court's order throwing out the lawsuit, the court of appeals explained that "the construction of a sewerage system is a governmental function[.]"[225] The court further remarked that the city's sale of sewer service to its citizens did not, by itself, remove the construction project from the governmental function category.[226]

---

220. *Id.* at 228.

221. Howland v. City of Asheville, 174 N.C. 749, 752 (1917). *See also* Mabe v. City of Winston-Salem, 190 N.C. 486, 488 (1925) ("A city may not be sued for loss sustained by fire, where the wrongful act charged was neglect in cutting off water from a hydrant, but for which the fire might have been extinguished, or in failing to keep a reservoir in repair, whereby the supply of water became inadequate, or because the pipes were not sufficient or out of order, or because the officers and members of the fire department were negligent in the performance of their duties.").

222. *Howland*, 174 N.C. at 752.

223. *See id.* ("[The plaintiff] was . . . served just as were other citizens of the same community, there being no extra charge made . . . for the use of water at fires, if such a payment would make any difference, which we do not decide, as it is not necessary to do so."). *See also* Peerless Indem. Ins. Co. v. City of Greensboro, No. 1:13CV1104, 2015 WL 2151898, at *6 (M.D.N.C. May 7, 2015) (unpublished) (applying the *Williams* test (see Section 2.6, *supra*) and holding that the city's allegedly negligent failure to provide water to the fire suppression line leading to sprinklers in the plaintiffs' building concerned a governmental function, in part because the city did not meter or charge for water used from the fire suppression line), *aff'd*, 628 F. App'x 202 (2016) (per curiam).

224. 6 N.C. App. 234, 240 (1969).

225. *Id.*

226. *Id.* at 240–41.

Whether the operation of a public sewer system amounts to a governmental function appears to depend on whether it is fee-based. By operating a free public sewer system, a unit acts governmentally.[227] The state supreme court has therefore held that governmental immunity bars personal injury claims arising from the activity.[228] The operation of a sewer system becomes proprietary when the unit sets fees and charges for the service, though not every relevant case expressly supports this position.[229] Moreover, as discussed in Section 9.1, *infra*, even when a unit does not charge for sewer service, governmental immunity will not shield the unit from a nuisance claim for property damage caused by its operation of such a system.[230]

Many of the cases involving the operation or maintenance of fee-based sewer systems concern property damage resulting from the overflow or backup of such systems. In one case, the plaintiffs sued the defendant city for negligence, nuisance, and trespass, alleging that an overflow from a manhole had caused thirty-nine inches of untreated sewage to enter their basement.[231] They further alleged that the city had failed to take any remedial action when informed of the problem. Additionally, the city had ignored prior complaints about other sewage discharges onto the plaintiffs' property. The court held that governmental immunity did not foreclose the plaintiffs' tort claims because, in operating and maintaining the sewer system, the city had undertaken a proprietary function.

---

227. Metz v. City of Asheville, 150 N.C. 748, 752 (1909).

228. *Id.* at 749 (holding that plaintiff should not prevail against the city on a wrongful death claim arising from the city's operation of its free public sewer system).

229. Harrison v. City of Sanford, 177 N.C. App. 116, 121 (2006) ("The law is clear in holding that the operation and maintenance of a sewer system is a proprietary function where the municipality sets rates and charges fees for the maintenance of sewer lines."). *See also* Bostic Packaging, Inc. v. City of Monroe, 149 N.C. App. 825, 829 (2002) ("[T]he *Pulliam* Court determined that the operation of the defendant[] [city's] sewer system, for which it charged rates, was a proprietary function . . . [W]e hold that defendant [city] is not immune from tort liability in the operation . . . of its sewer system . . . ."); Pulliam v. City of Greensboro, 103 N.C. App. 748, 754 (1991) ("[D]efendant city is not immune from tort liability in the operation of its sewer system . . . .").

In *Roach v. City of Lenoir*, 44 N.C. App. 608, 610 (1980), the court held that the defendant city had performed a "governmental function in the maintenance of a sewer system within its municipal jurisdiction" and so was not liable "for any damage arising out of the governmental activity[.]" Interestingly, the court's opinion in *Roach* devotes no attention to whether the city charged for sewer service.

230. The *Metz* case itself declares that plaintiffs may recover for property damage caused by the operation of free public sewer systems because, "[w]here, in the discharge of its governmental functions and police powers, the officers of a municipality invade property rights, the doctrine of respondeat superior applies, and the corporation is liable for their acts." *Metz*, 150 N.C. at 751.

231. *Harrison*, 177 N.C. App. at 117–18. The manhole was located on the plaintiffs' property but maintained by the city.

A recent case introduces a wrinkle into the law concerning governmental immunity and city sewer systems. In *Town of Sandy Creek v. East Coast Contracting, Inc.*, the plaintiff town sued a contractor over damage to its streets allegedly resulting from the contractor's construction of a sewer system for a nearby city.[232] The contractor brought the city into the lawsuit, essentially alleging that the city had negligently failed to provide adequate contract documents and had improperly certified the contractor's work as conforming to contract documents. Although *McCombs* labels the construction of sewer systems a governmental function, the court reasoned that the precise activity to be classified as either governmental or proprietary in *Sandy Creek* was the city's business relationship with the contractor. Because local governments act proprietarily when they contract with engineering or construction companies, the city could not invoke governmental immunity to prevent the contractor from bringing it into the lawsuit.[233] Chapter 7 considers the broader implications of *Sandy Creek*, but, at a minimum, the decision eliminates governmental immunity as a defense to contract-related tort claims brought against a city by a contractor it has hired to construct a sewer system.

3.4.3 Solid Waste Collection and Disposal (Governmental with Exception)

The collection of garbage by a unit within its territorial limits constitutes a governmental function.[234] Similarly, a unit undertakes a governmental function by operating a landfill for garbage collected within its territorial limits.[235] Thus, in one early case, the court held that the defendant city was not liable for injuries allegedly inflicted when a speeding garbage truck under the control of an employee in the city's sanitation department struck the plaintiff.[236]

---

232. 226 N.C. App. 576 (2013).

233. *Id.* at 582.

234. Koontz v. City of Winston-Salem, 280 N.C. 513, 520 (1972). *See also* Stephenson v. City of Raleigh, 232 N.C. 42, 46 (1950) (city acted governmentally in using its garbage truck to collect and remove prunings from shrubbery and trees from the homes of city residents); Edwards v. Akion, 52 N.C. App. 688, 691 (1981) ("Plaintiff has conceded . . . that the refuse collection service provided by the City is a governmental function.").

235. *Koontz*, 280 N.C. at 521. *See also* Scales v. City of Winston-Salem, 189 N.C. 469, 471 (1925) (city's construction of an incinerator used to burn garbage was a governmental function).

236. James v. City of Charlotte, 183 N.C. 630, 631 (1922). *See also* Reid v. Town of Madison, 137 N.C. App. 168, 170 (2000) (governmental immunity defeated the plaintiffs' negligence claims arising from an automobile accident involving a town garbage truck).

Although the city charged a fee to collect garbage, the court observed that fee-generated revenue merely covered the actual cost of removal.[237]

Governmental immunity can be lost if a unit contracts to pick up garbage outside its boundaries or to dispose of garbage collected outside its boundaries.[238] In *Koontz v. City of Winston-Salem*, the defendant city faced wrongful death and negligence claims arising from an explosion allegedly resulting from the buildup of methane gas coming from the city's landfill.[239] In classifying the city's operation of the landfill as proprietary, the court highlighted several factors.

- The city had entered a contract with Forsyth County under which licensed private contractors collected garbage outside the city limits and transported it to the landfill.
- By entering the contract, the city avoided having to exercise its statutory authority to remove, abate, or remedy conditions dangerous or prejudicial to public health within one mile of the city limits.[240] Of course, it also thereby avoided the expense of such actions.
- Although the city lost money on the landfill, it received enough revenue from the contract in the fiscal year immediately preceding the explosion to cover 9.39 percent of the cost of landfill operations during that year.[241] In making this last point, the court cited *Glenn v. City of Raleigh*,[242] which classified the operation of a city park as proprietary because park revenue covered 11.7 percent of the cost of park maintenance.[243]

In sum, then, a unit acts governmentally in collecting or disposing of solid waste. The imposition of a fee does not alter the governmental character of the activity, at least when fee revenue merely covers the cost of collection or disposal. A unit risks losing the protection of governmental immunity if it

---

237. *James*, 183 N.C. at 633.

238. *See* Smith v. City of Winston-Salem, 247 N.C. 349, 355 (1957) (cited in *Koontz*, 280 N.C. at 529) (city acted in proprietary capacity by providing sewer service to persons residing outside the city limits).

239. 280 N.C. at 514–17.

240. The source of this authority was G.S. 160-234, the forerunner of G.S. 160A-193.

241. Revenue from the contract apparently did not subsidize the solid waste services provided to city residents. The county paid the city one dollar per ton of garbage delivered to the landfill. *Koontz*, 280 N.C. at 516. The cost to the city of operating the landfill was approximately one dollar per ton of waste. *Id.* In other words, the payments the city received under the contract merely covered the cost of accepting the county's garbage.

242. 246 N.C. 469 (1957).

243. *See Koontz*, 280 N.C. at 529 (noting that "[i]n *Glenn*, as [in *Koontz*], the city received income which was not actual profit" and comparing the revenue-to-cost figures in both cases).

enters into a contract to collect or accept waste from outside its boundaries. The court's reliance on multiple factors in *Koontz*, however, suggests that such a contract will not transform the unit's collection or disposal of solid waste into a proprietary function unless there is evidence of an accompanying and significant financial benefit.

3.4.4 Airports (Proprietary)

As explained in Section 2.6.2.1, *supra*, the operation of a city airport is a proprietary function. The state supreme court has so held notwithstanding G.S. 63-50, which describes the construction, maintenance, and operation of municipal airports as "governmental and municipal functions exercised for a public purpose and matters of public necessity."

3.4.5 Stormwater Drainage (Proprietary with Exception)

The court of appeals has rejected arguments that the maintenance of city storm drains constitutes a governmental function.[244] For this reason, governmental immunity has not been a defense to lawsuits for property damage allegedly caused by flooding resulting from negligently maintained city drains.[245] Still, a conflict exists in the case law over whether governmental immunity can apply to a claim for personal injury or wrongful death arising from a city's negligence in maintaining its storm drainage system.[246] A recent case on point holds that a city is not immune to such a claim, a result in keeping with the appellate court's apparent classification of storm drain maintenance as a proprietary activity.[247]

A city does act governmentally by attempting to unclog a private storm drain.[248] (For liability purposes, a private storm drain is one the city did not

---

244. Kizer v. City of Raleigh, 121 N.C. App. 526, 528 (1996) ("[W]e hold that storm drain maintenance does not enjoy governmental immunity.") The court of appeals based this conclusion primarily on earlier cases in which, without expressly considering the issue of governmental immunity, the supreme court held cities or towns liable for negligent storm drain maintenance. *Id.* at 527–28 (citing Milner Hotels, Inc. v. Raleigh, 268 N.C. 535 (1966), *modified on reh'g*, 271 N.C. 224 (1967); Gore v. Wilmington, 194 N.C. 450 (1927); Pennington v. Tarboro, 184 N.C. 71 (1922); Williams v. Greenville, 130 N.C. 93 (1902)).

245. *Kizer*, 121 N.C. App. at 528; Bell v. City of New Bern, 233 N.C. App. 785 (2014) (unpublished).

246. *Compare* Jennings v. City of Fayetteville, 198 N.C. App. 698, 701 (2009) (governmental immunity did not defeat a wrongful death lawsuit alleging that decedent had drowned upon falling into a ditch and becoming stuck in a drainage pipe negligently maintained by the city), *with* Stone v. City of Fayetteville, 3 N.C. App. 261, 264 (1968) (interpreting state supreme court precedent to hold that governmental immunity will bar a claim against a city for personal injury or death arising from the city's negligent maintenance of a drainage ditch).

247. *Jennings*, 198 N.C. App. at 701.

248. Biggers v. John Hancock Mut. Life Ins. Co., 127 N.C. App. 199, 202 (1997).

construct and that it has neither adopted into its storm drainage system nor brought under its control and management.[249]) Accordingly, immunity barred a plaintiff's claim for flood damage allegedly caused by the city fire department's negligent response to a request that the department unclog drains in the parking area of an apartment complex.[250]

3.4.6 Electric Systems (Proprietary with Exception)

A city performs a proprietary function by selling electricity.[251] The North Carolina Supreme Court has therefore rejected governmental immunity as a defense in lawsuits filed over the deaths of individuals electrocuted by downed electric wires.[252]

Citing the proprietary nature of selling electricity, the court has further determined that a city may not refuse to supply electricity to inhabitants as a means of forcing them to comply with police power regulations.[253] In particular, the court ruled that a city could not withhold electric service merely to keep the plaintiff from placing a new tenant in a house the city had declared unfit for human habitation.[254]

The transmission of electricity on lines used solely for street lighting purposes qualifies as a governmental function,[255] even if the current comes from a power plant that also supplies electricity to paying customers.[256] Accordingly, a city was not liable for the death of a man electrocuted by a broken wire that was part of its street-lighting system.[257]

---

249. *Id.* at 202 (citing *Milner Hotels*).

250. *Id.*

251. Rice v. City of Lumberton, 235 N.C. 227, 235 (1952); Terrell v. City of Washington, 158 N.C. 282, 288 (1912); Fisher v. City of New Bern, 140 N.C. 506, 511–12 (1906).

252. *Rice*, 235 N.C. at 235; *Terrell*, 158 N.C. at 288; *Fisher*, 140 N.C. at 511–12.

253. Dale v. City of Morganton, 270 N.C. 567, 573 (1967).

254. *Id.* The court remarked, however, that the dangerous condition of the house's wiring justified the city's decision not to furnish electricity. *Id.*

255. Steelman v. City of New Bern, 279 N.C. 589, 591 (1971); Baker v. City of Lumberton, 239 N.C. 401, 408 (1953).

256. Beach v. Town of Tarboro, 225 N.C. 26, 27–28 (1945) (town employee performed governmental function by repairing streetlights powered by the same plant used to generate electricity sold to customers).

257. *Baker*, 239 N.C. at 408.

3.5 Human Services and Related County Functions (Governmental)

3.5.1 Public Health (Governmental)

"Each county in North Carolina is required by law to provide public health services."[258] A majority of counties satisfy this obligation by operating county health departments, though other organizational options are available.[259] The many public health services that counties provide include family planning assistance and processing septic tank permits. It is also common for counties to house their animal control programs in county health departments.[260]

3.5.1.1 Prescribing and Dispensing Contraceptives (Governmental)

In providing contraceptives at no cost through a family planning clinic, a county health department performs a governmental function.[261] Accordingly, a county was not liable for serious medical complications the plaintiff suffered after a physician in the county's family planning clinic inserted an intrauterine device in the plaintiff when she was sixteen years old. In reaching this outcome, the court observed that the clinic's free services benefitted the public by helping "to prevent unwanted pregnancies and provid[ing] proper health care to children, born and unborn, and their parents."[262] The court therefore classified those services as governmental for immunity purposes. It even suggested that the outcome would have been the same if the clinic had charged fees to cover the cost of the services provided.[263]

---

258. JILL D. MOORE, *Public Health, in* COUNTY AND MUNICIPAL GOVERNMENT IN NORTH CAROLINA 644 (Frayda S. Bluestein ed., 2d ed. 2014) (citing G.S. 130A-34).

259. *Id.* at 645, Fig. 38.2. In particular, a county may opt to fulfill its public health obligations through participation in a multi-county district health department, a public health authority, a consolidated human services agency, or by contracting with the state. *Id.* at 644.

260. AIMEE N. WALL, *Animal Control, in* COUNTY AND MUNICIPAL GOVERNMENT IN NORTH CAROLINA 569 (Frayda S. Bluestein ed., 2d ed. 2014) ("County animal control programs are often housed in county health departments because health directors have several statutorily mandated duties related to rabies control.").

261. Casey v. Wake Cty., 45 N.C. App. 522 (1980).

262. *Id.* at 524.

263. The court also attempted to explain why the outcome in *Casey* should not be seen as inconsistent with *Sides v. Cabarrus Memorial Hospital, Inc.*, 287 N.C. 14 (1975), wherein it had earlier held that the operation of a county hospital is a proprietary function. The court remarked that, whereas state law permits but does not require counties to operate hospitals, G.S. 130-13(a) required each county to have a health department. As noted in Section 2.6.2, *supra*, the courts tend to classify local government activities mandated by the legislature as governmental functions.

3.5.1.2 Septic System Permitting (Governmental)

A county health department's approval or denial of a septic tank permit is a governmental function, regardless of whether a fee is charged.[264] In one case, a married couple sued the county for negligent misrepresentation, alleging that an environmental health specialist from the county health department had incorrectly informed them that their application to add a second septic system to their property would be approved. The health department later denied the permit request, but not before the plaintiffs—who wished to subdivide their lot—had commenced the approval process with the county planning department, constructed a road, and bought a mobile home to place on their property. Nonetheless, because the denial or approval of a septic permit constitutes a governmental function, the court of appeals ruled that governmental immunity barred the plaintiffs' negligent misrepresentation claim.[265]

3.5.1.3 Animal Control (Governmental)

Counties act in a governmental capacity when they quarantine animals due to possible rabies exposure.[266] For this reason, governmental immunity barred negligence claims by plaintiffs against a county over the local board of health's decision to quarantine the plaintiffs' dog after it attacked a raccoon.[267]

3.5.2 Social Services (Governmental)

In responding to claims of child neglect or abuse as required by law, county departments of social services carry out governmental functions.[268] In one case, for example, the plaintiff sued the county for negligently training and supervising social workers involved in investigating unfounded allegations that the plaintiff had sexually abused his minor son.[269] According to the complaint, the abuse allegations led to criminal charges against the plaintiff,

---

264. Tabor v. Cty. of Orange, 156 N.C. App. 88, 91 (2003).

265. *Id.* Likewise, governmental immunity defeated the plaintiffs' negligent misrepresentation claims against the county health department, the county planning department, and the specialist in his official capacity.

266. Kitchin *ex rel.* Kitchin v. Halifax Cty., 192 N.C. App. 559 (2008).

267. *Id.* at 567.

268. Other functions assigned by law to the county social services director and executed with the aid of employees in the county department of social services include arranging and supervising the placement of children in foster care; investigating adoption cases and supervising adoptive placements; receiving and responding to reports of abuse, neglect, or exploitation of disabled adults; supervising adult care homes for aged or disabled persons; and serving as guardian for individuals adjudicated incompetent when appointed by the clerk of superior court to do so. AIMEE N. WALL, *Social Services,* *in* COUNTY AND MUNICIPAL GOVERNMENT IN NORTH CAROLINA 676 (Frayda S. Bluestein ed., 2d ed. 2014). Beyond doubt, these other functions also constitute governmental functions for purposes of governmental immunity.

269. Hare v. Butler, 99 N.C. App. 693 (1990).

charges ultimately dismissed for lack of evidence. In ruling that governmental immunity defeated the plaintiff's negligence claim against the county, the court said that "[i]nvestigations by a social service agency of allegations of child sexual abuse are in the nature of governmental functions."[270]

In another case, the plaintiff sued social workers in their official capacities over the death of her minor son.[271] The complaint alleged that the child had died in an automobile accident with his father, who was driving drunk at the time. It further asserted that the defendants had negligently failed to investigate abuse and neglect claims and to remove the child from the father's custody. The court held that the plaintiff could not proceed against the defendants because "[s]ervices provided by local Departments of Social Services are governmental functions to which governmental immunity applies."[272]

3.5.3 Mental Health Services (Governmental)

"Every county must provide mental health, developmental disabilities, and substance abuse . . . services through an area authority."[273] The courts have treated area authority activities as governmental functions. In one case, the plaintiff filed an official capacity lawsuit against an area authority employee over the death of a young woman who fatally burned herself by setting herself on fire two days after police transported her to the emergency room for treatment of a self-inflicted abdominal wound.[274] Although the woman's complaints indicated paranoia and disorientation, the doctor released her after calling the defendant, the woman's mental health caseworker. The court of appeals affirmed the trial court's order dismissing the lawsuit on governmental immunity grounds.[275]

The plaintiff in another case alleged negligence and slander claims based on an area authority's decision to revoke his provider status.[276] The area authority took the disputed action after an investigation by the county's department of social services substantiated a claim that the plaintiff had struck a disabled client in his care. Expressly assuming that the area authority's action was governmental in nature, the court of appeals turned to the plaintiff's contention that the area authority's immunity from tort claims had been waived by the county's purchase of liability insurance. The court noted that,

---

270. *Id.* at 699.

271. Whitaker v. Clark, 109 N.C. App. 379 (1993).

272. *Id.* at 381.

273. MARK F. BOTTS, *Mental Health Services, in* COUNTY AND MUNICIPAL GOVERNMENT IN NORTH CAROLINA 698 (Frayda S. Bluestein ed., 2d ed. 2014) (citing G.S. 122C-115(a)). "Today, North Carolina is served by nine multi-county area authorities . . . ." *Id.*

274. Warren v. Guilford Cty., 129 N.C. App. 836 (1998).

275. *Id.* at 838–39.

276. Clancy v. Onslow Cty., 151 N.C. App. 269 (2002).

whereas G.S. 153A-435 allows counties to waive their tort liability through a purchase of liability insurance, area authorities have independent statutory authority to waive their tort immunity under G.S. 122C-152. (Chapter 4 examines these statutes in more detail.) Given that separate statutes control immunity waivers by counties and area authorities, the court concluded that the county's purchase of liability insurance was "insufficient to constitute a waiver of immunity" by the area authority.[277]

3.5.4 Register of Deeds (Governmental)

"Registers of deeds are major custodians of county records," including real estate records (deeds, deeds of trust and mortgages, maps, and plats), marriage records, and birth and death certificates.[278] "[T]he operation and maintenance of a register of deeds office in a county courthouse is clearly a governmental function for which the county enjoys immunity from suit for negligence."[279] Thus, governmental immunity shielded a county from liability for the death of a woman who was fatally injured in a fall down a steep stairway in the register of deeds office, notwithstanding the plaintiff's allegations that the register was responsible for the removal of any barrier at the head of the stairway and for the placement of official records there.[280]

3.6 Other Local Government Activities

3.6.1 Alcoholic Beverage Control (Proprietary?)

In North Carolina, liquor is sold through alcoholic beverage control (ABC) stores operated by local ABC boards whose members are appointed by counties or cities following voter approval of the stores.[281] ABC stores provide significant revenue to local governments.[282]

While it may seem obvious that ABC stores undertake proprietary functions, the North Carolina Supreme Court declined an opportunity to say whether the operation of an ABC store constitutes a proprietary activity.[283] The court did conclude, though, that governmental immunity was no defense to allegations that the local ABC board had negligently damaged the plaintiff's

---

277. *Id.* at 274.

278. CHARLES SZYPSZAK, *Registers of Deeds, in* COUNTY AND MUNICIPAL GOVERNMENT IN NORTH CAROLINA 745 (Frayda S. Bluestein ed., 2d ed. 2014).

279. Robinson v. Nash Cty., 43 N.C. App. 33, 36 (1979).

280. *Id.*

281. MICHAEL CROWELL, *Alcoholic Beverage Control, in* COUNTY AND MUNICIPAL GOVERNMENT IN NORTH CAROLINA 619 (Frayda S. Bluestein ed., 2d ed. 2014).

282. *Id.*

283. Waters v. Biesecker, 309 N.C. 165, 166 (1983) ("The holding by the Court of Appeals that the operation of an ABC store is a proprietary function was not necessary for the resolution of the appeal; it is entirely obiter dictum and not approved by this Court . . . . We expressly refrain from ruling upon this interesting issue.").

property by failing to notify the plaintiff of an excavation made during the construction of an ABC store on an adjoining lot.[284] The excavation deprived the plaintiff's building of lateral support, in consequence of which "a crack in a plate glass window in [the plaintiff's] building appeared, a crack in the masonry wall widened, waterlines under the building separated, and the pillars supporting a back corner of the building shifted or moved."[285] In ruling for the plaintiff, the court seems to have based the outcome chiefly on a much earlier case holding a city liable for the collapse of walls caused by the city's negligence in lowering the grade of a nearby street.[286]

3.6.2 Arena or Coliseum (Proprietary)

A city or county engages in a proprietary function by operating an arena or coliseum, or by leasing such a facility to an event promoter, as means of producing revenue for the local government unit.[287] The plaintiff in one case alleged that a group of boys playing in a corridor at the city coliseum had fractured her ankle by knocking a hockey puck into it as she headed for the restroom during a hockey game. She further alleged that the city had prior notice of such play by young people inside the coliseum and had not taken reasonable steps to stop it. Evidence produced at trial showed that the city had leased part of the coliseum for hockey games, though it had retained control of the corridors and other spaces used for concessions, and that the lease agreement guaranteed the city a share of box office receipts. The state supreme court concluded that "the liability of the city . . . . to the plaintiff for injury, due to an unsafe condition of the premises, [was] the same as that of a private person or corporation."[288] "The mere execution [by the city] of [the]

---

284. The court held that the board could be liable for the damage to the plaintiff's property, even though an independent contractor hired by the board had carried out the excavation and construction. *Id.* at 169–70. "The general rule is that the employer is not liable for the torts of an independent contractor, so long as the employer has exercised ordinary care to secure a competent contractor to do the work." DAYE & MORRIS, *supra* note 1, § 23.30, at 565. Yet "[w]here a duty is held to be non-delegable, or the activity to be carried on is inherently dangerous, the employer may be vicariously liable for the torts of an independent contractor." *Id.* § 23.30[1], at 565. In line with prior case law, the court in *Waters* regarded the excavation of the lot adjoining the plaintiff's property as an inherently dangerous activity. *See* 309 N.C. at 168–69 (discussing Davis v. Summerfield, 133 N.C. 325 (1903)).

285. *Waters*, 309 N.C. at 166.

286. *Id.* at 169 (discussing Meares v. City of Wilmington, 31 N.C. 73 (1848)).

287. Aaser v. City of Charlotte, 265 N.C. 494, 497 (1965); Pierson v. Cumberland Cty. Civic Ctr. Comm'n, 141 N.C. App. 628, 634 (2000).

288. *Aaser*, 265 N.C. at 497.

lease [did] not free the city . . . from liability to a ticket holder injured in the corridor while in the Coliseum to attend a hockey game."[289]

3.6.3 City Streets (Proprietary?)

The maintenance of public roads and highways plainly merits classification as a governmental function.[290] Nonetheless, the state's appellate courts have consistently declined to recognize governmental immunity as a defense to negligence claims premised on a city's failure to keep its streets or sidewalks in proper repair.[291] Indeed, some cases even refer to a city's maintenance of its streets and sidewalks as a proprietary function.[292] Chapter 9 analyzes the relationship between street maintenance and governmental immunity at length.

3.6.4 Insect Extermination (Governmental)

In using a chemical fog to exterminate mosquitos and other insects, a city or county acts governmentally.[293] Governmental immunity therefore blocked a plaintiff's negligence claim against a city for personal injuries and property damage sustained in an automobile accident that occurred when a vaporized form of insecticide emitted by a city jeep enveloped the plaintiff's vehicle.[294]

---

289. *Id.* at 498. *See also Pierson*, 141 N.C. App. at 634 (governmental immunity did not bar the plaintiffs' private nuisance action against the defendant civic center commission alleging that the plaintiffs' property—located near the county coliseum—had suffered a substantial and permanent decrease in value due to heavy traffic going to and from the coliseum and the frequently disruptive behavior of event patrons).

290. DAYE & MORRIS, *supra* note 1, § 19.40[2][c][vii], at 467 ("Maintaining the public streets falls as neatly into the definition of 'governmental function' as any activity performed by city government.").

291. *E.g.*, Millar v. Town of Wilson, 222 N.C. 340, 342 (1942) ("While the maintenance of public roads and highways is generally recognized as a governmental function, exception is made in respect to streets and sidewalks of a municipality."); Kirkpatrick v. Town of Nags Head, 213 N.C. App. 132, 140 (2011) ("[A] municipality has an obligation to protect individuals from injury resulting from defective street and roadway conditions without being allowed to avoid liability for negligently performing its street and road maintenance obligations by relying on a governmental immunity defense . . . ."); Sisk v. City of Greensboro, 183 N.C. App. 657, 659 (2007) (quoting *Millar*, 222 N.C. at 342) ("Maintenance of a public road and highway is generally considered a governmental function; however, 'exception is made in respect to streets and sidewalks of a municipality.' ").

292. *Millar*, 222 N.C. at 342 ("[T]he maintenance of streets and sidewalks is classed as a ministerial or proprietary function."); *Kirkpatrick*, 213 N.C. App. at 140 (same). *But see* City of Reidsville v. Burton, 269 N.C. 206, 210 (1967) ("The construction and maintenance of public streets and of bridges constituting a part thereof are governmental functions of a municipality . . . .").

293. White v. Mote, 270 N.C. 544, 554 (1967); Clark v. Scheld, 253 N.C. 732, 737 (1960).

294. *Clark*, 253 N.C. at 737.

3.6.5 Parks and Recreation (Governmental and Proprietary)

Both cities and counties have express statutory authority to own and operate public parks and establish and conduct recreation programs.[295]

3.6.5.1 Public Parks (Governmental or Proprietary)

A considerable lack of clarity marks the case law on governmental immunity and injuries arising from unsafe conditions in city or county parks. Chapter 6 attempts to harmonize the relevant cases in light of *Estate of Williams v. Pasquotank County Parks & Recreation Department*.[296] In short, the operation of a public park is likely proprietary if the park generates more than incidental income for the city or county.

3.6.5.2 City Golf Course (Proprietary)

The operation of a city golf course is a proprietary function.[297] Accordingly, the court rejected the defendant city's argument that governmental immunity protected it from liability for injuries suffered by the plaintiff when he fell from a small bridge on a city golf course due to the bridge's defective condition.[298]

3.6.5.3 Free Youth Sports Programs (Governmental)

The court of appeals has held that a city carried out a governmental function by sponsoring a free youth tennis clinic at a public school.[299] The city thus avoided liability for injuries to a four-year-old boy who was struck by a car as he and other children tried to cross a street without supervision immediately after taking part in the tennis clinic.[300]

It is not clear that there would be a finding of immunity in a similar case if the free youth clinic took place in a public park that produced substantial revenue for the city or county.

3.6.6 Public Hospital (Proprietary)

"[T]he construction, maintenance and operation of a public hospital by either a city or a county is a proprietary function."[301] The county hospital in one case was thus potentially liable for the wrongful death of a patient alleged to

---

295. G.S. 160A-353.

296. 366 N.C. 195 (2012).

297. *See* Lowe v. City of Gastonia, 211 N.C. 565, 566 (1937) (city's contention that it was not liable for the plaintiff's injuries because "it owned and maintained the golf course in the exercise of a governmental function, [could] not be sustained").

298. *Id.*

299. Hickman v. Fuqua, 108 N.C. App. 80, 85 (1992).

300. *Id.*

301. Sides v. Cabarrus Mem'l Hosp., Inc., 287 N.C. 14, 25–26 (1975).

have died because hospital employees transfused blood of the wrong blood type into her body.[302]

3.6.7 Public Library (Governmental)

"The public library—whether city, county, or multi-county (regional)—traditionally has been the responsibility of local government."[303] "The operation of a public library meets the test of 'governmental function' . . . ."[304] Accordingly, a plaintiff could not obtain money damages for injuries she allegedly sustained in a fall when the heel of her shoe became lodged in a crack in one of the public library's front steps.[305]

3.7 Local School Administrative Units

Although this book's focus is the governmental immunity of cities and counties, a significant part of the case law on governmental immunity concerns public school districts. The case law addressing the immunity of public school districts to tort claims is summarized in Appendix B. As noted in Appendix B, the state's appellate courts have yet to classify any public school activity as proprietary. Recent case law also indicates that governmental immunity extends to charter schools.[306]

---

302. *Id.* at 26. *See also* Odom v. Lane, 161 N.C. App. 534, 536 (2003) (governmental immunity did not bar plaintiff's medical malpractice claim because the operation of a county hospital is a proprietary function).

303. ALEX HESS, *Public Library Services, in* COUNTY AND MUNICIPAL GOVERNMENT IN NORTH CAROLINA 593 (Frayda S. Bluestein ed., 2d ed. 2014).

304. Seibold v. Kinston-Lenoir Cty. Pub. Library, 264 N.C. 360, 361 (1965).

305. *Id.*

306. Yarbrough v. E. Wake Charter Sch., 108 F. Supp. 3d 331, 337–38 (E.D.N.C. 2015) ("In view of the statutory scheme and the policy reasons underpinning North Carolina's governmental immunity doctrine for public schools, this court predicts that the Supreme Court of North Carolina would hold that charter schools enjoy governmental immunity.").

Chapter 4

Waiver of Governmental Immunity

The courts have recognized that units of local government may waive governmental immunity through certain actions. By acting in any of those ways, a unit consents to be sued for any civil claims that fall within the scope of the waiver. The impact and major characteristics of each waiver mechanism are the focus of this chapter.

4.1 Means of Waiver

The actions by which a local government unit may waive governmental immunity—agree to be sued—include

- engaging in a proprietary activity,
- purchasing liability insurance, or
- entering into a valid contract.[307]

The extent to which the unit exposes itself to civil liability through any of the above actions depends on the means of waiver.

4.2 Alleging Waiver of Immunity

To take advantage of a unit's waiver of governmental immunity, a plaintiff must adequately allege the waiver in his or her complaint.[308] Chapter 10 sets out the law concerning such waiver allegations.

---

307. Fuller v. Wake Cty., ___ N.C. App. ___, ___, 802 S.E.2d 106, 113 (2017). *See also* AGI Assocs., Inc. v. City of Hickory, 773 F.3d 576, 578 (4th Cir. 2014) (North Carolina cases establish that a city or county may waive its immunity against civil actions in one of three ways: (1) by entering into a valid contract, (2) by acting in a proprietary capacity, or (3) by purchasing liability insurance.).

308. *E.g.*, Paquette v. Cty. of Durham, 155 N.C. App. 415, 418 (2002) ("In order to overcome a defense of governmental immunity, the complaint must specifically allege a waiver of governmental immunity.").

4.3 Proprietary Activities

In most respects, when a unit of local government undertakes a proprietary function—operating a city golf course, for example—it is liable for the tortious conduct of its personnel on essentially the same basis as a private employer.[309] Thus, if a unit's employees negligently execute a proprietary function and harm results, the unit can be forced to pay compensatory damages, that is, a monetary award calculated to "'compensate [the] plaintiff for actual injury or loss resulting, for instance, from bodily injury or property damage.'"[310]

Yet even when a unit undertakes a proprietary activity, its potential liability exposure differs from that of a private employer in at least one important respect. Governmental immunity protects local governments from having to pay punitive damages in lawsuits, except when a statute expressly authorizes the recovery of such damages from local governments.[311] The North Carolina

---

309. *See, e.g.,* Mosseller v. City of Asheville, 267 N.C. 104, 107 (1966) ("When a municipal corporation operates a system of waterworks for the sale by it of water for private consumption and use, it is acting in its proprietary or corporate capacity and is liable for injury or damage resulting from such operation to the same extent and upon the same basis as a privately owned water company would be."); Hodges v. City of Charlotte, 214 N.C. 737, 739 (1938) ("The decisions of this Court uniformly hold that . . . cities, when acting in their corporate character, or in the exercise of powers for their own advantage, may be liable for the negligent acts of their officers and agents . . . ."); Fussell v. N.C. Farm Bureau Mut. Ins. Co., Inc., 198 N.C. App. 560, 563 (2009) ("[A] municipal corporation that sells water for private consumption is acting in a proprietary capacity and can be held liable to the same extent as a privately owned water company.").

310. Dobrowolska v. Wall, 138 N.C. App. 1, 12 (2000) (quoting 22 AM. JUR. 2D *Damages* § 23 (1988)). In personal injury cases, factors commonly considered in compensatory damages calculations include the plaintiff's lost earnings, medical and other expenses incurred by reason of the injury, and pain and suffering. 3 DAN B. DOBBS ET AL., THE LAW OF TORTS § 479 (2d ed. 2011).

311. *See* Long v. City of Charlotte, 306 N.C. 187, 207 (1982) ("The general rule is that no punitive damages are allowed against a municipal corporation unless expressly authorized by statute."); Jackson v. Hous. Auth. of High Point, 316 N.C. 259, 263 (1986) ("[T]he statutory provision must remove the *immunity of municipal corporations,* not merely provide for punitive damages, before the immunity of the common law is abrogated."). *See also* Davis v. Blanchard, 175 F. Supp. 3d 581, 600 (M.D.N.C. 2016) ("Despite their classification as a body corporate, courts have held that [local boards of education] are generally immune from punitive damages.").

The court in *Long* offered several policy reasons for exempting local governments from punitive damages. The reasons take into account the purpose of punitive damages, which is not "to compensate the injured party, but rather to *punish* the tortfeasor whose wrongful action was intentional or malicious, and to *deter* him and others from similar extreme conduct." 306 N.C. at 207 (quoting Newport v. Facts Concerts, Inc., 453 U.S. 247, 266–67 (1981)). Regarding punishment, the court observed that an award of punitive damages against a local government penalizes the unit, not the individual(s) who engaged in misconduct. Indeed the consequences to a unit of a large punitive damages award could be a tax increase or reduction of public services. As for deterrence, the court expressed skepticism that "municipal officials, including those at the

Supreme Court has interpreted the state's wrongful death statute, Chapter 28A, Section 18-2 of the North Carolina General Statutes (hereinafter G.S.), to make punitive damages available against local governments in wrongful death cases.[312] Of course, even when a statute allows punitive damages against a unit, the plaintiff may not recover them without evidence that the harm complained of resulted from the kind of aggravated misconduct that punitive damages are intended to punish and deter.[313]

4.4 Liability Insurance

State law expressly authorizes cities and counties to waive their immunity to tort claims through the purchase of liability insurance.[314] Without this express authority, the purchase of liability insurance by a city or county would not waive governmental immunity.[315] Like other statutes that waive governmental immunity, the city waiver statute, G.S. 160A-485, and the county waiver statute, G.S. 153A-435, must be strictly construed to preserve governmental immunity to the degree consistent with their provisions.[316]

4.4.1 Reasons for Waiver

It might be asked why a city or county would ever purchase liability insurance if the effect is to waive governmental immunity. There are several reasons why a unit might choose to purchase liability insurance in spite of, or even because of, the resulting waiver.

- A city or county that lacks liability insurance exposes itself to considerable financial risk for injuries caused by activities that the courts deem proprietary. As noted above, governmental immunity

---

policymaking level, would be deterred from wrongdoing by the threat of large punitive awards against the wealth of their municipality and its taxpayers." *Id.* at 207–08.

312. *Jackson*, 316 N.C. at 265.

313. *See* G.S. 1D-15 (setting out the standards for recovery of punitive damages).

314. G.S. 160A-485(a) ("Any city is authorized to waive its immunity from civil liability in tort by the act of purchasing liability insurance."); 153A-435(a) ("A county may contract to insure itself and any of its officers, agents, or employees against liability for wrongful death or negligent or intentional damage to person or property or against absolute liability for damage to person or property caused by an act or omission of the county or of any of its officers, agents, or employees when acting within the scope of their authority and the course of their employment. . . . Purchase of insurance pursuant to this subsection waives the county's governmental immunity . . . .").

315. Stephenson v. City of Raleigh, 232 N.C. 42, 47 (1950) (city's purchase of liability insurance did not waive governmental immunity because, at that time, no statute authorized cities to waive immunity in that way).

316. *See* Guthrie v. N.C. State Ports Auth., 307 N.C. 522, 537–38 (1983) ("Waiver of sovereign immunity may not be lightly inferred and State statutes waiving this immunity, being in derogation of the sovereign right to immunity, must be strictly construed.").

does not apply to claims arising from proprietary acts. Moreover, because many local government activities have not yet been classified as governmental or proprietary, and because courts may change their minds regarding the proper classification of an activity, a unit cannot always know in advance whether governmental immunity attaches to a particular undertaking.

- Certain kinds of claims fall outside the scope of governmental immunity, such as constitutional claims, most statutory claims, and breach of contract claims. Cities and counties may want to purchase liability insurance to limit their financial exposure to such claims.
- By purchasing liability insurance, a city or county can supply its officers and employees with liability protection from lawsuits filed against them in their individual capacities for acts or omissions within the scope of their duties.
- The purchase of liability insurance can provide a means of compensating citizens who have been injured by the performance of governmental functions and who, for that very reason, would otherwise be left without a remedy.[317]

4.4.2 What Counts as Purchase of Insurance

There are three ways in which a city or county may waive governmental immunity through the purchase of liability insurance, each of which is discussed below. The first is by purchasing liability insurance from a company licensed to execute insurance in the state. The second is by participating in a local government risk pool pursuant to Article 23 of Chapter 58 of the General Statutes. The third pertains to cities or counties that set aside their own funds to pay tort claims. Although ordinarily such self-insurance does not waive governmental immunity, the city council or board of county commissioners may adopt a resolution that, for immunity purposes, treats the creation of its fund as the equivalent of purchasing liability insurance.[318]

4.4.3 Extent of Waiver by Liability Insurance

The waiver statutes grant cities and counties total discretion to decide which categories of tort claims and which of their officials, employees, or agents to cover or exclude.[319] Any waiver of governmental immunity by the purchase

---

317. BROWN-GRAHAM, *supra* note 119.

318. BAKER, *supra* note 127, at 103; G.S. 153A-435(a); 160A-485(a).

319. G.S. 160A-485(b) ("An insurance contract purchased pursuant to this section may cover such torts and such officials, employees, and agents of the city as the governing board may determine."); 153A-435(a) ("The board of commissioners shall determine what liabilities and what officers, agents, and employees shall be covered by any insurance purchased pursuant to this subsection.").

of liability insurance is limited to the extent of coverage.[320] Often, disputes over the extent of coverage in immunity cases have focused on whether (1) the plaintiff's tort claim was subject to an exclusion in the unit's insurance policy or (2) the amount of damages sought by the plaintiff fell outside the policy's monetary limits.

4.4.3.1 Policy Exclusions

An exclusion is a provision in an insurance policy "specifying the situations, occurrences or persons not covered by the policy."[321] When a plaintiff's tort claim is subject to an exclusion, the unit has not waived immunity as to the claim. In one case, the court ruled that no waiver had occurred because (1) the plaintiff's wrongful discharge claim concerned the sheriff's decision to fire the plaintiff and (2) the unit's liability policy excluded claims between law enforcement officers.[322]

The courts disfavor exclusions in insurance policies.[323] Although unambiguous exclusions must be enforced as written, the courts will construe any ambiguity in an exclusion against the insurance company and in favor of the insured.[324] The court of appeals adhered to these principles in the wrongful death case of a man who died of a heart attack while being held in the county

---

320. G.S. 160A-485(a) ("Immunity shall be waived only to the extent that the city is indemnified by the insurance contract from tort liability."); 153A-435 ("Purchase of insurance pursuant to this subsection waives the county's governmental immunity, to the extent of insurance coverage, for any act or omission occurring in the exercise of a governmental function.").

What happens if a tort claim is covered by the unit's insurance contract but the insurance company is unable to pay it? In *McDonald v. Village of Pinehurst*, 91 N.C. App. 633, 634 (1988) (cited in Daye & Morris, *supra* note 1, § 19.40[2][c][iii][A][a], at 459 n.415), the defendant municipality argued that its purchase of liability insurance did not waive immunity as to the plaintiff's wrongful death claim in that the insurance company had become insolvent. The court of appeals agreed in principle that a city's waiver of immunity is "negated" as soon as the city ceases to be indemnified by liability insurance purchased in accordance with G.S. 160A-485. It nonetheless reasoned that no such negation had been proved in *McDonald* inasmuch as, "to some extent and under certain conditions," the North Carolina Insurance Guaranty Association (NCIGA) assumed the indemnification obligations of liability insurance companies that became insolvent. *Id.* at 635. Because the court disposed of the waiver issue on other grounds, its remarks about waiver and the NCIGA are merely *dicta* and, thus, not binding in future cases.

321. Black's Law Dictionary 563 (6th ed. 1990).

322. Phillips v. Gray, 163 N.C. App. 52, 56–57 (2004).

323. *E.g.*, State Capital Ins. Co. v. Nationwide Mut. Ins. Co., 318 N.C. 534, 538 (1986) ("[P]rovisions which exclude liability of insurance companies are not favored . . . .").

324. *Id.* ("[A]ll ambiguous provisions [in an exclusion] will be construed against the insurer and in favor of the insured."); Doe v. Jenkins, 144 N.C. App. 131, 134 (2001) (quoting Nationwide Mut. Ins. Co. v. Mabe, 342 N.C. 482. 492 (1996)) ("If an insurance policy is not ambiguous, 'then the court must enforce the policy as written . . . .'").

jail's isolation cell. The complaint attributed the death partly to the negligent failure of sheriff's department employees to have the man medically examined. The sheriff argued that the plaintiff's negligence claim fell under an exclusion in the county's liability policy for claims arising from "the acts of any Covered Person 'while engaged in any form of health care.'"[325] In holding that the exclusion did not apply, the court observed that the exclusion concerned efforts to provide health care, whereas the claim at issue arose from a total failure to make health care available.[326]

4.4.3.1.1 Exclusion for Governmental Functions?

A city or county can purchase liability insurance without waiving governmental immunity at all. In *Patrick v. Wake County Department of Human Services*, the county's liability policy contained the following provision:

> "'[T]his policy provides coverage only for occurrences or wrongful acts for which the defense of governmental immunity is clearly not applicable or for which, after the defense[] is asserted, a court of competent jurisdiction determines the defense of governmental immunity not to be applicable.'"[327]

According to the North Carolina Court of Appeals, the provision unambiguously excluded coverage for any tort claims that governmental immunity would defeat in the absence of liability insurance. The upshot was that the county had not actually waived its immunity from tort claims by purchasing the policy. Governmental immunity therefore barred the minor plaintiff's claims for negligence and negligent infliction of emotional distress against the county's human services department for failing to protect the plaintiff from domestic sexual abuse.[328]

The reasoning in *Patrick* is open to criticism. In a later case, the court of appeals referred to the "arguably circular nature of the logic employed in *Patrick*," while still acknowledging the decision's status as binding precedent.[329] The court has followed *Patrick* in several other cases construing

---

This rule of interpretation creates something of an inconsistency in the law on waiver of governmental immunity. Whereas the waiver statutes must be strictly construed in order to preserve immunity to the maximum extent consistent with their provisions, any ambiguity in an insurance policy purchased pursuant to one of those statutes must be resolved in favor of coverage, that is, in favor of waiver.

325. Myers v. Bryant, 188 N.C. App. 585, 590 (2008).

326. *Id.*

327. 188 N.C. App. 592, 596 (2008).

328. *Id.* at 596–97.

329. Estate of Earley v. Haywood Cty. Dep't of Soc. Servs., 204 N.C. App. 338, 343 (2010).

> We acknowledge the arguably circular nature of the logic employed in *Patrick*. . . . [T]he legislature [has] explicitly provided [in G.S. 153A-435] that governmental immunity is waived to the extent of insurance

liability policies with similar or identical exclusion provisions.[330] In *Wright v. Gaston County*, for example, governmental immunity blocked the plaintiffs' wrongful death and related tort claims arising from the alleged negligence of 911 operators because the county's liability policy excluded claims subject to governmental immunity.[331]

4.4.3.1.2 Supplemental Insurance

Local governments often purchase insurance that supplements the coverage provided by their general liability policies. Depending on its terms, a supplemental policy may waive governmental immunity as to a plaintiff's claims, even when the claims are subject to an exclusion in the unit's general liability policy. In one case, a county's general liability policy excluded claims arising from the acts or omissions of public officials. Citing this exclusion, the county insisted that governmental immunity shielded it from liability for the department of social services' allegedly negligent supervision of a juvenile who had fatally stabbed her neighbor. The court held that, even if the general liability policy excluded the plaintiff's claim, the county had waived immunity from the claim by purchasing supplemental insurance that covered claims against its officials of the sort alleged by the plaintiff.[332]

4.4.3.2 Insurance Policy Monetary Limits

Liability insurance policies cap the amount payable for covered claims. The purchase of liability insurance by a city or county does not operate to waive governmental immunity for damages in excess of the policy limits. It is also common for liability insurance policies to exclude all claims below a

---

> coverage, but the [county's] insurance contract eliminates any potential waiver by excluding from coverage claims that would be barred by sovereign immunity. Thus, the logic in *Patrick* boils down to: Defendant retains immunity because the policy doesn't cover his actions and the policy doesn't cover his actions because he explicitly retains immunity. Nonetheless in this case, as in *Patrick*, where the language of both the applicable statute and the exclusion clause in the insurance contract are clear, we must decline Plaintiff's invitation to implement "policy" in this matter. Any such policy implementation is best left to the wisdom of our legislature.

Id.

330. Bullard v. Wake Cty., 221 N.C. App. 522, *discretionary review denied*, 336 N.C. 409 (2012); Lunsford v. Renn, 207 N.C. App. 298 (2010); Owen v. Haywood Cty., 205 N.C. App. 456 (2010); Wright v. Gaston Cty., 205 N.C. App. 600 (2010); Pryor v. City of Raleigh, ___ N.C. App. ___, 788 S.E.2d 684 (2016) (unpublished); White v. Stokes Cty. Dep't of Soc. Servs., 207 N.C. App. 378 (2010) (unpublished). *See also* Hagans v. City of Fayetteville, No. 5:14-CV-717-F, 2015 WL 4414929, at *3 (E.D.N.C. July 17, 2015) (governmental immunity barred the plaintiff's tort claims because the defendant city's insurance policy expressly provided that it should not be construed to waive such immunity).

331. 205 N.C. App. at 607–08.

332. Fulford v. Jenkins, 195 N.C. App. 402, 407–09 (2009).

designated amount, often referred to as a *retention* or *retained limit*.[333] Policies with this feature are often referred to as *excess insurance* because they provide coverage only for damages above the retention amount.[334] A unit whose only liability insurance is excess insurance has waived governmental immunity with regard to covered claims only to the extent that a claimant's damages fall within the policy's monetary parameters. Thus, a city with insurance coverage for claims in excess of $2 million but less than $4 million waived immunity only as to claims inside that range.[335] Likewise, because a county's liability policy excluded claims under $250,000, governmental immunity foreclosed a plaintiff's claims against the county for $73,000 in damages.[336]

Depending on the precise terms of the policy, a unit's retained limit can render the purchase of liability insurance ineffective as a waiver of governmental immunity. In a series of cases decided by the court of appeals, the policies specified that the insurance companies did not have to indemnify the units for damages in excess of the retained limits until the units had paid out the full retention amounts.[337] Because immunity protected the units from liability for damages below their retentions, they did not pay out the full retention amounts, leaving the insurance companies without any legal obligation to indemnify the units for excess damages. With the units effectively lacking coverage for damages above the retained limits, the court determined that no waiver of governmental immunity had occurred as to the plaintiffs' claims.[338]

Obviously, if a unit's liability insurance has a high retention, some individuals harmed by the unit's performance of a governmental function could find themselves without legal recourse. (The same may be said, though, of anyone whose claim is barred by an immunity defense.) Whether in the interest of justice or to promote good will, units sometimes settle personal injury or property damage claims not covered by their liability insurance. Such settlements typically provide financial compensation to the claimants, who in return agree to release the units from any liability.[339] Units do not

---

333. Jones v. Kearns, 120 N.C. App. 301, 303 (1995).

334. The term *excess insurance* is used more generically to refer to coverage that pays amounts beyond the limit another carrier is required to pay.

335. Dobrowolska v. Wall, 138 N.C. App. 1, 8 (2000). *See also* Clayton v. Branson, 153 N.C. App. 488, 493 (2002) (allegation by the plaintiff that he suffered more than $3 million in damages put his lawsuit within the limits of the city's liability insurance, which covered claims for more than $2 million but less than $4 million).

336. McIver v. Smith, 134 N.C. App. 583, 590 (1999).

337. Bullard v. Wake Cty., 221 N.C. App. 522, 531, *discretionary review denied*, 336 N.C. 409 (2012); Arrington v. Martinez, 215 N.C. App. 252, 264 (2011); Magana v. Charlotte-Mecklenburg Bd. of Educ., 183 N.C. App. 146, 148 (2007).

338. *Bullard*, 221 N.C. App. at 532; *Arrington*, 215 N.C. App. at 265; *Magana*, 183 N.C. App. at 149.

339. *See, e.g.*, Jones v. City of Durham, 183 N.C. App. 57, 60–61 (2007) (describing the city's approach to settling tort claims).

waive governmental immunity by entering into settlements of this sort.[340] Consequently, if a claimant were to file suit in violation of the terms of his or her settlement, the unit could still assert governmental immunity as a defense.[341] As discussed in Chapter 8, decisions by units to settle some claims subject to governmental immunity but not others have prompted constitutional challenges.

4.4.4 Local Government Risk Pools

According to the city and county waiver statutes, a unit's participation in a local government risk pool pursuant to Article 23, Chapter 58 of the General Statutes counts as the purchase of liability insurance.[342] In other words, like the purchase of liability insurance, participation in a local government risk pool waives governmental immunity for cities and counties to the extent of coverage. More precisely, the waiver is limited to the extent to which a unit is indemnified under its risk-pool agreement.

Many of the relevant cases concern whether the particular liability-sharing arrangement in dispute qualifies as a local government risk pool under Article 23, Chapter 58. The cases highlight key features of qualifying risk pools.

- The only units of local government authorized to form qualifying risk pools are cities, counties, and housing authorities.[343]
- A qualifying risk pool is required "to pay all claims for which each member [unit] incurs liability during each member's period of membership, except where a member has individually retained the risk, where the risk is not covered, and except for [the] amount of claims above the coverage provided by the pool."[344]
- A qualifying risk pool must include at least two units of local government. Thus, a city did not join a risk pool by organizing a corporation to pay tort claims against the city of $1,000,000

---

340. *See id.* at 60 ("Nor does the City's practice of executing settlement contracts with certain claimants constitute a waiver of [governmental] immunity in those cases.").

341. *See id.* at 61 ("[S]hould a tort claimant violate the settlement agreement by suing the City after executing the settlement contract, the City would be entitled to raise any applicable defense, including satisfaction and accord or [governmental] immunity.").

342. G.S. 153A-435(a) ("Participation in a local government risk pool pursuant to Article 23 of General Statute Chapter 58 shall be deemed to be the purchase of insurance for the purposes of this section."); 160A-485(a) (same).

343. Lyles v. City of Charlotte, 344 N.C. 676, 680 (1996) (citing G.S. 58-23-1) ("Only counties, cities, and housing authorities are defined as local governments for purposes of joining a local government risk pool.").

344. Dobrowolska v. Wall, 138 N.C. App. 1, 8 (2000) (quoting G.S. 58-23-15(3)).

or less because no other local government unit took part in the corporation.[345]

- A qualifying risk pool is one in which the member units actually pool their risks.[346] An arrangement that requires each member to reimburse the pool for payments made on claims against it does not satisfy Article 23, Chapter 58.[347]

If the court determines that a particular arrangement is not a qualifying risk pool, then the unit has not waived governmental immunity unless its agreement amounts to a contract for liability insurance.

4.4.5 Self-Insurance (Funded Reserve)

Cities and counties may opt to use funded reserves. By so doing, they self-insure. They may self-insure entirely or, if they have liability insurance or risk-pool coverage, for damages outside their policy limits. For instance, if a unit's liability insurance includes a retention of $500,000, the unit may choose to cover the retained limit through self-insurance.[348]

The use of a funded reserve does not automatically waive a unit's governmental immunity. If the city council or board of county commissioners so desires, it may adopt a resolution equating its creation of a funded reserve with the purchase of liability insurance.[349] When a unit adopts such a resolution, the wording of the resolution determines the parameters of the waiver for purposes of the funded reserve.[350] In one case, the resolution adopted by the board restricted the waiver to claims voluntarily settled prior to the filing of any legal proceedings. In light of that language, the court held that

---

345. Blackwelder v. City of Winston-Salem, 332 N.C. 319, 322 (1992) ("The City of Winston-Salem has not joined with any local government unit in the operation of [the Risk Acceptance Management Corporation]. It is not participating in a risk pool.").

346. *Lyles*, 344 N.C. at 680 ("As we read [G.S. 58-23-5], the risks of the parties must be put in one pool for the payment of claims in order to have a local government risk pool.").

347. *Id.* ("[General Statute] 58-23-15 provides that a local government risk pool agreement must contain a provision that the pool pay all claims for which a member incurs liability. We do not believe the pool has paid a claim if it is reimbursed for it."). *See also Dobrowolska*, 138 N.C. App. at 8 ("[I]mmunity is not waived when a claim is paid for which the pool is reimbursed, because the pool has not paid the claim and the [indemnification] requirements of [G.S.] 160A-485 have not been met.").

348. Bullard v. Wake Cty., 221 N.C. App. 522, 529 (county chose to cover its retained limit of $500,000 through self-insurance as allowed by G.S. 153A-435(a)), *discretionary review denied*, 336 N.C. 409 (2012).

349. G.S. 153A-435(a); 160A-485(a).

350. G.S. 153A-435 ("Adoption of such a resolution waives the county's governmental immunity only to the extent provided in the board's resolution . . . ."); 160A-485(a) (same for cities).

the county had not waived its immunity from the negligent inspection and negligent misrepresentation claims asserted in the plaintiffs' lawsuit.[351]

No waiver by resolution may exceed the funds available in the unit's funded reserve for the payment of claims.[352] In other words, waiver by resolution cannot expose the unit to liability greater than the funds it allocates for the payment of tort claims.

4.4.6 Cities with Populations Over 500,000

A separate statute, G.S. 160A-485.5, allows any city with a population of 500,000 or more to waive governmental immunity by adopting a resolution expressing the city's intent to subject itself to the Tort Claims Act (TCA). When a city takes such action, the TCA's limit of $1,000,000 per claim applies to tort claims against the city.[353] The city may provide for the payment of tort claims by obtaining liability insurance or creating a self-funded reserve.[354] Although the TCA invests the North Carolina Industrial Commission with jurisdiction over negligence claims against the state, jurisdiction over claims against a city lies with the superior court of the county in which the city is principally located.[355]

Charlotte is the only city in North Carolina large enough to qualify under the statute.[356] It has in fact elected to put itself under the TCA.

4.4.7 Litigating Coverage Questions

When a plaintiff's ability to proceed with a tort claim is contingent on a unit's waiver of governmental immunity through the purchase of liability insurance, the trial judge must resolve all issues regarding the unit's coverage.[357] Issues regarding the impact of a policy's terms on governmental immunity usually come to the judge fairly early during litigation in the form of a unit's motion to dismiss (MTD), motion for judgment on the pleadings, or motion for summary judgment. Chapter 10 discusses MTDs on immunity grounds in more detail. A party may move for judgment on the pleadings only after all necessary pleadings—usually the complaint and the defendant's

---

351. *Bullard*, 221 N.C. App. at 530.

352. G.S. 153A-435(a); 160A-485(a).

353. G.S. 143-299.2 (state's liability for injury or damage to any one person arising out of any one occurrence is limited to $1,000,000); 160A-485.5(b)(3) (limitation on payments in G.S. 143-299.2 applies to claims made against city that has waived immunity under G.S. 160A-485.5).

354. G.S. 160A-485.5(c).

355. G.S. 160A-485.5(b)(1).

356. With a population of more than 440,000, Raleigh may soon qualify.

357. Plaintiffs may not take advantage of a unit's waiver of governmental immunity unless they agree to have the trial judge decide all issues of law or fact relating to insurance. G.S. 153A-435(b); 160A-485(d).

answer—have been filed.[358] The trial court may grant such a motion only if the pleadings do not disclose any unresolved issues of material fact and the moving party is entitled to prevail as a matter of law.[359] Motions for summary judgment look beyond the pleadings to the parties' forecast of evidence. As with motions for judgment on the pleadings, the trial court may not grant a motion for summary judgment unless there are no genuine issues of material fact and, when applied to the undisputed facts, the law compels a ruling in favor of the moving party.[360]

A motion that asserts governmental immunity usually includes a copy of the unit's insurance policy, if the unit has one, along with an affidavit from the finance officer or other appropriate individual verifying that the unit has no other applicable coverage.[361] If the plaintiff has quantified his or her damages in response to a request for statement of monetary relief sought or to some other discovery request, the unit will submit that information to the court as well.[362] If the plaintiff seeks damages beneath the retention amount, the unit prevails and the case ends without a trial on the plaintiff's tort claims against the unit. If the plaintiff seeks damages above the retention, or if the plaintiff has not quantified the damages sought, the unit may obtain partial summary judgment as to any damages outside the policy's monetary limits.[363]

---

358. G. Gray Wilson, North Carolina Civil Procedure § 12-13, at 12-40 (3d ed. 2007). If matters outside the pleadings are presented to the court and the court considers them, it must treat the motion for judgment on the pleadings as one for summary judgment. N.C. R. Civ. P. 12(c).

359. Wilson, *supra* note 358, § 12-13, at 12-41 to 12-42.

360. N.C. R. Civ. P. 56(c).

361. *E.g.*, Parker v. Town of Erwin, 243 N.C. App. 84, 90 (2015) (town submitted affidavits from its finance officer and former town manager in support of motion to dismiss (MTD) based on governmental immunity); Hinson v. City of Greensboro, 232 N.C. App. 204, 212 (2014) (city supported MTD on immunity grounds with affidavit from the executive director of its insurance advisory committee).

362. Under Rule 8 of the North Carolina Rules of Civil Procedure,

> at any time after service of the claim for relief, any party may request of the claimant a written statement of the monetary relief sought, and the claimant shall, within 30 days after such service, provide such statement, which shall not be filed with the clerk until the action has been called for trial or entry of default entered.

For an example of a unit's use of a plaintiff's response to a request for statement of monetary relief sought, see *McIver v. Smith*, 134 N.C. App. 583, 584 (1999).

363. Blackwelder v. City of Winston-Salem, 332 N.C. 319 (1992) (city was entitled to partial summary judgment on the plaintiff's claims in that it had no liability insurance for claims of $1,000,000 or less). *See also* Young v. Woodall, 119 N.C. 132, 136 (1995) (because city's liability insurance did not indemnify for damages of $2,000,000 or less, city "would ordinarily be entitled to partial summary judgment for any claims . . . up to and including that amount"), *rev'd on other grounds*, 343 N.C. 359 (1996).

If the case makes it to trial on the plaintiff's tort claims, no one may read, display, or mention any document or exhibit related to the unit's liability insurance in the jury's presence.[364] Similarly, the jury must be absent during any testimony involving the unit's insurance coverage.[365] Any unresolved issues related to insurance coverage must be heard and decided by the judge, away from the jury.[366] None of these restrictions on jury involvement apply, however, if the unit has requested a jury trial on insurance coverage issues, an option available to cities and counties under the waiver statutes.[367]

If the jury awards the plaintiff damages greater than the policy limits on tort claims that governmental immunity would bar in the absence of liability insurance, the trial court must reduce the award to the maximum policy limits before entering judgment.[368]

4.4.8 Waivers by Other Units of Local Government

4.4.8.1 *Local Boards of Education*

Like cities and counties, local boards of education may waive governmental immunity for their respective school districts by purchasing liability insurance, with any such waiver limited to the extent of coverage.[369] The waiver statute for school boards, G.S. 115C-42, differs from city and county waiver statutes in major respects, including the following.

- It declares that any liability policy purchased by a local board of education must "adequately insure the . . . board . . . against any and all liability for any damages by reason of death or injury to person or property proximately caused by the negligent acts or torts of [the board's] agent and employees . . . ."[370] The apparent implication is that school boards do not have the same freedom that cities and counties enjoy when making decisions on the scope and amount of liability insurance. Nonetheless, the court of appeals has rejected a plaintiff's argument that, if a school board chooses to buy liability insurance,

---

364. G.S. 153A-435(b); 160A-485(d); 160A-485.5(d).

365. G.S. 153A-435(b) (counties); 160A-485(d) (cities). The city waiver statute goes so far as to prohibit "the plaintiff, his counsel, or anyone testifying in his behalf [to] directly or indirectly convey to the jury any inference that the city's potential liability is covered by insurance." *See also* G.S. 160A-485.5(d) (same for city that waives immunity under G.S. 160A-485.5).

366. G.S. 153A-435(b); 160A-485(d); 160A-485.5(d).

367. G.S. 153A-435(b); 160A-485(d); 160A-485.5(d).

368. G.S. 160A-485(c). The county waiver statute does not explicitly so provide, but the court would have to reduce an award against the county to the policy limits given that, as with cities, a county's waiver of immunity through purchase of liability insurance is confined to the extent of coverage. G.S. 153A-435(a).

369. G.S. 115C-42.

370. *Id.*

the insurance must cover *all* tort claims arising from the negligence of its employees. The court explained that, notwithstanding the adequacy requirement in G.S. 115C-42, a school board "may exercise its discretion to determine for which, if any, of its potential liabilities to purchase insurance and thereby limit its waiver of liability."[371]

- There is no mention of risk pools in the waiver statute for school boards. For this reason, a school board does not waive governmental immunity by participating in a risk pool. In particular, it does not waive immunity through participation in the North Carolina School Boards Trust.[372]
- The statute omits any reference to self-insurance. Presumably, this means that, even if a school board elects to self-insure, it may not waive immunity as to its funded reserve.

In enacting G.S. 115C-524(b), the General Assembly placed an important restraint on the capacity of school boards to waive immunity through the purchase of liability insurance. Paragraph (b) of G.S. 115C-524 authorizes school boards to adopt rules under which they may enter into agreements allowing non-school groups to use school property for non-school purposes. It further states that "[n]o liability shall attach to any board of education or to any individual board member for personal injury suffered by reason of the use of such school property pursuant to such agreements." According to the court of appeals, this non-liability provision renders a school board's waiver by insurance ineffective as to personal injury claims arising from the use of school property by a non-school group pursuant to G.S. 115C-524(b).[373]

4.4.8.2 Special Purpose Governments

Although cities, counties, and public school districts carry out most local government functions in North Carolina, special purpose governments exist in the form of sanitary districts, rural fire protection districts, housing authorities, water and sewer authorities, airport authorities, and mental health area authorities.[374] Several cases address the impact of liability insurance on the governmental immunity of special purpose governments.

---

371. Overcash v. Statesville City Bd. of Educ., 83 N.C. App. 21, 25 (1986).

372. Johnson v. Avery Cty. Bd. of Educ., 221 N.C. App. 669, ___ (2012) (participation in the North Carolina School Board Trust does not waive a local school board's right to assert governmental immunity); Willett v. Chatham Cty. Bd. of Educ., 176 N.C. App. 268, 269 (2006) (same); Ripellino v. N.C. Sch. Bds. Ass'n, Inc., 158 N.C. App. 423, 428 (same), *cert. denied*, 358 N.C. 156 (2004); Lucas v. Swain Cty. Bd. of Educ., 154 N.C. App. 357, 363 (2002) (same).

373. Lindler v. Duplin Cty. Bd. of Educ., 108 N.C. App. 757, 761 (1993).

374. LAWRENCE, *supra* note 44, at 8. "Generally, *special districts* are special purpose governments with taxing power, and *authorities* are such governments without taxing power." *Id.* (emphases in original).

In *Evans v. Housing Authority of the City of Raleigh*, the state supreme court held that the city waiver statute does not apply to city housing authorities primarily because the definition of "city" found in G.S. Chapter 160A, which contains the primary statutes for cities, expressly excludes "municipal corporations organized for a special purpose."[375] Nonetheless, the court determined that the state's Housing Authorities Law (HAL) grants housing authorities the power to waive governmental immunity by purchasing liability insurance. In support of this conclusion, the court quoted language in the HAL that allows housing authorities "'to sue and be sued'" and "to insure or provide for insurance of the property or operations of the authority against such risks as the authority may deem advisable."[376] The implication is that a city's other special purpose governments may not waive governmental immunity through the purchase of liability insurance unless a state law separate from the city waiver statute authorizes their action.

In *Clancy v. Onslow County*, the court of appeals held that a plaintiff who wishes to pursue tort claims against a mental health area authority must allege that the authority itself has purchased liability insurance covering the plaintiff's claims.[377] It is not enough to allege that liability insurance has been purchased by the county or counties in which the area authority operates. As grounds for its decision, the court pointed to the relative independence of area authorities from county control and to G.S. 122C-152, which expressly permits area authorities to waive their governmental immunity by securing liability insurance. It is not clear from *Clancy* whether, or under what circumstances, a county may waive the immunity of other special purpose governments operating at the county level.

4.4.9 Official Bonds

State law mandates that certain county officials post bonds, including, for example, sheriffs and registers of deeds.[378] Pursuant to G.S. 58-76-5, anyone injured by "the neglect, misconduct, or misbehavior in office" of any such official may file suit against the official and the bond's surety, both of whom "shall be liable to the person injured."

In cases applying G.S. 58-76-5 to claims against sheriffs or officers in their departments, the courts have held that a sheriff's bond waives governmental immunity as to official capacity claims.[379] This makes sense in light of the

---

375. 359 N.C. 50, 56 (2004) (quoting G.S. 160A-1(2)).

376. *Id*. at 56–57 (quoting G.S. 157-9(a)).

377. 151 N.C. App. 269, 274 (2002).

378. G.S. 162-9 (sheriffs); 166-4 (registers of deeds).

379. *E.g.*, Messick v. Catawba Cty., 110 N.C. App. 707, 715 (1993) ("Governmental immunity, however, does not preclude an action against the sheriff and the officers sued in their official capacities. . . . The statutory mandate that the sheriff furnish a bond works to remove the sheriff from the protective embrace of governmental immunity . . . .");

bond's purpose, which is "to ensure that persons have an adequate remedy for wrongs done to them by a sheriff or other officers of the department notwithstanding governmental immunity."[380]

Plaintiffs will not consider the bond to be an adequate remedy in many cases. The waiver of immunity effected by the bond is limited to the extent of coverage,[381] and state law caps the amount of a sheriff's bond at $25,000.[382] Obviously, lawsuits for serious bodily injuries and major property damage will often involve damages exceeding the bond amount. If the county has purchased liability insurance that covers the sheriff, the insurance will supplement the bond, unless the plaintiff's claims fall within one or more of the policy's exclusions.[383]

To recover on the sheriff's bond, the plaintiff must join the surety as a party to the lawsuit.[384] If the plaintiff fails to name the surety as a party, the oversight "is easily corrected by amendment to the complaint."[385]

4.4.10 Waiver by Insurance and Equitable Claims

Although this book focuses on the immunity of local governments to tort claims, governmental immunity can protect units from contract-related equitable claims such as unjust enrichment and "contract implied in law." Chapter 7 analyzes the relationship between governmental immunity and such equitable claims. These equitable claims should not be confused with direct claims for breach of contract, which are taken up in Section 4.5, *infra*.

There is good reason to doubt whether the purchase of liability insurance can waive a unit's immunity from contract-related equitable claims.

Summey v. Barker, 142 N.C. App. 688, 691 (2001) ("Defendants [sheriff and the chief jailer] are not immune from suit because of the existence of the bond which operates to remove the protection of governmental immunity.").

380. BROWN-GRAHAM, *supra* note 119, at 3-25 (1999) (citing Smith v. Phillips, 117 N.C. App. 378 (1994)).

381. *E.g.*, Greene v. Barrick, 198 N.C. App. 647, 652 (2009) (noting that the defendant sheriff, "in his official capacity, [was] immune from liability, except to the extent that the immunity was waived by the surety bond"); Myers v. Bryant, 188 N.C. App. 585, 588 (2008) (sheriff waived immunity "for Plaintiffs' claims up to $25,000, the amount of his official bond").

382. G.S. 162-8.

383. *See Myers*, 188 N.C. App. at 591 (trial court correctly denied sheriff's summary judgment motion because the evidence did not show that plaintiffs' claims were subject to exclusion in county's liability policy). *See also id.* at 588 (quoting *Smith*, 117 N.C. App. at 383) ("Where a sheriff is covered by his county's liability insurance purchased pursuant to [G.S.] 153A-435(a) and his official bond, the county's liability insurance 'serves to complement the purpose of the bond statute, insuring an adequate remedy for wrongs done to the plaintiff if . . . the bond does not provide an adequate remedy.' ").

384. *Messick*, 110 N.C. App. at 715.

385. *Id.*

No express reference to equitable claims appears in the waiver statutes. The city statute refers specifically to a waiver "in tort."[386] The term *tort* does not appear in the county waiver statute, but the statute's description of the kinds of claims to which a county's waiver by insurance may apply—"wrongful death or negligent or intentional damage to person or property"—seems to authorize waiver only with regard to tort claims.[387] Strictly construed, the statutes offer no grounds for concluding that cities or counties may waive immunity to equitable claims through the purchase of liability insurance.

4.5 Valid Contracts

In *Smith v. State*, the North Carolina Supreme Court held that, when the state enters into a valid contract, it implicitly consents to be sued for damages for its breach of that contract.[388] Inasmuch as governmental immunity is a diluted version of the state's sovereign immunity, the courts have aptly recognized that governmental immunity will not shield a unit of local government that has entered into a valid contract from a claim for breach.[389] Like the state, "where [a city or county] enters into a valid contract, [it] 'implicitly consents to be sued for damages on the contract in the event it breaches the contract.'"[390] Thus, because a former county employee's claim for unpaid wages was "contractual, rather than tortious, in nature," governmental immunity did not bar the claim.[391]

The court of appeals has further opined that the remedies available to a party under waiver by contract are not restricted to breach-of-contract claims; a party to a valid contract with the state may seek a declaratory judgment from a court of competent jurisdiction if the parties' respective obligations under the contract are in dispute.[392] It follows that parties to valid

---

386. G.S. 160A-485(a). Similarly, the waiver statute for local school boards authorizes the boards to waive their immunity in "negligence or tort" by purchasing liability insurance. G.S. 115C-42.

387. G.S. 153A-435(a).

388. 289 N.C. 303, 320 (1976) ("We hold, therefore, that whenever the State of North Carolina, through its authorized officers and agencies, enters into a valid contract, the State implicitly consents to be sued for damages on the contract in the event it breaches the contract.").

389. Wray v. City of Greensboro, 370 N.C. 41, 47 (2017); Data Gen. Corp. v. Cty. of Durham, 143 N.C. App. 97, 100 (2001).

390. *Data Gen. Corp.*, 143 N.C. App. at 100 (quoting *Smith*, 289 N.C. at 320).

391. Paquette v. Cty. of Durham, 155 N.C. App. 415, 420 (2002).

392. Atl. Coast Conference v. Univ. of Md., 230 N.C. App. 429, 442 (2013) ("The Court's holding in *Smith* explicitly waived the State's sovereign immunity in 'causes of action on contract' and we can discern no sound reason to limit that language to breach of contract claims when the Court's stated rationale is equally persuasive with respect to declaratory relief actions seeking to ascertain the rights and obligations owed under an alleged contract.").

contracts with local governments may pursue declaratory judgments in disputes over their contractual obligations. Were it otherwise, governmental immunity would provide local governments with greater liability protection than the state enjoys under the doctrine of sovereign immunity.

Chapter 5

Governmental Immunity and Premises Liability

Many lawsuits filed against cities, counties, or other units of local government allege injuries sustained in falls or similar mishaps on government property. Such lawsuits commonly assert that the unit caused the injuries by negligently failing to keep the premises in a safe condition or to warn of hidden dangers, the legal duty of care that property owners owe to lawful visitors.[393] Local governments frequently raise governmental immunity as a defense to this kind of premises liability.

This chapter examines the relationship between governmental immunity and claims of negligent property maintenance. In particular, it explores the impact of *Estate of Williams v. Pasquotank County Parks & Recreation Department*[394] on governmental immunity as a defense to these claims.[395]

---

393. North Carolina law requires landowners to exercise reasonable care to keep their premises safe for lawful visitors and to warn lawful visitors of hidden dangers on their property. Rolan v. N.C. Dep't of Agric. & Consumer Servs., 233 N.C. App. 371, 382–83 (2014). In this context, the term "landowners" includes all possessors of real property. The reasonable care standard obliges a landowner to make a reasonable inspection of the premises for hidden defects and perils. DAYE & MORRIS, *supra* note 1, § 17.30[2], at 311. It extends to all parts of the property a visitor may be expected to use, including parking lots, for example. *Id.* § 17.30[2], at 315. The precise measures that a landowner must take to satisfy the reasonable care standard can vary based on many factors, such as the use to which the property is being put or the mental capacity of a lawful visitor, if the landowner knows or should know that the visitor might be incapable of taking precautions for his or her own safety. *Id.* § 17.30[2], at 312–13.

To sustain a claim for negligence based on unsafe premises, a lawful visitor must show an actionable breach of the reasonable care standard. The visitor may establish such a breach by proving that the landowner negligently created the condition that led to his or her injury or negligently failed to correct that condition despite having actual or constructive notice of its existence. *Rolan*, 233 N.C. App. at 382.

Generally speaking, landowners do not owe a duty of care to trespassers and may not be held liable for injuries to them. G.S. 38B-2. *But see* G.S. 8-B-3 (setting forth the conditions under which a landowner may be liable for a trespasser's injuries).

394. 366 N.C. 195 (2012).

395. This chapter incorporates material from Allen, *supra* note 62.

5.1 Premises Liability and Governmental Immunity: The Basic Approach

North Carolina's courts have usually tied the availability of governmental immunity as a defense in a negligent maintenance lawsuit to the purpose served by local government property. When, for instance, a city or county has used a building for a governmental function, the courts have regarded maintenance of the building as a *governmental* function, and governmental immunity has barred unsafe premises claims. Several cases cited in Chapter 3 illustrate this approach. In one such case, the court held that governmental immunity foreclosed the plaintiff's attempt to recover damages for injuries she allegedly sustained in a fall down the public library's front steps.[396] In rejecting the plaintiff's negligence claim, the court explained that the operation of a public library is a governmental function akin to "the operation of a fire department, the operation of a fogging machine to eradicate insects, the maintenance of a police force, or the operation of public schools."[397] In another case, the court evaluated a county's liability for the death of a woman who fell down a stairway in the office of the register of deeds.[398] The court held that "the operation and maintenance of a register of deeds office in a county courthouse is clearly a governmental function for which the county enjoys immunity from suit for negligence."[399]

On the other hand, when a building has been reserved for a proprietary function, the judiciary has deemed its upkeep a *proprietary* function and has ruled that the local government may be liable for injuries resulting from its failure to keep the premises reasonably safe. In one of several cases cited in Chapter 3 that support this view, the court held that a city had acted proprietarily in operating a coliseum to generate revenue from sporting events; consequently, "the liability of the city . . . to the plaintiff for injury, due to an unsafe condition of the premises, [was] the same as that of a private person or corporation."[400]

---

396. Seibold v. Kinston-Lenoir Cty. Pub. Library, 264 N.C. 360, 360 (1965), discussed in Section 3.6.7, *supra*.

397. *Id.* at 361.

398. Robinson v. Nash Cty., 43 N.C. App. 33, 36 (1979), discussed in Section 3.5.4, *supra*.

399. *Id.*

400. Aaser v. City of Charlotte, 265 N.C. 494, 497 (1965), discussed in Section 3.6.2, *supra*.

5.2 The Basic Approach and *Williams*

How does *Estate of Williams v. Pasquotank County Parks & Recreation Department*[401] fit into the framework just described? In short, *Williams* provides the test a trial judge must now employ to evaluate whether local government property was being used for a governmental undertaking or a proprietary endeavor. Once this initial determination has been made, the judiciary's traditional approach to unsafe premises claims against local governments will dictate whether governmental immunity bars the plaintiff's lawsuit. Nonetheless, it appears that *Williams* has already had and will continue to have a big impact on the exposure of local governments to liability, especially for unsafe building conditions. In *Bynum v. Wilson County*, the first post-*Williams* case involving a local government building to reach the North Carolina Supreme Court, the court applied *Williams* to arrive at a holding that could significantly limit local government liability for injuries allegedly caused by the failure to keep buildings reasonably safe.[402] The case posed a question the court had not yet answered: When a building houses both governmental and proprietary endeavors, should a unit's maintenance of the building be regarded as governmental or proprietary?

5.2.1 Bynum v. Wilson County

The plaintiff in *Bynum v. Wilson County*[403] visited a county office building to pay his water bill. After leaving the water department, he fell down the building's front steps and suffered serious injuries, including paralysis in his legs and right arm. The plaintiff filed suit against the county, alleging that the county had negligently failed to inspect, maintain, and repair the steps.[404] He later died, allegedly due to his injuries, but the administratrix of his estate continued the lawsuit.

The county asserted that governmental immunity barred the claims against it. In addition to housing the water department, the building contained the planning department, the finance department, the human resources department, the county manager's office, and the board of commissioners' meeting room—governmental functions all. The court of appeals rejected the county's immunity argument, holding that the lawsuit was not subject to governmental immunity inasmuch as (1) the state supreme court had previously ruled that a water department's sale of water for private consumption is a proprietary

---

401. 366 N.C. 195 (2012).
402. 367 N.C. 355 (2014).
403. 228 N.C. App. 1 (2013), *rev'd in part, remanded*, 367 N.C. 355 (2014).
404. The lawsuit also alleged that the county had failed to install a required handrail and to meet the requirements of the North Carolina Building Code. 367 N.C. at 357.

activity and (2) Mr. Bynum had gone to the county office building on the date of his fall to pay his water bill.[405]

All seven justices of the North Carolina Supreme Court voted to reverse the court of appeals, but three of the justices did not join the majority opinion for reasons explained in a concurring opinion. According to the majority, the court of appeals' approach in *Bynum* would erroneously base the availability of governmental immunity on a plaintiff's reason for visiting a city or county facility. That standard, the majority explained, is contrary to *Williams*, "which mandates that the analysis should center upon the governmental act or service that was allegedly done in a negligent manner."[406] In *Bynum*, it was not the county's operation of the water department that allegedly inflicted injury; it was the failure to keep the building's steps in good repair. The critical question, then, was whether the county's maintenance of the building constituted a governmental or a proprietary function.

Taking the *Williams* inquiry's first two steps in reverse order, the majority reasoned that the upkeep of the building was a governmental function inasmuch as the building was used for discretionary, legislative, and public functions only the county could perform.[407] The majority also held that the General Assembly has designated as a governmental function the locating, supervising, and maintaining of county buildings that serve discretionary, legislative, or public functions. In support of this conclusion, the court cited Chapter 153A, Section 169 of the North Carolina General Statutes (hereinafter G.S.),[408] which directs the board of commissioners to supervise the

---

405. Bynum v. Wilson Cty., 228 N.C. App. 1, 13 (2013). Curiously, although the court of appeals cited *Williams* in its discussion of governmental immunity, it did not attempt to apply the case's three-step inquiry in *Bynum*.

406. *Bynum*, 367 N.C. at 359.

407. Aside from the water department, all of the operations listed in *Bynum* as housed in the office building—the planning and inspection departments, for instance—constituted governmental functions. *See, e.g.*, City of Raleigh v. Fisher, 232 N.C. 629, 635 (1950) ("In enacting and enforcing zoning regulations, a municipality acts as a governmental agency . . . .").

408. G.S. 153A-169 provides:

> The board of commissioners shall supervise the maintenance, repair, and use of all county property. The board may issue orders and adopt by ordinance or resolution regulations concerning the use of county property, may designate and redesignate the location of any county department, office, or agency, and may designate and redesignate the site for any county building, including the courthouse. Before it may redesignate the site of the courthouse, the board of commissioners shall cause notice of its intention to do so to be published once at least four weeks before the meeting at which the redesignation is made.

The majority opinion in *Bynum* also cites G.S. 153A-351 and 153A-352, which collectively address the authority of counties to establish inspection departments and enforce state and local laws dealing with building construction.

maintenance, repair, and use of all county property.[409] Having found that the county's maintenance of the building qualified as a governmental function under the first two steps of the *Williams* inquiry, the majority did not proceed to the third step.

5.2.1.1 The Bynum Concurrence

The three concurring justices in *Bynum* agreed with the result reached by the majority but set out perceived problems with the majority's reasoning. Their chief worry was that the majority opinion would be interpreted to create "a categorical rule barring *any* premises liability claims against counties or municipalities for harms that occur on government property."[410] Such a rule, the concurring opinion argued, would be at odds with the court's many precedents demonstrating that a case-by-case inquiry is necessary to decide whether tort claims arising from unsafe property conditions are barred by governmental immunity.

Notwithstanding the concerns expressed in the concurring opinion, the *Bynum* majority pretty clearly did not intend to prohibit all premises liability claims against cities or counties. In the first place, the majority opinion nowhere states that the upkeep of local government property is always a governmental function. It holds that counties—and presumably other units of local government—perform a governmental function when they locate, supervise, or maintain "buildings that provide [discretionary, legislative, and public] functions."[411] A local government building devoted entirely to a proprietary function would not fall into this category. If the office building in *Bynum* had been occupied solely by the water department, there can be little doubt that the court would have classified its upkeep as a proprietary activity.

Similarly, the use of precedent in the majority opinion demonstrates that the majority did not mean to cloak all property maintenance by local governments in governmental immunity. The majority opinion approvingly cites the court's earlier decision holding that governmental immunity protected a county from a negligence claim based on the unsafe condition of the steps at the public library.[412] In that case, as the *Bynum* majority observed, the

---

409. The majority's reading of the statute is noticeably restrictive. As construed by the majority, G.S. 153A-169 classifies the upkeep of county buildings devoted to legislative, discretionary, or public functions as a governmental function. On its face, however, the statute applies to all county buildings. The majority appears to have interpreted the statute narrowly in *Bynum* to avoid the conclusion that a county undertakes a governmental function whenever it maintains or repairs a county building, including one dedicated exclusively to proprietary functions.

410. *Bynum*, 367 N.C. at 361 (Martin, J., concurring) (emphasis in original).

411. *Id.* at 360.

412. *Id.* (citing Seibold v. Kinston-Lenoir Cty. Pub. Library, 264 N.C. 360, 361 (1965)).

outcome turned not merely on the county's ownership of the property but on the property's service as a public library. The majority also cited *Williams* extensively without so much as hinting that the park's status as county property automatically entitled the county in that case to governmental immunity.

5.2.2 Governmental Immunity and Premises Liability after *Williams* and *Bynum*

Consistent with precedent, *Bynum* recognizes that when a local government facility serves a governmental function, maintenance of the facility becomes a governmental function and governmental immunity may bar personal injury claims arising from an alleged failure to maintain the premises in a reasonably safe condition. The *Bynum* decision expands on precedent by clarifying that, when a building houses both governmental and proprietary functions, the upkeep of the building will generally be deemed a governmental function, regardless of the plaintiff's reason for being there. Any local government unit that houses governmental and proprietary undertakings in the same facility is a potential beneficiary of the state supreme court's application of *Williams* in *Bynum*.

Although the *Bynum* majority probably did not intend to say that the maintenance of local government property is always a governmental function, a panel of the North Carolina Court of Appeals may have adopted something close to that interpretation in *Bellows v. Asheville City Board of Education*.[413] There the court held that governmental immunity barred claims against the school board for injuries the plaintiff had allegedly suffered in a fall from her wheelchair caused by unsafe conditions on school grounds. Citing *Bynum* as controlling authority, the court opined that the General Assembly had designated the ownership, maintenance, and repair of school property as governmental functions. It pointed to G.S. 115C-40 and 115C-521, which together invest school boards with responsibility for "the ownership and control of all school real and personal property, . . . [and] the maintenance and care thereof."[414] While noting the *Bynum* concurrence's worry about the potential breadth of the *Bynum* majority's opinion, the court of appeals did not consider itself "free to disregard the [*Bynum*] majority's reasoning."[415]

The subsequent decision by the North Carolina Supreme Court in *Meinck v. City of Gastonia* calls the soundness of the *Bellows* reasoning into question.[416] In *Meinck*, the plaintiff sued over injuries allegedly sustained in a

---

413. 243 N.C. App. 229 (2015).

414. *Id*. at 232.

415. *Id*. at 232 n.3.

416. The validity of *Bellows* is suspect for other reasons. The court of appeals' opinion omits any reference to G.S. 115C-524, arguably the statute most directly on point. Under G.S. 115C-524, school boards have a duty "to keep all school buildings in

fall down unsafe steps at a building the city was leasing to a nonprofit arts organization. The city had entered into the lease as part of a downtown redevelopment and revitalization effort. After examining the facts of the case in light of the *Williams* inquiry, the supreme court characterized the lease as a governmental activity for purposes of governmental immunity. If the court had understood *Bynum* to designate the upkeep of local government buildings as a governmental function in every situation, it would not have bothered analyzing whether the city's use of the building amounted to a governmental activity. The *Bynum* decision, then, should not be read to extend governmental immunity to the maintenance of local government buildings that are being used solely for proprietary endeavors.

---

good repair to the end that all public school property shall be taken care of and be at all times in proper condition for use." Subject to certain requirements, however, the statute exempts school boards from liability for personal injuries arising from the use of school property by non-school groups for non-school purposes or the use of outdoor school property by the public for recreational purposes. If it is correct to say that G.S. 115C-40 and 115C-521 make school maintenance a governmental function, then one may wonder why the General Assembly saw any need for the liability protections in G.S. 115C-524.

Chapter 6

Governmental Immunity for Public Parks

One of the more problematic topics in governmental immunity is the liability of cities and counties for injuries alleged to have resulted from unsafe conditions in public parks. This chapter analyzes the case law on this subject, paying special attention to the impact of *Estate of Williams v. Pasquotank County Parks & Recreation Department*[417]—itself a public park case—on the availability of governmental immunity as a defense to claims of negligent park maintenance.[418]

6.1 Liability for Park-Related Negligence Pre-*Williams*

In 1937, the North Carolina Supreme Court issued its first opinion on the relevance of governmental immunity to negligence claims arising from the operation of public parks. The plaintiff in *White v. City of Charlotte* alleged that a minor had been fatally injured when she fell—or was thrown—from a defective swing in a city park.[419] The city disputed liability, partly contending that its operation of the park amounted to a governmental function. Rejecting the city's argument, the supreme court reasoned that, even if the city's operation of the park constituted a governmental function, the city might still be held liable if the minor's death resulted from the breach of a legal duty to maintain the park in a reasonably safe condition.[420] The city charged fees for the use of certain facilities at the park, but the court did not highlight that fact in its opinion.

While describing the operation of public parks as a governmental function, the *White* decision left open the possibility that governmental immunity might not apply to tort claims arising from a local government's upkeep of a public park. Such an outcome would have been unusual but not

---

417. 366 N.C. 195 (2012).

418. This chapter incorporates material from Allen, *supra* note 62.

419. 211 N.C. 186 (1937).

420. The court speculated but did not rule outright that such a duty existed. *Id.* at 188–89. Furthermore, it went on to hold that the trial judge's dismissal of the lawsuit was proper because the plaintiff could not produce any evidence that negligence by the city had led to the minor's death. *Id.* at 189.

unprecedented. The court had previously held that the governmental nature of street maintenance does not protect a city from tort claims stemming from its failure to keep its streets in a reasonably safe condition.[421]

Roughly eight years after *White*, the General Assembly enacted Chapter 160, Section 156 of the North Carolina General Statutes (hereinafter G.S.), declaring that the establishment and operation of a "recreation system" is a "governmental function and a necessary expense as defined by . . . the Constitution of North Carolina."[422] It is tempting to assume that G.S. 160-156 represented a legislative response to *White*, but there are reasons to question this assumption. In the first place, the proximity of the terms "governmental function" and "necessary expense" in G.S. 160-156 suggests that the legislature had in mind not tort liability but constitutional challenges to the expenditure of public funds on local recreation programs.[423] Additionally, the statute's description of a recreation system as a "governmental function" did nothing to undermine the holding of *White*. The supreme court in *White* had conceded that the operation of a public park is a governmental function; the problem for cities and counties was that the court had then implied that they could still face tort liability for injuries resulting from unsafe park conditions. Presumably, if the General Assembly had wished to abrogate *White*, it would have added language to G.S. 160-156 unambiguously shielding local governments from park-related tort claims. Finally, although G.S. 160-156 referred to a "recreation system," public parks were not specifically mentioned in the statute. It might be expected that a legislature dissatisfied with *White* would have inserted an express reference to public parks into G.S. 160-156.

The state supreme court had a chance to consider the impact of G.S. 160-156 on park-related tort claims in *Glenn v. City of Raleigh*.[424] While picnicking in a city park, the plaintiff was struck in the head by a rock ejected from a lawnmower operated by a city employee.[425] According to evidence produced at trial, the park generated $18,531.14 in revenue for the fiscal year in which

---

421. Speas v. City of Greensboro, 204 N.C. 239, 241 (1933) ("The exercise of due care to keep its streets in a reasonably safe and suitable condition is one of the positive obligations imposed upon a municipal corporation. The discharge of this obligation cannot be evaded on the theory that in the . . . maintenance of its streets the municipality acts in a governmental capacity."). See Chapter 9 for more on the relationship between governmental immunity and the maintenance of city streets.

422. S.L. 1945, Ch. 1052, § 1.

423. For a case that discusses G.S. 160-156 in the funding context, see *Purser v. Ledbetter*, 227 N.C. 1 (1946).

424. 246 N.C. 469 (1957).

425. The mower was missing its front guard at the time of the incident, and the park superintendent testified that he had seen mowers throw rocks in the park on many prior occasions. *Id.* at 471.

the plaintiff was injured.[426] During that same year, the city spent a total of $43,995.96 on activities and maintenance at the park and $158,247.95 on maintenance and activities for its entire park system.[427]

The city argued that governmental immunity barred the plaintiff's negligence claims. The state supreme court agreed that if the operation of the park constituted a governmental activity, the plaintiff's negligence claims would be subject to governmental immunity. The court nonetheless concluded that the city's operation of the park did not qualify as a governmental function because (1) the park had produced more than "incidental income" and (2) the "pecuniary profit" to the city was large enough to transform the park into a proprietary undertaking.[428] In reaching this holding, the court did not explicitly compare the city's income from the park to the cost of operating the park.[429] Although the court noted the existence of G.S. 160-156, the statute played no discernible role in its analysis.[430]

The *Glenn* decision deviated from *White* in two important respects. First, the supreme court acknowledged in *Glenn* that governmental immunity could bar tort claims premised on unsafe park conditions. As previously noted, the court had suggested in *White* that immunity might not be available for park operations, even those regarded as governmental functions. Second, *Glenn* made the applicability of governmental immunity to park-related tort claims contingent on the revenue generated by the park. By contrast, in *White* the court had shown no interest in the fees charged by the city for certain park facilities.

---

426. Members of the public could take advantage of the picnic area for free. *Id.* at 472. The park did charge for the use of a train, merry-go-round, and swimming pool located in its amusement section. *Id.*

427. Adjusted for inflation, the income generated by the park during fiscal year 1952–1953 comes to about $172,166 in 2018 dollars, while the amount spent on maintenance and activities at Pullen Park, the site of the plaintiff's injury, totals approximately $408,745 and the system-wide amount comes to roughly $1,470,236. *See* U.S. Dep't of Labor, Bureau of Labor Statistics, CPI Inflation Calculator, www.bls.gov/data/inflation_calculator.htm.

428. *Glenn*, 246 N.C. at 477.

429. In the much more recent case of *Meinck v. City of Gastonia*, which did not involve public parks, the North Carolina Supreme Court interpreted the *Glenn* decision to say that the earlier court did not consider the city's evidence of the cost of park maintenance and activities. No. 130PA17, 2018 WL 5310160, at *10 n.7 (N.C. Oct. 26, 2018). While not repudiating the approach taken in *Glenn*, the supreme court approved the trial court's consideration of relevant city revenues and expenditures in *Meinck*. *Id.* For more on *Meinck*, see Section 3.3.3, *supra*.

430. Here is the court's only comment about G.S. 160-156 in *Glenn*: "We are advertent to G.S. 160-156, which is a declaration of State Public Policy as to adequate recreational programs and facilities . . . ." 246 N.C. at 477.

In 1971, the General Assembly recodified G.S. 160-156 as G.S. 160A-351, altering the statutory text in the process.[431] In contrast to its predecessor, G.S. 160A-351 expressly designates the establishment and operation of "public parks"—not just recreation programs—as a governmental function. Moreover, the "necessary expense" reference in G.S. 160-156 is omitted in G.S. 160A-351. It is unclear what prompted these changes. Perhaps the legislature intended to signal that, notwithstanding *Glenn*, park operations should be deemed governmental functions for immunity purposes, regardless of the income they generate. If that was indeed its intent, the legislature could have achieved its objective more effectively by straightforwardly exempting cities and counties from liability for injuries allegedly caused by unsafe park conditions.

The state supreme court issued an opinion in another park case not long after the enactment of G.S. 160A-351. The complaint in *Rich v. City of Goldsboro* alleged that the minor plaintiff had been injured in a fall from a seesaw in a city park and that her fall had resulted from the city's negligent failure to install handholds or other stabilizing devices.[432] The only income the city had derived from the park during the fiscal year of the plaintiff's injury was a $1,200 donation from the local Kiwanis Club, which operated a Kiddie Train in the park.[433] For that same year, the recreation program's total cost to the city was $167,912.66.[434] The supreme court reasoned that, unlike the revenue generated in *Glenn*, the Kiwanis donation plainly qualified as incidental income and, consequently, "was insufficient to constitute a waiver of [the city's] governmental immunity against suit."[435] The court did not discuss the potential relevance of G.S. 160-156 or the newly enacted G.S. 160A-351 to the city's immunity defense.

Prior to *Estate of Williams v. Pasquotank County Parks & Recreation Department*, then, the operation of a public park could qualify as a governmental function for immunity purposes, unless the park produced more than incidental income for the city or county in comparison with the total amount spent by the unit on park activities and maintenance. Aside from the specific dollar amounts at issue in *Glenn* and *Rich*, the case law did not offer local governments much guidance on the dividing line between incidental and substantial park revenue. Yet, as *Glenn* demonstrated, a park could operate at a financial loss and still be a proprietary function. Furthermore, though the General Assembly had twice enacted statutes describing recreation

---

431. S.L. 1971-698, §§ 1–2.

432. 282 N.C. 383 (1972).

433. The Kiddie Train was the only park activity for which there was a charge. *Id.* at 384.

434. In 2018 dollars, the donation amounts to about $7,235, and expenses for the city's recreation program equal roughly $1,012,320. *See* U.S. Dep't of Labor, Bureau of Labor Statistics, *supra* note 427.

435. *Rich*, 282 N.C. at 387.

programs as a governmental function, the judiciary seemed unmoved by its pronouncements.

6.2 The Approach to Park-Related Tort Claims in *Williams*

On its face, *Williams* represents a major departure from *Glenn* and *Rich*.[436] Whereas the earlier cases summarily discounted or ignored the legislature's description of park operations as a governmental function, *Williams* required the trial court to begin by considering the potential impact of G.S. 160A-351 on the defendant county's assertion that governmental immunity barred the plaintiff's wrongful death claim. Of course, *Williams* also states that G.S. 160A-351 will not always control the outcome of governmental/proprietary determinations in cases involving unsafe park conditions because not everything that occurs at a public park is covered by the statute.

The *Williams* opinion does not identify the criteria the lower courts should use to determine whether the specific activity that led to a plaintiff's injury in a particular case falls within the scope of G.S. 160A-351. The state supreme court could have provided some guidance on this score by deciding whether the statute encompassed the county's operation of the swimming area in which the decedent in the case had drowned, but it declined to rule on the matter. Alternatively, the court could have listed a few examples of the kinds of activities the statute likely encompasses. The lack of guidance as to what park activities fall within the ambit of G.S. 160A-351 handicapped the court of appeals when it confronted its first park case following *Williams*.

6.3 Application of *Williams* to Subsequent Park Cases

In *Horne v. Town of Blowing Rock*, the complaint alleged that the minor plaintiff was injured at a municipal park when he stepped into a drain hole that had been completely obscured by overgrown grass and grass clippings.[437] The complaint further alleged that the defendant town caused the plaintiff's injuries by negligently failing to maintain the grass around the drain hole.[438] The town argued that governmental immunity foreclosed the plaintiff's negligence claims because (1) G.S. 160A-351 classifies the operation of public parks as a governmental function and (2) there was nothing in the record showing that the town had received a profit or derived substantial income from the park.[439]

---

436. For a discussion of the *Williams* facts and holding, see Section 2.6, *supra*.

437. 223 N.C. App. 26 (2012).

438. The plaintiff also alleged that the town had negligently failed to inspect the premises and to warn visitors of hidden perils or unsafe conditions. *Id.* at 27.

439. The town further argued that the public policy of North Carolina favored a ruling that its operation of the park was a governmental function entitled to the

The court of appeals recognized that, under *Williams*, it first had to consider whether, and to what degree, the legislature had classified the specific activity that led to the plaintiff's injury as governmental or proprietary. It ruled that G.S. 160A-351 did not resolve the issue because, as observed in *Williams*, the statute does not cover "every nuanced action that could occur in a park[.]"[440] The court then turned to the other steps in the *Williams* test (see Section 2.6, *supra*), devoting special attention to the revenue factors found in step three. It viewed these factors and the ones relied upon in *Glenn* and *Rich* as essentially identical and concluded that it should evaluate the town's immunity defense in light of the two earlier cases. According to the court of appeals, *Glenn* and *Rich* establish that

- a local government's operation of a free public park for the recreation of its citizens is a governmental function for which ordinarily governmental immunity will apply and
- governmental immunity for park operations will be lost if a local government derives more than incidental revenue from either the operation of the park or the conduct of activities within the park.

Applying these principles, the court of appeals held that no governmental immunity determination could be made in *Horne* without evidence of the revenue the town had received from the park's operation. Such evidence, the court pointed out, could be obtained through the discovery process and presented to the trial court, enabling it to make an evidence-based assessment of the town's immunity defense.

6.3.1 The Treatment of G.S. 160A-351 in *Horne*

The rationale for the outcome in *Horne* is not wholly persuasive. For one thing, the opinion's treatment of G.S. 160A-351 is problematic. The court of appeals held that G.S. 160A-351 did not bar the negligence claims against the town, largely because *Williams* holds that the statute does not cover every *nuanced action* that could happen in a public park. Of course, the mere fact that G.S. 160A-351 will not *always* control the classification of a park activity does not mean that it will *never* do so. Like *Williams*, though, *Horne* says little about how a court should go about analyzing whether G.S. 160A-351 covers the specific park activity alleged to have harmed the plaintiff in a given lawsuit.

---

protection of governmental immunity. *Id.* at 32. The court of appeals did not address the merits of this contention, but the argument is not without foundation. The best statutory support for it is found in G.S. 160A-351, which states that "*the policy* of North Carolina [is] to forever encourage, foster, and provide" public parks and recreation programs for the state's citizens. G.S. 160A-351 (emphasis added).

440. *Horne*, 223 N.C. App. at 34 (quoting *Williams*, 366 N.C. at 202).

Interestingly, the *Horne* opinion offers a good reason for thinking that, contrary to its holding, G.S. 160A-351 encompasses a local government's upkeep of park lawns.

> [The] attempt to distinguish the particular activity of lawn maintenance from the general undertaking of operating the public park . . . is meaningless, as lawn maintenance of a public park is an indispensable aspect of establishing and operating such park.[441]

It stands to reason that if lawn maintenance is an indispensable aspect of operating a public park, it must be covered by G.S. 160A-351, or the statute is effectively meaningless. Put differently, if the broad language of the statute does not encompass the very activities necessary to operate a public park, then it does not cover park operations at all for purposes of governmental immunity. This conclusion seems at odds with the emphasis placed in *Williams* on the statute's relevance to immunity decisions in public park cases.

Additionally, the *Horne* opinion's reliance on *Glenn* and *Rich* might not be justified. In neither of those cases did the state supreme court consider in any substantive way the General Assembly's classification of park activities as a governmental function. The *Williams* decision does not expressly overrule *Glenn* or *Rich*—it actually cites *Glenn* approvingly—but it is not obvious that the outcome in *Glenn* would have been the same under the three-step inquiry mandated by *Williams*. At a minimum, if confronted with a case substantially similar to *Glenn*, the supreme court would need to explain in more detail than the court of appeals did in *Horne* why the legislature's designation of park operations as a governmental function did not apply to the city's maintenance of a public park.

6.4 Governmental Immunity and Park Cases: The Rules after *Williams* and *Horne*

After *Williams* and *Horne*, it is unclear when, if ever, G.S. 160A-351 will compel a court to designate the specific park-related undertaking that led to a plaintiff's injury as a governmental function. The state of the law seems to be that when a plaintiff alleges injury due to an unsafe condition at a city or county park, the court will deem the operation of the park a governmental function if the park is completely free to the public. In such cases, governmental immunity will shield the city or county from the plaintiff's claims, unless the unit has waived immunity through the purchase of liability insurance or participation in a government risk pool. If the unit receives income from the park—usually in the form of facilities or activity fees—the court will have to analyze whether the income qualifies as incidental, with the amounts at

---

441. *Id.* at 35.

issue in *Glenn* and *Rich*, adjusted for inflation, providing guidance. Incidental income will not transform the operation of the park into a proprietary function and thus will not deprive the unit of governmental immunity. If the park generates substantial income, the court will categorize its operation as a proprietary function, exposing the unit to liability on the same basis as a private landowner.

Chapter 7

Governmental Immunity and Contract-Related Claims

As explained in Chapter 4, governmental immunity is not a defense to claims that a unit of local government has breached its obligations under a valid contract. The law recognizes an array of contract-related claims aside from breach of contract, however. They fall broadly into two categories: (1) equitable claims potentially available to parties to invalid contracts and (2) negligence claims connected to a party's negotiation or performance of a contract.

This chapter explores the extent to which governmental immunity is a defense to contract-related claims other than breach of contract. It pays special attention to the impact of *Estate of Williams v. Pasquotank County Parks & Recreation Department*[442] on governmental immunity in this context.[443]

7.1 Governmental Immunity and Equitable Claims

7.1.1 Equitable Claim Basics

When a party furnishes goods or services to another only to find no payment forthcoming, and the existence of a valid contract is in doubt, the injured party can attempt to obtain compensation through one or more of the equitable remedies created by the courts to prevent a party from unjustly profiting at another's expense.[444] The measure of damages for unjust enrichment is the reasonable value of the goods and services provided to the defendant.[445]

---

442. 366 N.C. 195 (2012).

443. This chapter incorporates material from Trey Allen, *The Impact of* Williams v. Pasquotank County *on Local Government Liability: Part II: Contract-Related Claims*, Loc. Gov't L. Bull. No. 138 (Sept. 2015), https://www.sog.unc.edu/sites/www.sog.unc.edu/files/reports/2015-09-29_20150488.pdf.

444. *See* Britt v. Britt, 320 N.C. 573, 577 (1987) (quoting Restatement (First) of Restitution § 1 (1937)) (noting the legal principle that "'a person who has been unjustly enriched at the expense of another is required to make restitution'"). To establish a claim for unjust enrichment, the generic form of many such remedies, a plaintiff must show that (1) it conferred a benefit on the defendant; (2) the benefit was not conferred by an officious or unjustified interference in the defendant's affairs; (3) the benefit was not provided gratuitously, that is, for free; (4) the benefit is measurable; and (5) the defendant consciously accepted the benefit. JPMorgan Chase Bank, Nat'l Ass'n v. Browning, 230 N.C. App. 537, 541–42 (2013).

445. Booe v. Shadrick, 322 N.C. 567, 570 (1988).

Decisions by both the North Carolina Supreme Court and the North Carolina Court of Appeals characterize unjust enrichment claims as claims in "quasi contract" or "contract implied in law."[446] When a plaintiff alleges a quasi contract or contract implied in law for the reasonable value of services provided to the defendant, the claim is often described as one for *quantum meruit*—Latin for "as much as he deserved."[447] When the claim is for materials or other goods furnished to the defendant, the expression *quantum valebant*—"as much as they were worth"—is sometimes used.[448] A plaintiff may not pursue an unjust enrichment claim if a valid contract between the plaintiff and the defendant governs the transaction at issue.[449]

---

446. *E.g.*, Whitfield v. Gilchrist, 348 N.C. 39, 42 (1998) (describing circumstances in which the courts will "impose a quasi contract or a contract implied in law in order to prevent an unjust enrichment"); Bain v. Unitrin Auto & Home Ins. Co., 210 N.C. App. 398, 417 (2011) (internal quotation marks omitted) (citations omitted) ("It is well settled . . . that a claim for unjust enrichment is a claim in quasi contract or a contract implied in law . . . .").

As the terms "quasi contract" and "contract implied in law" suggest, the defendant's obligation to pay the plaintiff on a claim of unjust enrichment "is not based on a promise but is imposed by law to prevent an unjust enrichment." *Britt*, 320 N.C. at 577.

> A quasi-contractual obligation is one that is created by the law for reasons of justice, without any expression of assent and sometimes even against a clear expression of dissent, and generally, quasi or constructive contracts rest on the equitable principle that a person shall not be allowed to enrich himself unjustly at the expense of another, and on the principle that whatsoever it is certain that a man ought to do, that the law supposes him to have promised to do. The obligation to do justice rests on all persons, and if one obtains money or property of others without authority, the law, independently of express contract, will compel restitution of compensation.

Root v. Allstate Ins. Co., 272 N.C. 580, 583 (1967) (internal quotation marks omitted) (citations omitted).

447. *Whitfield*, 348 N.C. at 42 ("*Quantum meruit* is a measure of recovery for the reasonable value of services rendered in order to prevent unjust enrichment.").

The term *quantum meruit* has occasionally been defined to include equitable claims for materials as well as services. *E.g.*, Potter v. Homestead Pres. Ass'n, 330 N.C. 569, 578 (1992) ("*Quantum meruit*, a measure of recovery for the reasonable value of material and services rendered by the plaintiff, is an equitable remedy based upon a contract implied in law."); Data Gen. Corp. v. Cty. of Durham, 143 N.C. App. 97, 103 (2001) ("*Quantum meruit* operates as an equitable remedy based upon a quasi contract or a contract applied in law, such that a party may recover for the reasonable value of materials and services rendered in order to prevent unjust enrichment.").

448. *E.g.*, Coats v. Sampson Cty. Mem'l Hosp., Inc., 264 N.C. 332, 334 (1965) ("Plaintiffs furnished to defendant there all the material and labor the value of which they now seek to recover in *quantum valebant* and in *quantum meruit*.").

449. *See, e.g., Britt*, 320 N.C. at 577 ("If there is a contract between the parties the contract governs the claim and the law will not imply a contract."). *See also Whitfield*, 348 N.C. at 42 ("An implied contract is not based on an actual agreement, and

Another equitable remedy that a plaintiff may employ when a contract is of doubtful validity is estoppel. Estoppel by acceptance of benefits, for example, prevents a party that has accepted the benefits arising under a contract from later denying the contract's validity.[450] Similarly, estoppel by misrepresentation keeps a party from denying the enforceability of a contract if that party "'intentionally or through culpable negligence'" induced the other party to believe that their contract was binding and the other party relied on this belief to its detriment.[451]

7.1.2 Governmental Immunity and Equitable Claims Pre-*Williams*

When it abolished sovereign immunity as a defense to breach of contract claims in *Smith v. State*, the North Carolina Supreme Court did not address whether sovereign immunity bars contract-related equitable claims against the state.[452] The court took up that issue for the first time in *Whitfield v. Gilchrist*.[453] There, at the request of the local district attorney, the plaintiff law firm brought public nuisance actions against two corporations, each of

---

quantum meruit is not an appropriate remedy when there is an actual agreement between the parties."); *Potter*, 330 N.C. at 578 ("*Quantum meruit* is not an appropriate remedy when the plaintiff has alleged an express, oral contract.").

450. Brooks v. Hackney, 329 N.C. 166, 172 n.3 (1991). For an instance of this use of estoppel, see *Capital Outdoor Advertising, Inc. v. Harper*, 7 N.C. App. 501, 505 (1970) (Inasmuch as "[t]he contract has been fully and wholly executed by the lessor by constructing and erecting the highway signs according to the terms of the lease . . . the defendant, having accepted the benefits of these signs, will not now be heard to repudiate the validity of the lease[.]").

451. Gaston-Lincoln Transit, Inc. v. Md. Cas. Co., 285 N.C. 541, 548 (1974) (quoting Boddie v. Bond, 154 N.C. 359, 365 (1911)). For there to be a valid claim of equitable misrepresentation,

> there must exist a false representation or concealment of material facts, with a knowledge, actual or constructive, of the truth. The other party must have been without such knowledge, or, having the means of knowledge of the real facts, must not have been culpably negligent in informing himself. It must have been intended or expected that the representation or concealment should be acted upon, and the party asserting the estoppel must have reasonably relied on it or acted upon it to his prejudice.

Boddie, 154 N.C. at 365–66. *See also* Hawkins v. M & J Fin. Corp., 238 N.C. 174, 177–78 (1953) (setting forth the factors to be considered when determining whether estoppel by misrepresentation applies).

452. 289 N.C. 303, 320 (1976), discussed in Section 4.3, *supra*.

453. 348 N.C. at 40 ("The question presented for review is whether the doctrine of sovereign immunity bars recovery in *quantum meruit* upon an action based on a contract implied in law against the State of North Carolina.").

which owned a motel or hotel in Charlotte.[454] After those actions resulted in the abatement of the nuisances, the plaintiff filed suit against the state alleging claims of *quantum meruit* for the value of its services in the nuisance actions.[455] The state argued that sovereign immunity barred the plaintiff's claims.

Ruling in the state's favor, the supreme court stressed that the outcome in *Smith* had turned on its conclusion that, "'when the state enters into a [valid] contract[,] it does so voluntarily and authorizes its liability'" for damages upon its breach of the contract.[456] Put differently, each time the state enters into a valid contract, it signals a willingness to be sued for breach. To hold that the state has consented to be sued over a contract implied in law would require the court "first [to] imply a contract in law where none exist[ed] in fact, [and] then use that implication to support the further implication that the State ha[d] intentionally waived its sovereign immunity and consented to be sued for damages for breach of the contract it never entered in fact."[457] The court pronounced itself unwilling to pile up inferences in that way.[458]

By holding that sovereign immunity bars equitable claims against the state, *Whitfield* left open the possibility that governmental immunity could protect local governments from equitable claims. In cases decided prior to *Whitfield*,

---

454. Chapter 19 of the North Carolina General Statutes (hereinafter G.S.) covers certain public nuisances defined therein. It encompasses, *inter alia*, the erection or use of any building or place for prostitution, gambling, the illegal possession or sale of alcoholic beverages, the illegal possession or sale of controlled substances, or the illegal possession or sale of obscene or lewd matter. G.S. 19-1(a). When such a nuisance exists, the attorney general, the district attorney, county, municipality, "or any private citizen of the county" may bring a lawsuit to abate the nuisance and perpetually to enjoin all persons from maintaining the nuisance, except that a private citizen may not initiate proceedings under Chapter 19 if the nuisance involves the illegal possession or sale of obscene or lewd matter. G.S. 19-2.1.

455. It appears that the plaintiff did not allege breach of contract. This may have been because, as the state supreme court remarked in its opinion, the district attorney could not have lawfully entered into a contract to pay the plaintiff for legal services without having first obtained the approval of other state officials. *Whitfield*, 348 N.C. at 43–45.

456. *Id.* at 42 (quoting *Smith*, 289 N.C. at 322).

457. *Id.* at 42–43. Fiscal concerns appear to have influenced the outcome in *Whitfield*. When the state enters into a contract, the court observed, it has the ability, "with a fair degree of accuracy, [to] estimate the extent of its liability for a breach of contract." *Id.* at 42 (quoting *Smith*, 289 N.C. at 322). The state would find it much harder, if not impossible, to estimate its potential liability for unjust enrichment claims, largely because the state would have no way of identifying every unjust enrichment claim that might be alleged against it.

458. *Id.* at 43 (emphases in original) ("Only when the State has implicitly waived sovereign immunity by *expressly* entering into a *valid* contract through an agent of the State expressly authorized by law to enter into such contract may a plaintiff proceed with a claim against the State upon the State's breach.").

the state supreme court had repeatedly held that local governments may be liable for claims of *quantum meruit,* but apparently governmental immunity was not raised as a defense in any of those cases.[459] Almost exactly three years after *Whitfield,* the North Carolina Court of Appeals considered the effect of governmental immunity on equitable claims in *Data General Corp. v. County of Durham.*[460] The plaintiff company alleged breach of contract, *quantum meruit,* estoppel, and negligent misrepresentation over the defendant county's refusal to make further payments for computer hardware and software the county had kept following the expiration of its lease agreement with the plaintiff.[461]

The county argued that governmental immunity barred the plaintiff's claims because the contract did not comply with G.S. 159-28. Under that statute, a city or county must satisfy certain "preaudit" requirements before it may incur a financial obligation accounted for in the budget ordinance or project ordinance.[462] If the obligation is reduced to writing or evidenced by a written purchase order, the preaudit statute dictates that the agreement or purchase order include a preaudit certificate on its face.[463] (The preaudit certificate is written confirmation that all preaudit requirements have been

---

459. *E.g.,* Charlotte Lumber & Mfg. Co. v. City of Charlotte, 242 N.C. 189, 195 (1955) (in the absence of a valid contract, plaintiff could recover "on basis of *quantum meruit* for the reasonable and just value of the sewer system" taken over by city); Hawkins v. Town of Dallas, 229 N.C. 561, 564 (1948) (internal quotation marks omitted) (citations omitted) (when a construction contract is rendered illegal due to noncompliance with statutory bidding requirements, plaintiff may nonetheless recover "on a *quantum meruit* for the reasonable and just value of the work and labor done and material furnished" if it has completed the project and its work has been accepted by the defendant municipality); Abbot Realty Co. v. City of Charlotte, 198 N.C. 564, 568 (1930) ("Notwithstanding the failure of plaintiff to sustain its contention that defendant is liable to it on the contract alleged in the complaint, the defendant . . . is liable for the reasonable and just value of the sewers, if . . . after their construction defendant took them over and incorporated them into its municipal sewerage system."); McPhail v. Bd. of Comm'rs of Cumberland Cty., 119 N.C. 330, 335 (1896) ("As the repairs [to the bridge] have been actually made and accepted, the county is bound on a *quantum meruit* for the reasonable and just value of the work and labor done and material furnished, but not for the attempted contract of Harrison and McNeill, which, under the law, they had and could have no authority to make so as to bind the county.").

460. 143 N.C. App. 97 (2001).

461. "The tort of negligent misrepresentation occurs when a party justifiably relies to his detriment on information prepared without reasonable care by one who owed the relying party a duty of care." Raritan River Steel Co. v. Cherry, Bekaert & Holland, 322 N.C. 200, 206 (1988).

462. *See generally* GREGORY S. ALLISON & KARA A. MILLONZI, *Managing and Disbursing Public Funds, in* INTRODUCTION TO LOCAL GOVERNMENT FINANCE 212–19 (Kara A. Millonzi ed., 4th ed. 2018) (explaining preaudit requirements).

463. The preaudit statute specifies that the preaudit certificate must be worded substantially as follows:

fulfilled.) An obligation incurred in violation of the preaudit statute is "invalid and may not be enforced."[464]

Although the preaudit statute applied to the lease agreement in *Data General*, there was no evidence of any preaudit certificate. The court of appeals therefore held that no valid contract existed between the plaintiff and the county. Turning to the plaintiff's *quantum meruit* and estoppel claims, the court ruled that governmental immunity defeated the plaintiff's efforts to recover in equity.

> In *Whitfield* . . . , our Supreme Court declined to imply a contract in law in derogation of sovereign immunity to allow a party to recover under a theory of quantum meruit, and we decline to do so here. . . . On this same basis, we conclude that [the plaintiff] may not defeat a claim of . . . governmental immunity upon a theory of estoppel.[465]

The court also held that the plaintiff could not "recover under an equitable theory such as estoppel" because the lease agreement failed to satisfy the preaudit statute and "parties dealing with governmental organizations are charged with notice of all limitations upon the organizations' authority, as the scope of such authority is a matter of public record."[466]

In disposing of the plaintiff's equitable claims, the court took no notice of whether the county had interacted with the plaintiff in a governmental or a proprietary capacity. The court did, however, use the governmental/proprietary distinction to evaluate whether governmental immunity barred the plaintiff's claim for negligent misrepresentation. In particular, it determined that the county's entry into the lease agreement with the plaintiff qualified as a proprietary activity and, consequently, that governmental immunity did not block the plaintiff's claim for negligent misrepresentation. Presumably, given the court's ruling that the county had undertaken a proprietary function, application of the governmental/proprietary distinction to the plaintiff's equitable claims would have led the court to find that the county was not immune to those claims. The collective holdings in *Data General* thus suggest that governmental immunity can bar equitable claims without regard to whether the activity that produced the plaintiff's injury was governmental or proprietary.

This instrument has been preaudited in the manner required by the Local Government Budget and Fiscal Control Act.

———————————————————
(Signature of finance officer)

G.S. 159-28(a1).

464. G.S. 159-28(a2).
465. *Data General*, 143 N.C. App. at 103–04.
466. *Id.* at 104.

In *Wing v. Town of Landis*,[467] the court of appeals once more examined the availability of equitable claims against units of local government. The plaintiff in *Wing* sought reimbursement for the cost of engineering plans for the extension of the defendant town's water service to a proposed housing development expansion. The court of appeals agreed that in certain situations a unit may be liable on a claim of *quantum meruit*, provided adequate evidence supports the claim.[468] Yet the court took pains to observe that, because the town had not asserted governmental immunity as a defense, its opinion did not consider how that defense might have affected the plaintiff's claim.[469]

In *M Series Rebuild, LLC v. Town of Mount Pleasant*,[470] the court of appeals issued its last major decision in advance of *Estate of Williams v. Pasquotank County Parks & Recreation Department*[471] on equitable remedies and governmental immunity. The plaintiff alleged claims against the defendant town for breach of contract and unjust enrichment over unpaid repairs to the town's firetruck. While admitting that its agreement with the town lacked a preaudit certificate, the plaintiff insisted that its claim of unjust enrichment was viable under *Wing* and state supreme court precedents acknowledging the liability of cities for unjust enrichment. The town argued that *Data General* foreclosed the plaintiff's unjust enrichment claim.

The court of appeals concluded that *Data General* indeed controlled the outcome. It held that the absence of a preaudit certificate meant that the parties had not entered into a valid contract and, thus, the town had not waived its immunity for breach of contract. Although *Data General* involved a claim of *quantum meruit* and not, as in *M Series Rebuild*, for unjust enrichment, the court observed that both are "claim[s] in quasi contract or contract implied in law."[472] Accordingly, "based on the reasoning in *Data General* and *Whitfield*," governmental immunity upended the plaintiff's attempt to recover for unjust enrichment.[473]

Once again, the court's ruling that governmental immunity precluded a contract-related equitable claim did not turn on whether the defendant local

---

467. 165 N.C. App. 691 (2004).

468. *Id.* at 693–94 ("A party may recover from a municipality under a *quantum meruit* theory upon a proper showing.").

469. Ultimately, the court of appeals affirmed summary judgment in favor of the defendant municipality because the evidence showed neither that the plans had been drafted in expectation of payment by the municipality nor that the municipality had benefited from completion of the plans. *Id.* at 695.

470. 222 N.C. App. 59 (2012).

471. 366 N.C. 195 (2012).

472. 222 N.C. App. at 67 (internal quotation marks omitted) (citations omitted).

473. *Id.* The court explained that *Wing* was inapposite for two reasons: (1) the defendant in *Wing* did not assert an immunity defense and (2) *Wing* did not concern a contract subject to preaudit requirements.

government had acted in a governmental capacity. This perhaps added to an impression made by *Data General* that the governmental/proprietary distinction is not a factor when a unit raises governmental immunity as a defense to an equitable claim.

7.1.3 Governmental Immunity and Equitable Remedies Post-*Williams*

In *Estate of Williams v. Pasquotank County Parks & Recreation Department*[474]—as explained more fully in Chapter 2—the state supreme court reformulated the standards for distinguishing governmental activities from proprietary undertakings. Less than two years later, the court of appeals again considered governmental immunity as a defense to equitable claims in *Viking Utilities Corp., Inc. v. Onslow Water & Sewer Authority*.[475] According to the complaint, the defendant water and sewer authority entered into an agreement to purchase the plaintiffs' wastewater system. The agreement specified that the authority would receive a credit of $250,000 toward the purchase price in return for allowing the plaintiffs to connect to the wastewater system at any location served by the authority without paying a connection—or "tap"—fee. The complaint alleged that the authority had subsequently required the plaintiffs to pay tap fees anyway. It sought damages not only for breach of contract but also for a range of equitable claims: restitution, *quantum meruit*, unjust enrichment, and estoppel. The authority moved to dismiss the lawsuit and appealed after the trial court denied its motion.

Instead of relying on *Data General* and *M Series Rebuild*, the court of appeals looked to *Williams* for guidance. It quoted the supreme court's remark in *Williams* that governmental immunity "covers only the acts of a municipality or a municipal corporation committed pursuant to its governmental functions" and "does not . . . apply when [a] municipality engages in a proprietary function."[476] The court of appeals took this remark to mean that immunity would not bar the plaintiffs' equitable claims if they stemmed from the authority's performance of a proprietary function. It further reasoned that the *Williams* test had to be employed to ascertain whether the author-

---

474. 366 N.C. 195 (2012).

475. 232 N.C. App. 684 (2014). A water and sewer authority is a kind of special purpose government created under G.S. Chapter 162A. LAWRENCE, *supra* note 44, at 8. It is formed by resolution of a board of county commissioners or by resolution of any two or more political subdivisions. G.S. 162A-3, -3.1. For purposes of forming a water and sewer authority, a "political subdivision" is "any county, city, town, incorporated village, sanitary district or other political subdivision or public corporation of this State now or hereafter incorporated." G.S. 162A-2(7). A water and sewer authority enjoys a wide range of powers related to the provision of water and sewer services, though it lacks taxing power. G.S. 162A-6; LAWRENCE, *supra*, at 8.

476. *Viking Utilities*, 232 N.C. App. at 687 (quoting *Williams*, 366 N.C. at 199 (internal quotation marks omitted)).

ity's undertaking was governmental or proprietary. In particular, the court explained, properly assessing the authority's immunity defense would require the trial court to

> consider the pertinent statutory provisions as well as factual evidence regarding [the] plaintiffs' allegations, fees charged by [the] defendant, whether the fees cover[ed] more than the operating costs of the water authority, and any other evidence relevant to the issue of whether, in executing and interpreting its contract with [the] plaintiffs, [the] defendant was acting in a governmental or proprietary capacity.[477]

Because the trial court had been without all of the information necessary to conduct the full *Williams* inquiry, the court of appeals ruled that it had properly refused to dismiss the plaintiffs' claims at the outset of the litigation.

On the surface, *Viking Utilities* might seem at odds with *Data General* and *M Series Rebuild*. It is unclear whether the judges who decided *Viking Utilities* regarded their ruling as a departure from those earlier cases: no reference to *Data General* or *M Series Rebuild* appears in the court's opinion. Such was the uncertain state of the law when the United States Court of Appeals for the Fourth Circuit decided *AGI Associates, Inc. v. City of Hickory*.[478]

AGI Associates concerned an agreement between Profile Aviation and the defendant city for aviation services at Hickory Regional Airport. Profile obtained a leasehold interest in certain parcels of land at the airport under the agreement and used that interest as security to obtain financing from a bank, which in turn assigned its rights to the plaintiff. Profile defaulted on its repayment obligations and declared bankruptcy, and the bankruptcy court put the city in possession of the airport. The plaintiff asserted that, under the agreement between the city and Profile, the city should not have taken possession without first having cured Profile's default. It further maintained that the city owed it rental payments that the city had collected from airport tenants after taking possession. The plaintiff filed suit against the city in federal district court, alleging equitable claims for disgorgement of rents and unjust enrichment.[479] The city unsuccessfully moved to dismiss the plaintiff's claims, asserting governmental immunity.

---

477. *Id.* at 689.

478. 773 F.3d 576 (4th Cir. 2014).

479. As a corporation from another state, the plaintiff had the option of pursuing relief against the City of Hickory in federal court rather than state court, despite the lack of any federal claims in the complaint. *See* 28 U.S.C. § 1332. In such a case, when resolving a question of North Carolina law, the Fourth Circuit follows the decisions of the North Carolina Supreme Court. *AGI Associates*, 773 F.3d at 580. If the issue is one that the supreme court has not addressed, the Fourth Circuit looks to the decisions of the North Carolina Court of Appeals to try to predict how the supreme court would rule, though it may disregard those decisions if it concludes, based on other persuasive

On appeal, the plaintiff argued that the city had waived immunity by engaging in a proprietary function, namely, the operation of an airport.[480] The city countered that "North Carolina law limits waiver of governmental immunity under the proprietary function theory to contract and tort cases only."[481] In other words, the city maintained that a waiver of immunity for a proprietary undertaking does not extend to equitable claims. It cited *M Series Rebuild* and *Data General* as the foundation for its position.

In affirming the trial court's order, the Fourth Circuit deemed the city's reliance on *Data General* and *M Series Rebuild* to be misplaced. Regarding *M Series Rebuild*, the court pointed out that the "proprietary function theory" of waiver is not discussed in the opinion of the North Carolina Court of Appeals.[482] The Fourth Circuit conceded, though, that *Data General* bolstered the city's argument. After all, "if immunity from equitable claims can properly be waived under the proprietary function theory, the court [in *Data General*] could have upheld the quantum meruit and estoppel claims on the same basis that it had upheld the negligent misrepresentation claim: that [the county] had acted in a proprietary capacity."[483]

Yet the Fourth Circuit ultimately concluded that *Data General* should not be afforded "controlling weight."[484] It reasoned that *Viking Utilities* had called the soundness of *Data General* into question by making the applicability of governmental immunity to equitable claims there depend on whether the defendant water and sewer authority had acted in a proprietary capacity. The Fourth Circuit saw *Viking Utilities* as consistent with *Williams* and, as the court of appeals had done in *Viking Utilities*, quoted *Williams* for the proposition that governmental immunity is confined to governmental functions.[485]

In short, then, *AGI Associates* views *Data General* as outdated in view of *Williams* and *Viking Utilities*. If this is correct, when a future case materially

---

information, that the supreme court would disagree with the court of appeals. *Id.* at 580–81.

480. It has long been held that a local government's operation of an airport is a proprietary function. See Section 3.4.4, *supra*.

481. *AGI Associates*, 773 F.3d at 580.

482. The Fourth Circuit's discussion of *M Series Rebuild* begs the question. The plaintiff in *M Series Rebuild* did not allege any tort claims, so if engaging in a proprietary function does not waive immunity against equitable claims, the North Carolina Court of Appeals had no reason to evaluate whether the defendant municipality had undertaken a proprietary activity.

483. *AGI Associates*, 773 F.3d at 580.

484. *Id.* at 581.

485. The Fourth Circuit ended by opining that the rationale behind the governmental/proprietary distinction supports the waiver of immunity from equitable claims arising from a proprietary function. That rationale, according to the court, is that local government units warrant special protection from civil liability when they fulfill their governmental responsibilities but not when they act as corporations. *Id.* at 582.

similar to *Data General* comes before the North Carolina Court of Appeals, the court should rule that governmental immunity does not defeat the plaintiff's equitable claims. As discussed below, there is reason to think that the Fourth Circuit was wrong about the ongoing reliability of *Data General*.

7.1.4 Current Rules on Immunity and Equitable Claims

Although it is easy to understand why the Fourth Circuit perceived a conflict between *Data General* and *Viking Utilities*, the two cases can be reconciled. The key to harmonizing them is recognizing that the preaudit statute was a factor in *Data General* but not in *Viking Utilities*. When this distinction is carefully evaluated in light of relevant precedents, two complementary principles emerge.

- *First Principle: When the failure to comply with preaudit requirements invalidates a contract, governmental immunity will bar equitable claims arising from the contract, regardless of whether it concerns a proprietary function.*

If *Data General* is construed to hold that governmental immunity blocks all contract-related equitable claims against local governments, the decision plainly is at odds with *Viking Utilities*. The former decision can and should be read more narrowly, however. Two factors dictated the outcome in *Data General*: (1) the state supreme court's declaration in *Whitfield* that sovereign immunity defeats equitable claims against the state and (2) the disputed lease's noncompliance with preaudit requirements. In *M Series Rebuild*, the court confirmed that the preaudit statute had influenced its handling of the equitable claims alleged in *Data General*. The court expressly distinguished *Data General* from *Wing v. Town of Landis*,[486] wherein it had approved the pursuit of an equitable claim against a local government, by noting that, unlike the equitable claim alleged in *Wing*, the equitable claims asserted in *Data General* arose from a contract invalidated by the preaudit statute.

By declaring that contracts entered into in contravention of its provisions are invalid and unenforceable, the preaudit statute reflects the General Assembly's judgment that local governments should not be bound by agreements executed in violation of preaudit requirements. Given the close relationship between claims for breach of contract and equitable claims, allowing a plaintiff to recover in equity when noncompliance with preaudit requirements forecloses a claim for breach would undermine the legislative intent behind the preaudit statute.[487] The court of appeals said as much in *Finger*

---

486. 165 N.C. App. 691 (2004).

487. It can be argued that this same logic should have prompted the court of appeals in *Data General* to ignore the governmental/proprietary distinction in its treatment of the defendant county's immunity defense to the plaintiff's claim of

v. Gaston County,[488] a decision issued after *Data General* but before *M Series Rebuild*. The plaintiff, a former police officer, alleged breach of contract and estoppel claims over the defendant county's refusal to pay the supplemental retirement benefit specified in the parties' memorandum of understanding.[489] The court of appeals held that the lack of a preaudit certificate invalidated the memorandum and that *Data General* precluded the plaintiff's estoppel claim. It further justified its unwillingness to let the plaintiff proceed on a claim of estoppel as follows:

> Our General Assembly has in [the preaudit statute] made a policy determination to forbid counties from entering into contracts for payment of money that lack a preaudit certificate. To permit a party to use estoppel to render a county contractually bound despite the absence of the certificate would effectively negate [the statute]. We are not free to allow a party to obtain a result indirectly that the General Assembly has expressly forbidden.[490]

Consistent with *Finger*, the rejection of the equitable claims in *Data General* and *M Series Rebuild* should be viewed as judicial deference to the General Assembly's wishes. Rightly understood, then, *Data General* stands for the proposition that governmental immunity applies to equitable claims

---

negligent misrepresentation. Like the plaintiff's equitable claims, the negligent misrepresentation claim rested on alleged facts surrounding the contract between the plaintiff and the defendant county.

While this argument unquestionably has merit, preexisting case law pretty clearly made the county's immunity to the plaintiff's negligent misrepresentation claim contingent on the governmental/proprietary distinction. Long before *Data General*, it was settled law in North Carolina that a tort claim's susceptibility to governmental immunity hinged on whether the conduct that produced the plaintiff's injury was governmental or proprietary. If the legislature wants noncompliance with G.S. 159-28 to bar tort claims along with claims for breach and equitable claims, an express declaration to that effect is probably necessary.

488. 178 N.C. App. 367 (2006).

489. The supplemental retirement benefit in question was the special separation allowance for law enforcement officers provided for in G.S. 143-166.41.

490. *Finger*, 178 N.C. App. at 371. The court echoed this point in *Transportation Services of North Carolina v. Wake County Board of Education*, 198 N.C. App. 590, 591 (2009). Local boards of education are bound by the preaudit requirements of G.S. 115C-441(a), which are "essentially identical" to those of G.S. 159-28(a). In *Transportation Services*, the defendant school board entered into a contract with the plaintiff for the transport of special needs students. When the board refused to pay for students who had not actually been transported, the plaintiff filed suit against the board alleging breach of contract and estoppel. Inasmuch as no preaudit certificate appeared on the contract, the court of appeals ruled that, under *Data General*, governmental immunity barred the plaintiff's claims. The court went on to state that "applying estoppel to hold the Board liable would allow [the plaintiff] to escape the purpose of the legislature in enacting [G.S.] 115C-441(a)." *Id.* at 599.

arising from transactions subject to the preaudit statute, not to all equitable claims against local governments.

- *Second Principle: When a contract is not subject to preaudit requirements, governmental immunity will not foreclose equitable claims that stem from the contract if the claims arise from a proprietary function.*

Both *Viking Utilities* and *AGI Associates* assume that ordinarily the distinction between governmental functions and proprietary activities will determine whether a city, county, or other unit may invoke governmental immunity to block equitable claims. *AGI Associates* is probably mistaken insofar as the decision views *Data General* as wholly superseded by *Viking Utilities*. On the other hand, it seems safe to conclude that, so long as compliance with preaudit requirements is not an issue, a court should employ the *Williams* test (see Section 2.6, *supra*) when analyzing whether immunity defeats an equitable claim.

7.2 Governmental Immunity and Contract-Related Negligence Claims

Lawsuits filed by contractors alleging breach of contract claims against local governments also commonly allege negligence in connection with the agreements between the parties. As with other tort claims, whether governmental immunity can bar a claim of contract-related negligence depends partly on whether the activity that allegedly harmed the plaintiff was governmental or proprietary in character. A post-*Williams* decision by the North Carolina Court of Appeals calls into question whether a local government's actions in entering or performing a contract can ever qualify as governmental.

7.2.1 Basics of Contract-Related Negligence

The case law on contract-related negligence is complex, and a detailed review of it lies beyond the scope of this chapter, but a few points deserve attention.

- "Contractual obligations and tort duties are separate sources of liability."[491] It follows that a mere breach of contract will not sustain a claim of negligence. To prevail on a negligence claim, the plaintiff must show damages caused by the defendant's violation of the duty that the law imposes on everyone who undertakes an activity to exercise reasonable care to avoid harming others.[492]
- The courts are most disposed to find that a defendant's breach of contract involved negligence when the defendant's conduct resulted

---

491. DAYE & MORRIS, *supra* note 1, § 16.60[2][a], at 232.
492. *Id.*

in bodily injury or property damage.[493] Take the example of a plaintiff whose roof is damaged when the defendant hired by her to remove a tree performs the task carelessly. In addition to a claim for breach of contract, the plaintiff unquestionably has a negligence claim for the damage to her home.[494] On the other hand, the courts have been reluctant to concede that a breach of contract will sustain a negligence claim if the harm resulting from the breach is purely economic.[495]

- Allegations of negligent misrepresentation in contract cases usually focus on the negotiation—not the performance—of contractual obligations. Like equitable claims, negligent misrepresentation is often alleged when a plaintiff has concerns about the validity of its purported contract with the opposing party. Unlike most claims of negligence in the performance of a contract, negligent misrepresentation enables a plaintiff to recover for pecuniary loss without any showing of bodily injury or property damage.[496]

7.2.2 Governmental Immunity and Negligent Contract Performance

In *Town of Sandy Creek v. East Coast Contracting, Inc.*,[497] the court of appeals considered the immunity of local governments from claims of negligent contract performance following *Estate of Williams v. Pasquotank County Parks & Recreation Department*.[498] The City of Northwest hired East Coast Contracting (ECC) to construct a sewer system. The nearby Town of Sandy Creek subsequently filed suit against ECC alleging that the construction of Northwest's sewer system had damaged Sandy Creek's streets. ECC brought Northwest into the lawsuit, alleging breach of contract, negligence, contribution, and indemnity. In essence, ECC contended that Northwest had violated

---

493. City of Wilson v. Carolina Builders of Wilson, Inc., 94 N.C. App. 117, 119 (1989) ("The North Carolina courts have only recognized breach of contract as the basis for an action in tort where a promisor's negligent or willful act or omission in the course of performance of the contract results in personal injury or physical damage to property.").

494. DAYE & MORRIS, *supra* note 1, § 16.60[2][a], at 233.

495. *Id.* § 16.60[2][a], at 237 ("Outside the sale of goods, the [N.C. Supreme Court] has often denied recovery in tort for purely economic losses."). *But see id.* (noting the existence of cases to the contrary allowing recovery in tort when the only damage is to the property that is the subject of the contract).

496. Howard v. Cty. of Durham, 227 N.C. App. 46, 55 (2013) ("A claim for negligent misrepresentation must allege pecuniary loss."). *See also* Raritan River Steel Co. v. Cherry, Bekaert & Holland, 322 N.C. 200, 214–16 (1988) (describing the extent of an accountant's liability under the tort of negligent misrepresentation for financial harm attributable to a negligently prepared audit).

497. 226 N.C. App. 576 (2013).

498. 366 N.C. 195 (2012).

its duty of reasonable care to ECC by (1) failing to provide adequate contract documents, (2) improperly certifying that ECC's work conformed to contract documents, and (3) failing to retain sufficient contract funds to pay for the repair of Sandy Creek's streets.

Northwest argued that governmental immunity barred ECC's claims because the construction of a municipal sewer system is a governmental function.[499] While acknowledging that sewer system construction had been deemed a governmental activity, the court of appeals identified Northwest's handling of a contract and business relationship with ECC as the real focus of ECC's tort claims. The court categorized those activities as proprietary and affirmed the trial court's order denying Northwest's motion to dismiss the claims alleged by ECC. Northwest sought review by the North Carolina Supreme Court, which remanded the case to the court of appeals for reconsideration in light of *Williams*. On remand, the court of appeals, without explicitly going through the *Williams* test step-by-step, again held that Northwest's alleged negligence concerned a proprietary undertaking. The court "remain[ed] convinced that a local governmental unit acts in a proprietary function when it contracts with engineering and construction companies, regardless of whether the project under construction will be a governmental function once it is completed."[500]

The holding in *Sandy Creek* invites criticism. Many cities lack sufficient resources to construct sewer systems on their own.[501] A city in this category that wishes to offer wastewater services may have no choice but to hire a contractor. It can plausibly be argued that, when hiring a contractor is necessary to undertake a governmental function, such as the construction of a sewer system, a unit's dealings with the contractor should themselves be viewed as governmental for immunity purposes.

Whatever its merits, *Sandy Creek* is binding precedent for now, which makes it worthwhile to evaluate the decision's implications for the civil liability of local governments. At first glance, *Sandy Creek* might appear to expand that liability significantly. Read broadly it eliminates governmental immunity as a defense to a claim that a city, county, or other unit of local government has negligently performed its contractual obligations to a contractor, even if the contractor was hired to undertake a governmental function. The absence of immunity creates an incentive for contractors to accuse units of

---

499. Northwest cited *McCombs v. City of Asheboro*, 6 N.C. App. 234 (1969), which is discussed in Section 3.4.2, *supra*.

500. *Sandy Creek*, 226 N.C. App. at 582.

501. According to figures available from the North Carolina League of Municipalities, the entire population of Northwest amounts to just under 825 residents. *See* NC League of Municipalities, "Who We Are, Municipal Directory: Northwest," https://www.nclm.org/who-we-are/municipal-detail?org=fac7cdca-9ba5-de11-830f-005056a07b49.

contract-related negligence when the contractors find themselves sued by third parties for harms attributable to the contractors' own acts or omissions. As in *Sandy Creek*, the contractor in such a situation would probably argue that the local government contributed to the plaintiff's injury by negligently failing to furnish the contractor with important information or adequate direction.

Yet the long-term effect of *Sandy Creek* on local government liability might not be as great as it initially appears. It is possible to assess the decision's potential impact more precisely by separately analyzing the various legal claims alleged in *Sandy Creek*.

7.2.2.1 Negligent Contract Performance in Sandy Creek

The thrust of ECC's negligence claim against Northwest was that, by negligently performing its contractual duties, Northwest had exposed ECC to economic loss in the form of ECC's potential liability to Sandy Creek. Although *Sandy Creek* holds that governmental immunity does not bar claims of this sort, a contractor in a similar position could find it difficult to prevail on a claim of negligence. A ruling that immunity does not foreclose a negligence claim is not the same thing as a ruling that the unit acted negligently. To obtain an award for damages, the contractor still has to defeat any other defenses asserted by the unit and prove by a preponderance of the evidence that the unit actually engaged in negligent conduct to the contractor's detriment. At least two big legal hurdles can prevent the contractor from ultimately winning its lawsuit.

- Historically, as noted above, North Carolina's courts have been reluctant to allow a party asserting purely economic losses to recover for another party's negligent performance of a contract. In other words, the contractor might succeed in overcoming an immunity defense only to have the court later rule that its claim for negligent contract performance is legally deficient.
- In North Carolina, contributory negligence can be a complete bar to a negligence claim.[502] Thus, when a contractor's own negligence in performing a contract with a local government renders the contractor liable to a third party, the defense of contributory negligence can stop the contractor from using the law of negligence to force the unit to reimburse it for damages paid to the third party.

---

502. Love v. Singleton, 145 N.C. App. 488, 491 (2001). "Contributory negligence occurs when [the injured party] fails to exercise due care for his or her own safety, such that the [injured party's] failure to exercise due care is a proximate cause of his or her injury." *Id.* (internal quotation marks omitted) (citations omitted).

7.2.2.2 Contribution and Indemnity in Sandy Creek

Like its negligence claim, ECC's claims against Northwest for contribution and indemnity were founded on Northwest's allegedly negligent performance of its contractual duties. Contribution and indemnity are remedies frequently pursued by "joint tortfeasors," a term that once referred only to those "who acted in concert in producing the plaintiff's harm" but that nowadays also encompasses "those who commit separate wrongs without concert of action or unity of purpose, when the acts are concurrent as to place and time, and unite in setting in operation a single destructive and dangerous force that produces a single and indivisible injury."[503]

The purpose of contribution and indemnity is to allocate financial responsibility between or among tortfeasors for the harm suffered by an injured party. The right of contribution may be asserted by a tortfeasor to force other tortfeasors "to divide their mutual obligation to the injured party among themselves, usually in equal shares."[504] "Unlike contribution, indemnity shifts the entire liability to another wrongdoer. Indemnity is an all-or-nothing approach that transfers liability completely to one party, rather than dividing the liability among tortfeasors."[505]

There can be little doubt that *Town of Sandy Creek v. East Coast Contracting, Inc.*[506] has increased the vulnerability of local governments to contribution or indemnity claims brought by their contractors. Even when a unit hires a contractor to perform a governmental function, governmental immunity will not be a defense to a claim of contribution or indemnity premised on the unit's negligence in its business dealings with the contractor. Nonetheless, significant legal limitations on contribution and indemnity can hinder or derail a contractor's effort to obtain compensation from a unit.

- The right to contribution exists only when it can be shown that the injured party has a direct claim for negligence against each of

---

503. Daye & Morris, *supra* note 1, § 22.30, at 528.

504. *Id.* § 22.60, at 536. The rules for contribution are contained in the Uniform Contribution among Tort-Feasors Act. G.S. 1B-1, -7. For a detailed discussion of the act's provisions, see Daye & Morris, *supra* note 1, §§ 22.60[1]–[5], at 537–42.

505. Daye & Morris, *supra* note 1, § 22.70, at 542–43. The form of indemnity discussed here is a common law tort remedy. For a thorough discussion of the common law rules of indemnification, see *id.* § 22.70, at 542–48.

Business contracts frequently include indemnity provisions, but such provisions concern the law of contracts not of torts. State law places an important limitation on contractual indemnity provisions. Specifically, G.S. 22B-1 renders void and unenforceable any contract provision that would "insulate a party from its own negligence under a construction indemnity agreement." Norma R. Houston, North Carolina Local Government Contracting: Quick Reference and Related Statutes 44 (2014).

506. 226 N.C. App. 576 (2013).

the joint tortfeasors. Put differently, a contractor has no right to contribution from a local government unless the unit negligently played a role in causing the injury for which the contractor is liable.[507]

- A joint tortfeasor has no right to contribution if it intentionally caused or contributed to the harm to the injured party.[508] Thus, even assuming negligence on the part of a local government, a contractor that inflicted injury through intentional rather than negligent conduct does not have a valid contribution claim.

- In general, no right to indemnity exists among joint tortfeasors.[509] An exception to this limitation occurs when one tortfeasor is actively negligent and the other is merely passively negligent.[510] Whether ECC could have carried this burden in *Sandy Creek* is uncertain, inasmuch as doing so would have required ECC to show that Northwest was "primarily liable" for the damage to the plaintiff's streets.[511] Many contractors in similar cases could find the burden too heavy to bear.

- The right to contribution and the right to indemnification are mutually exclusive.[512] Consequently, a contractor may not obtain both remedies from a local government for the same injury.[513]

7.2.3 Governmental Immunity and Negligent Misrepresentation

Although the plaintiff did not allege negligent misrepresentation in *Sandy Creek*, the court's opinion plainly has implications for attempts by contractors to hold local governments liable for negligent misrepresentation. If a unit's actions under a contract constitute a proprietary function vis-à-vis the contractor, even when the contractor is hired to carry out a governmental function, then it seems obvious that units act proprietarily in negotiating such contracts. The apparent upshot? Governmental immunity cannot be a defense to allegations that a unit's negligent misrepresentations persuaded a contractor to enter into an invalid contract with the unit.

A look back at *Data General Corp. v. County of Durham*[514] helps illustrate the significance of this last point. Noncompliance with the preaudit statute

---

507. *See* DAYE & MORRIS, *supra* note 1, § 22.60, at 537 ("Joint liability is a prerequisite to the recovery of contribution.").

508. G.S. 1B-1(c).

509. Ingram v. Smith, 16 N.C. App. 147, 151 (1972).

510. *Id.*

511. *In re* Huyck Corp. v. C.C. Mangum, Inc., 309 N.C. 788, 793 (1983) (cited in DAYE & MORRIS, *supra* note 1, § 22.70, at 543).

512. *Ingram*, 16 N.C. App. at 151 ("The rights of contribution and indemnity are mutually inconsistent; the former assumes joint fault, the latter only derivative fault.").

513. DAYE & MORRIS, *supra* note 1, § 22.70, at 543. A contractor may plead both in the alternative, however. *Id.*

514. 143 N.C. App. 97 (2001).

prevented the contractor from pursuing its claim for breach of contract and associated equitable claims. The court allowed the contractor's negligent misrepresentation claim to proceed, however, after determining that it involved a proprietary activity. If a unit always acts proprietarily in negotiating with a contractor, then negligent misrepresentation may provide a way around governmental immunity in many cases where noncompliance with the preaudit statute bars breach of contract and equitable claims. This result seems inconsistent with the General Assembly's evident desire to invalidate any financial obligations assumed in violation of preaudit requirements.

7.2.4 Governmental Immunity and Contract-Related Negligence after *Sandy Creek*

The court of appeals' decision in *Town of Sandy Creek v. East Coast Contracting, Inc.*[515] has probably eliminated governmental immunity as an obstacle to a contractor who asserts claims against a unit of local government for negligence, contribution, or indemnity arising from a contract between the parties. This development by no means guarantees that the contractor will succeed in holding the unit liable, however. Other legal limitations on the availability of contract-related negligence claims, contribution, and indemnity could make it difficult for the contractor to prevail.

---

515. 226 N.C. App. 576 (2013).

Chapter 8

Governmental Immunity Constitutional Issues

This chapter explores two constitutional issues associated with governmental immunity. The first is whether the availability of the immunity as a defense to tort claims limits a local government's ability to have state constitutional claims thrown out under the adequate state remedy doctrine. The second concerns the degree to which due process and equal protection requirements constrain local government decisions to settle some tort claims but not others.

8.1 Governmental Immunity and Adequate State Remedies

The Declaration of Rights in Article I of the North Carolina Constitution sets out "individual and personal rights entitled to protection against state action," such as the right to free speech and freedom of the press.[516] The case law unambiguously allows a person to maintain "a direct action under the State Constitution against state officials for violation of rights guaranteed by the Declaration of Rights."[517] Likewise, violations of state constitutional rights by local government officials or employees can give rise to claims directly under the Declaration of Rights.[518]

Significantly, a plaintiff may bring claims directly under the North Carolina Constitution "only if there is no other adequate state remedy."[519] When an adequate state remedy exists, a unit of local government is entitled to prevail on the plaintiff's state constitutional claims, regardless of their validity.

By "adequate state remedy," the courts usually have in mind a tort claim that offers a redress for the plaintiff's injury, provided the plaintiff can prove

---

516. Corum v. Univ. of N.C., 330 N.C. 761, 782 (1992).

517. *Id.* at 783.

518. *E.g.*, Craig v. New Hanover Cty. Bd. of Educ., 363 N.C. 334, 342 (2009) (plaintiff could proceed with claim that school board violated his state constitutional right to an education free from harm and psychological abuse).

519. DAYE & MORRIS, *supra* note 1, § 12.10, at 136. *See also Corum*, 330 N.C. at 782 (a direct claim under the state constitution for a violation of state constitutional rights exists only "in the absence of an adequate state remedy"). This rule is probably attributable to the judiciary's general preference to avoid addressing constitutional issues.

his or her case.[520] For example, the prospect of relief in the form of claims for negligence, gross negligence, and willful and wanton conduct blocked the plaintiff in *Wilcox v. City of Asheville* from pursuing state constitutional claims arising from gunshot wounds she suffered when police officers opened fire on the automobile in which she was a passenger.[521]

It perhaps seems obvious that a tort claim barred by governmental immunity is not an adequate substitute for a constitutional claim. Still, the state supreme court found it necessary to clarify this point in *Craig v. New Hanover County Board of Education*.[522] The plaintiff alleged both negligence and state constitutional claims over the alleged failure of school personnel to stop another student from sexually assaulting him. The high court held that the plaintiff's negligence claim against the board did not constitute an adequate state remedy because "it [was] entirely precluded by the application of the doctrine of [governmental] immunity."[523]

An interesting issue can arise at the outset of litigation when the plaintiff puts forward both constitutional and tort claims arising from the same conduct. What happens if (1) the plaintiff's complaint alleges that the defendant city or county has waived governmental immunity as to the tort claims and (2) the unit files a motion to dismiss (MTD) the state constitutional claims based on the availability of an adequate state remedy? Should the trial court grant the unit's MTD? After all, if there really has been a waiver, then governmental immunity does not totally preclude the plaintiff's tort claims, and consequently, the plaintiff may not obtain money damages directly under the North Carolina Constitution. On the other hand, if the court grants the MTD and the waiver allegation turns out to be wrong, the plaintiff could end up without any remedy.

The court of appeals confronted essentially this scenario in *Bigelow v. Town of Chapel Hill*.[524] The complaint alleged that the town had fired the plaintiff

---

520. To be adequate, the alternative remedy "must provide *the possibility* of relief under the circumstances." *Craig*, 363 N.C. at 340 (emphasis added). In other words, the alternative remedy is adequate so long as it affords the plaintiff a chance to prove his or her case, even if the plaintiff ultimately loses. *Id*. at 339–40 ("[T]o be considered adequate in redressing a constitutional wrong, a plaintiff must have at least the opportunity to enter the courthouse doors and present his claim."); Wilcox v. City of Asheville, 222 N.C. App. 285, 299–300 (2012) ("[A]dequacy [of a remedy] is found not in success, but in chance."). *See also* Richmond v. City of Asheville, 242 N.C. App. 252, ___ (2015) (deeming the plaintiff's malicious prosecution claim an adequate state remedy, even though the plaintiff could not prevail due to her failure to produce evidence of malice).

521. The plaintiff alleged that the police had violated her state constitutional right "to be free from seizure by the use of excessive or unreasonable force." *Wilcox*, 222 N.C. App. at 301.

522. 363 N.C. 334 (2009).

523. *Id*. at 342.

524. 227 N.C. App. 1 (2013). The author previously discussed *Bigelow* in Trey Allen, Bigelow v. Town of Chapel Hill: *When May State Constitutional Claims Against Local*

sanitation workers for taking part in statutorily protected union activities, reporting unsafe working conditions, and—in the case of one plaintiff—filing a grievance over racially discriminatory hiring practices. The claims asserted in the complaint included the tort of wrongful discharge and violations of the plaintiffs' rights to free speech, due process, and equal protection under the North Carolina Constitution.[525] The complaint further alleged that the town had waived governmental immunity through the purchase of liability insurance.

The town filed a motion asking the trial court to throw out the plaintiffs' state constitutional claims given the availability of an adequate state remedy, namely, the plaintiffs' wrongful discharge claims. On appeal from the trial court's order granting the town's motion, the court of appeals ruled that, "[a]s long as [the Town's] [governmental] immunity defense remains potentially viable for any or all of Plaintiffs' wrongful discharge-related claims, our Supreme Court's decision in *Craig* . . . dictates that Plaintiffs' associated North Carolina constitutional claims are not supplanted by those claims."[526] Put differently, the court of appeals read *Craig* to say that a tort claim is not an adequate state remedy so long as governmental immunity lurks as a possible barrier to the claim.

Of course, neither *Craig* nor *Bigelow* prevents a trial court from dismissing tort claims or state constitutional claims when the complaint fails to allege facts sufficient to establish the existence of a tort or constitutional violation. In such situations, the potential applicability of governmental immunity to the plaintiff's tort claims is immaterial. Dismissal is proper because the complaint's own allegations reveal the absence of a valid legal claim.[527]

Governments Be Dismissed?, COATES' CANONS: NC LOC. GOV'T L. blog (May 20, 2013), https://canons.sog.unc.edu/bigelow-v-town-of-chapel-hill-when-may-state-constitutional-claims-against-local-governments-be-dismissed/.

525. "An employee-at-will has a cause of action for wrongful discharge if the dismissal violates important public policy." DAYE & MORRIS, *supra* note 1, § 12.20, at 136. Article I, Section 14 of the North Carolina Constitution provides: "Freedom of speech and of the press are two of the great bulwarks of liberty and therefore shall never be restrained, but every person shall be held responsible for their abuse." Article I, Section 19 declares that no person may be deprived of life, liberty, or property "but by the law of the land." The "law of the land" clause is the state constitution's equivalent to the Due Process Clause in the Fourteenth Amendment to the U.S. Constitution. Yancey v. N.C. State Highway & Pub. Works Comm'n, 222 N.C. 106, 108 (1942). Article I, Section 19 further provides that "[n]o person shall be denied the equal protection of the laws; nor shall any person be subjected to discrimination by the State because of race, color, religion, or national origin."

526. *Bigelow*, 227 N.C. App. at 15.

527. *See* Doe v. Charlotte-Mecklenburg Bd. of Educ., 222 N.C. App. 359 (2012) (notwithstanding *Craig*, trial court should have granted school board's MTD plaintiff's state constitutional claims inasmuch as the complaint's allegations of negligence were insufficient to establish violations of plaintiff's constitutional rights).

Similarly, even if the complaint successfully alleges causes of action both in tort and under the North Carolina Constitution, the trial court must grant a unit's motion for summary judgment on any tort claim not supported by the undisputed material facts.[528]

Furthermore, *Craig* and *Bigelow* do not forbid the dismissal of state constitutional claims when a plaintiff's own action or inaction makes it impossible to obtain relief in tort.[529] So, for instance, a plaintiff may not proceed under the North Carolina Constitution if the reason the plaintiff cannot pursue a negligence claim for the same injuries is that he or she failed to file suit within the three-year statute of limitations.[530]

The North Carolina Court of Appeals has held that a tort claim can be an adequate state remedy when the plaintiff has the opportunity to pursue it against a party other than the defendant local government unit.[531] In such cases, dismissal of the plaintiff's tort claims against the unit will not totally deprive the plaintiff of the ability to seek damages for his or her injury. Thus, in *Wilcox*, referenced in the text at note 521, *supra*, the trial court properly granted the city's motion to dismiss the tort claims against it on immunity grounds because the plaintiff's identical tort claims against several police officers in their individual capacities remained viable.[532]

8.2 Constitutional Restraints on Settlements

Many units of local government have adopted policies under which they settle claims for personal injury or property damage despite the availability of governmental immunity as a defense to those claims. Although units enjoy broad discretion when deciding whether to settle particular claims and under what

---

528. *See, e.g.*, Adams v. City of Raleigh, ___ N.C. App. ___, ___, 782 S.E.2d 108, 114 (2016) ("Because a finding of probable cause necessarily defeats plaintiff's claims for false arrest and malicious prosecution, we need not address governmental immunity as there is no liability.").

529. *Bigelow*, 227 N.C. App. at 15 ("The reasoning in *Craig* clearly does not extend to situations where a plaintiff has lost the right to pursue an adequate state remedy due to his own action.").

530. *Craig*, 363 N.C. at 340 ("[T]he facts presented here are distinguishable from a case in which a plaintiff has lost his ability to pursue a common law claim due to expiration of the statute of limitations, for example.").

531. Taylor v. Wake Cty., ___ N.C. App. ___, ___, 811 S.E.2d 648, 650 (2018) ("We hold that [the adequacy of an alternative remedy] depends upon recovery for the plaintiff's injury, without regard to the party from whom recovery may be obtained.").

532. Wilcox v. City of Asheville, 222 N.C. App. 285, 300 (2012) (because plaintiff still had a chance to obtain relief through her tort claims against the individual defendants in their individual capacities, plaintiff's "claims against the Individual Defendants in their individual capacities serve[d] as an adequate remedy").

terms, they may not choose to settle some tort claims while arbitrarily invoking governmental immunity to defeat others.[533]

In *Dobrowolska v. Wall*, the plaintiffs alleged that the defendant city had violated their due process and equal protection rights under the federal and state constitutions by invoking governmental immunity to bar their negligence claims despite the city's practice of compensating similarly situated individuals in other cases.[534] The negligence claims concerned injuries the plaintiffs had sustained when a police officer drove a city vehicle into their automobile. The trial court granted the city's motion for summary judgment on the plaintiffs' negligence and constitutional claims, whereupon the plaintiffs appealed. The court of appeals overturned the trial court's ruling in part, holding that governmental immunity barred the plaintiffs' negligence claims but that genuine issues of material fact precluded summary judgment for the city on the plaintiffs' constitutional claims.

The appellate court noted that the Due Process and Equal Protection Clauses of the Fourteenth Amendment to the United States Constitution prohibit units of local government from acting arbitrarily and capriciously, even when they elect to confer benefits that they are not legally required to provide. Arbitrary and capricious actions encompass decisions that do not treat similarly situated individuals alike or that categorize persons based on differences bearing no rational relationship to valid government objectives.[535]

According to the evidence available at summary judgment, the city had a practice of settling claims for personal injury and property damage, even in cases where it may have had no legal obligation to pay the claimants anything because of governmental immunity. Consistent with the plaintiffs' allegations, some of the claims settled arose from circumstances similar to the events leading to the plaintiffs' injuries. City officials with settlement authority did not employ "any uniform rule of action" when deciding whether to resolve or fight particular claims; rather, they exercised "total discretion" in such matters, though the city's legal department had a set of factors it examined when called upon to make settlement determinations.[536] Moreover, the city

533. BAKER, *supra* note 127, at 114.

534. 138 N.C. App. 1 (2000).

535. A higher standard applies when government action violates a fundamental right or operates to the peculiar disadvantage of a suspect class. In such a case, the government must do more than show a rational relationship to legitimate government objectives. White v. Pate, 308 N.C. 759, 766 (1983); Clayton v. Branson, 170 N.C. App. 438, 455 (2005). Ordinarily, for such an action to survive a substantive due process or equal protection challenge, the government must demonstrate that the action was necessary to further a compelling governmental interest. *See White*, 308 N.C. at 766 ("The 'strict scrutiny' standard requires that the government demonstrate that the classification it has imposed is necessary to promote a compelling governmental interest.").

536. *Dobrowolska*, 138 N.C. App. at 16–18.

failed to explain how its disparate treatment of claimants advanced legitimate government goals. In light of the evidence, the court of appeals concluded, the plaintiffs could proceed with their claims that the city's settlement practices violated their due process and equal protection rights.[537]

The *Dobrowolska* decision prompted many units to review their settlement practices and adopt or revise settlement policies to limit staff discretion in settling tort claims.[538] Perhaps due partly to this reaction, *Dobrowolska* appears to be the high water mark for constitutional challenges to the use of governmental immunity as a defense in lawsuits. In subsequent decisions, the court of appeals has taken pains to limit the impact of *Dobrowolska*.[539]

In *Clayton v. Branson*, a lawsuit brought against the same city sued in *Dobrowolska*, the court made it clear that, even when a *Dobrowolska* claim survives a summary judgment motion, the plaintiff will find it difficult to prove that a constitutional violation actually occurred.[540] The jury in *Clayton* found that the city had denied the plaintiff's due process and equal protection rights by asserting governmental immunity to block the plaintiff from seeking damages for injuries sustained when the driver of the patrol car in which the plaintiff was a passenger slammed on the breaks and swerved abruptly to avoid colliding with another vehicle. The city filed a motion for judgment notwithstanding the jury's verdict and then appealed the trial court's denial of the motion.

In reversing the trial court, and overturning the jury's verdict, the court of appeals ruled that the plaintiff had not proved that the city's settlement policies or practices violated his due process or equal protection rights.[541] Turning first to the plaintiff's due process claim, the court applied the "rational relationship" test. In other words, the court analyzed whether there was a rational relationship between the city's settlement policies or practices and a legitimate government objective. The court listed the factors on which the city generally based its decisions about whether to settle with tort claimants:

    a. Whether there was a negligent act by an employee of the City;

    b. Whether there was an intentional tort by a City employee;

    c. What, if any, defenses were available for the City, including the defenses of governmental immunity and contributory negligence;

    d. Whether any defenses, including governmental immunity, were available for the employee in his individual capacity;

---

537. *Id*. at 19.

538. BAKER, *supra* note 127, at 114.

539. Hagans v. City of Fayetteville, No. 5:14-CV-717-F, 2015 WL 4414929, at *9 n.5 (E.D.N.C. July 17, 2015) (unpublished) ("[S]ubsequent panels of the North Carolina Court of Appeals have taken pains to distinguish *Dombrowlska* [sic] or limit its holding").

540. 170 N.C. App. 438 (2005).

541. *Id*. at 459.

e. Whether the employee of the City violated any departmental regulation;

f. The cost of defending the case;

g. Goodwill on behalf of the citizens; and

h. The best use of taxpayer's money in a cost effective manner.[542]

Interestingly, the same factors are listed in *Dobrowolska* as the criteria used by that city's legal department to evaluate tort claims referred to it for review.[543] The *Clayton* opinion suggests that the city had begun to apply the criteria to its settlement decisions generally, not just to claims handled by the legal department.[544] Although the court had disapprovingly characterized some of the factors as "subjective" in *Dobrowolska*—for example, "goodwill on behalf of the citizens"[545]—it concluded in *Clayton* that "each of [the] factors, standing alone or considered collectively, clearly [bore] a rational relationship to legitimate governmental goals."[546] It therefore rejected the plaintiff's due process claim.

With regard to the equal protection claim, the court held that the plaintiff had failed to prove that claimants to whom the city had made settlement offers were similarly situated to him in all relevant respects. The plaintiff's evidence consisted of a list of claims for harms allegedly caused by city employees driving city vehicles in the performance of governmental functions. For each claim, the list named the department involved, briefly described the incident (e.g., "allegedly struck claimant's parked vehicle"), and recorded the outcome (settlement or denial).[547] As the court pointed out, the plaintiff seemed to assume that "any two claimants [were] 'similarly situated' as long as their claims both involve[d] damage caused by a city employee's operation of a city vehicle."[548] Yet as shown by its settlement criteria, the city made settlement determinations based on information far more nuanced and detailed than the data on the plaintiff's list. Moreover, the list omitted many kinds of information that any judge or jury would need to assess whether the plaintiff and other claimants were similarly situated, such as each claimant's specific factual allegations, the results of any investigation or physical tests, and the availability of credible witnesses.

---

542. *Id.* at 456.

543. *Dobrowolska*, 138 N.C. App. at 17.

544. *See Clayton*, 170 N.C. App. at 456 ("The evidence at trial establishes that the city's decisions about whether to offer a monetary settlement to a tort claimant are generally based on the following factors: . . .").

545. *Dobrowolska*, 138 N.C. App. at 17.

546. *Clayton*, 170 N.C. App. at 456.

547. *Id.* at 458.

548. *Id.*

In comments plainly intended to discourage future *Dobrowolska* claims, the court explained that the complexity and subjectivity of settlement decisions make it highly unlikely that a plaintiff will be able to succeed on a due process or equal protection challenge:

> [D]iscretionary decisions such as whether to make a settlement offer necessarily implicate a host of subjective factors rightfully reserved for city administrators and elected officials, and it is almost inevitable that any two claimants will be dissimilar as regards one or more factors relevant to settlement offers. Thus, as a practical matter, it would be exceedingly difficult for a plaintiff to show disparate treatment of "similarly situated" claimants . . . .[549]

The court of appeals continued to narrow the impact of *Dobrowolska* in *Jones v. City of Durham*, another case involving personal injuries arising from a police officer's operation of a patrol car.[550] The plaintiff alleged that the defendant city had a policy or practice of "waiving" governmental immunity in some cases but not others, that certain city employees exercised unbridled discretion over such waiver decisions, and that the city had violated the plaintiff's state due process and equal protection rights by waiving immunity for similarly situated claimants but not for her.[551]

In ruling that the city was entitled to summary judgment on the plaintiff's constitutional claims, the court of appeals noted the plaintiff's failure to present any evidence that the city took governmental immunity into account when deciding whether to pay or deny claims for personal injury or property damage. The uncontroverted evidence showed that the city made payment decisions based on the merits of each claim, including whether "(1) the claimant assert[ed] a legally cognizable cause of action; (2) investigation show[ed] the claim to be meritorious; and (3) the damages ha[d] been documented."[552] Whenever a claimant unhappy with the city's resolution of his or her claim resorted to litigation, the city would invariably at that point assert governmental immunity as a defense. Thus, contrary to the plaintiff's allegations, nothing in the evidence showed that the city had a practice of selectively waiving governmental immunity. The court contrasted this system of handling tort claims with the defendant city's approach in *Dobrowolska*, which was to assert governmental immunity as a defense to every claim and then waive immunity and execute settlement agreements in some cases. The court further observed that the plaintiff had failed to prove that she was treated differently from similarly situated claimants. As in *Clayton*, the evidence

---

549. *Id.* at 458–59.
550. 183 N.C. App. 57 (2007).
551. *Id.* at 60.
552. *Id.*

omitted key information necessary to establish legally significant similarity between the plaintiff's personal injury claim and claims the city had settled. Without evidence of selective waiver and disparate treatment of similarly situated individuals, the plaintiff could not prove violations of her due process and equal protection rights.

Following *Clayton* and *Jones*, the court of appeals has repeatedly rejected due process or equal protection challenges to units' assertions of governmental immunity.[553] Doubtless plaintiffs will continue to bring such challenges, but all indications are that they will rarely prove successful. Even if a plaintiff were to prevail on a *Dobrowolska* claim, the state supreme court has indicated that the remedy would be quite limited:

> Finally, the plaintiff contends that the City has violated the Equal Protection Clause of the Fourteenth Amendment to the Constitution of the United States and Article I, Section 19 of the Constitution of North Carolina. He says this is so because the City, through [its Risk Acceptance Management Corporation], can pick and choose what claims it will pay, thus depriving the plaintiff of the equal protection of the law. We decline to pass on this constitutional question because of its posture in this case. If we were to hold the City has acted unconstitutionally in the way it administers RAMCO, it would not mean the City had waived its governmental immunity. The most we could do is strike down RAMCO. A decision involving this constitutional question would not resolve this case and we do not consider it.[554]

Although the court's comments are *dicta*, and thus not binding in future cases, lower courts may well defer to them because of their source. If the remarks correctly state the law, the only remedy available to a plaintiff who prevails on a *Dobrowolska* claim is a court order striking down the unit's settlement program as unconstitutional. Governmental immunity would still bar the plaintiff's tort claims.

---

553. *E.g.*, Baltzell v. Dowdy, 202 N.C. App. 147 (2010) (unpublished).
554. Blackwelder v. City of Winston-Salem, 332 N.C. 319, 325–26 (1992).

Chapter 9

Governmental Immunity Exceptions

The preceding chapters demonstrate that the case law on governmental immunity is shot through with inconsistencies. This chapter briefly takes up three important exceptions to the immunity's fundamental principles.

9.1 Nuisance Claims

"A local government that engages in an activity that substantially and unreasonably interferes with the use and enjoyment of someone's land commits a tort called *nuisance*."[555] Although generally governmental immunity bars tort claims arising from governmental functions, it is no defense to nuisance claims, even when they result from governmental activities.[556] The reason for this deviation from standard immunity principles is that frequently a nuisance attributable to a local government "is, in a constitutional sense, a

---

555. BAKER, *supra* note 127, at 98. *See also* Glace v. Town of Pilot Mountain, 265 N.C. 181, 183 (1965) ("If a municipal corporation, by the construction and operation of a sewage disposal system or other facility, pollutes the air or otherwise creates a nuisance, permanent in character, thereby diminishing the value of property in proximity to the operation, the municipality is liable for the damage done."); Hughes v. City of High Point, 62 N.C. App. 107, 109 (1983) ("If a governmental entity builds and maintains a structure which is permanent in nature and the maintenance of the structure causes a diminution in value to a person's real estate, the structure is considered a nuisance and the landowner is entitled to compensation.").

556. *See, e.g.,* Hines v. City of Rocky Mount, 162 N.C. 409, 412 (1913) (citations omitted) (ordinarily cities "may not be held civilly liable to individuals for . . . neglect in performing, duties governmental in their nature," but "[t]his general principle is subject to the limitation that neither a [city] nor other governmental agency [may] establish and maintain a nuisance causing appreciable damage to the property of a private owner without being liable for it"); Donnell v. City of Greensboro, 164 N.C. 330, 334 (1913) ("[T]he right [to recover damages for a nuisance] is not affected by the fact that the acts complained of were done in the exercise of governmental functions . . . ."); Roach v. City of Lenoir, 44 N.C. App. 608, 610 (1980) (lawsuit for damages to the plaintiffs' home caused by backup of city's sewer system was barred by governmental immunity because plaintiffs "neither allege[d] facts sufficient to support a nuisance claim nor [was] their claim based on a theory of nuisance").

taking" of private property without just compensation.[557] In other words, the tort of nuisance provides a remedy for government invasions of constitutionally protected property rights.[558] Because governmental immunity typically is not a defense to constitutional claims, it will not defeat nuisance actions.

Much of the case law on nuisance claims against local governments stems from problems with city sewer systems. In one such case, the North Carolina Supreme Court ruled that the plaintiffs could pursue their nuisance claim against the defendant city for the permanent reduction to the value of the plaintiffs' home caused by the foul and persistent smell of nearby city lagoons.[559] In another case, the court held that the plaintiffs were entitled to a trial on their claim that the intermittent overflow of raw sewage from the defendant city's sewer system into their home for several years constituted a nuisance.[560]

Damages in a nuisance action "are confined to the diminished value of the property affected."[561] It follows that a nuisance claim is not the proper

557. City of Raleigh v. Edwards, 235 N.C. 671, 674 (1952). *See also* Long v. City of Charlotte, 306 N.C. 187, 198 (1982) ("Often where nuisance has been alleged, this Court has found the gravamen of the complaint to be a taking of property.").

558. *Hines*, 162 N.C. at 412 (a nuisance established and maintained by a local government "is regarded and dealt with as a taking or appropriation of the property, and it is well understood that such an interference with the rights of ownership may not be made or authorized except on compensation first made pursuant to the law of the land"); *Donnell*, 164 N.C. at 334 ("[D]amage arising from the impaired value of the property is to be considered and dealt with to that extent as a 'taking or appropriation,' and brings the claim within the constitutional principle that a man's property may not be taken from him even for the public benefit except upon compensation duly made.").

559. *Glace*, 265 N.C. at 185. *See also* Gray v. City of High Point, 203 N.C. 756, 767 (1932) (no error in judgment awarding plaintiff damages for diminished property value attributable to foul odors emitted by city sewage and disposal plant located on adjoining property).

Nowadays a plaintiff with a similar claim would probably pursue an inverse condemnation action. BAKER, *supra* note 127, at 99 (inverse condemnation claims are used to obtain compensation for government activities that permanently and substantially reduce the value of private land). *See also Long*, 306 N.C. at 197 (inverse condemnation, not nuisance, provided sole remedy for decrease in the value of plaintiffs' property allegedly caused by aircraft passing over or near their home on the way to or from a nearby city airport).

560. *Hughes*, 62 N.C. App. at 111. The court held that the plaintiffs' nuisance claim did not accrue until the city notified the plaintiffs that it would not take any more steps to correct the overflow problem. *Id.* at 109 ("We do not believe the defendant was maintaining a nuisance so long as it was attempting to repair or change the sewage system so that it would not overflow on the plaintiffs' property. When the defendant notified the plaintiffs that it would no longer attempt to correct the problem but would maintain the system in its then existing condition, we believe defendant started to maintain a nuisance.").

561. *Hines*, 162 N.C. at 412.

vehicle for obtaining damages for personal injuries.[562] Of course, if the unit acted negligently in creating, maintaining, or attempting to correct the nuisance, the plaintiff may be able to recover damages for bodily harm through a negligence claim, if the unit's negligence caused the plaintiff's injury and governmental immunity does not bar the claim.

9.2 Street Maintenance and Construction

9.2.1 Street and Sidewalk Maintenance

The courts have long recognized that cities have a legal duty to keep their streets in " 'proper repair'; that is, in such condition as that the people passing and repassing over them might at all times do so with reasonable ease, speed and safety."[563] For purposes of this duty, "a city street comprehends everything existing on land over which the city has an easement of passage," including "sidewalks, the grass plot between street and sidewalk, the street proper, trees or other objects located on the right-of-way, public alleys, and wharfs."[564] The legislature has largely codified this duty in Chapter 160A, Section 296 of the North Carolina General Statutes (hereinafter G.S.), which obliges cities to "keep the public streets, sidewalks, alleys, and bridges in proper repair [and] open for travel and free from unnecessary obstructions."[565]

The failure to satisfy the "proper repair" standard can leave a city liable for bodily injuries or property damage caused by its negligence.[566] This potential liability represents an "illogical exception" to the principles of governmental

---

562. *See id.* (sickness attributable to a nuisance could not properly be considered as a direct element of damages).

563. Bunch v. Town of Edenton, 90 N.C. 431, 434 (1884).

564. Joseph S. Ferrell, *Civil Liability of North Carolina Cities and Towns for Personal Injury and Property Damage Arising from the Construction, Maintenance, and Repair of Public Streets*, 7 WAKE FOREST L. REV. 143, 145 (1971). The duty can also extend to any private street over which a city has exercised control and has treated like a city street. *Id.* at 146. It does not extend to streets under the authority and control of the State Board of Transportation, even if the city has contracted to repair them. DAYE & MORRIS, *supra* note 1, § 19.40[2][c][vii], at 468–69.

565. G.S. 160A-296(a)(1), (2). The references to alleys and bridges in G.S. 160A-296 does not necessarily represent an expansion of the duty proclaimed by the courts. Preexisting case law construed the duty to impose obligations regarding "all bridges, dangerous pits, embankments, dangerous walls and the like perilous places and things very near and adjoining the streets[.]" *Bunch*, 90 N.C. at 434.

566. *E.g.*, Rhodes v. City of Asheville, 230 N.C. 134, 138 (1949) ("[I]t has been uniformly held in this jurisdiction that municipalities may be held liable in tort for failure to maintain their streets in a reasonably safe condition . . . ."). *See also* DAYE & MORRIS, *supra* note 1, § 19.40[2][c][vii], at 467 ("It is universally known, however, that cities are not immune from liability for negligence [in maintaining public streets], at least where plaintiff seeks recovery for personal injury or property damage.").

immunity.[567] Although the maintenance of public roads and highways plainly merits classification as a governmental function,[568] the state's appellate courts have consistently declined to recognize governmental immunity as a defense to negligence claims premised on a city's failure to keep its streets or sidewalks in proper repair.[569] Indeed, some cases even refer to a city's maintenance of its streets and sidewalks as a proprietary function.[570]

The failure to maintain city streets should not be confused with a failure to prevent their improper or unlawful use. "The condition of the street or walk . . . is one thing, and the manner of its use by the public is quite a different thing."[571] Governmental immunity will shield a city from a negligence claim premised on the public's wrongful use of a street, as it did when a city's allegedly negligent refusal to stop boys from playing baseball on its streets resulted in the death of a motorist who was fatally struck by a baseball.[572]

9.2.1.1 Exceptions to the Street-Maintenance Exception

The exception for street maintenance in the case law on governmental immunity is itself subject to several exceptions.

- *Original Plan Doctrine.* Some older cases hold that cities are not liable for injuries caused by hazardous street designs as opposed to

---

567. Millar v. Town of Wilson, 222 N.C. 340, 342 (1942); Ferrell, *supra* note 558, at 143.

568. DAYE & MORRIS, *supra* note 1, § 19.40[2][c][vii], at 467 ("Maintaining the public streets falls as neatly into the definition of 'governmental function' as any activity performed by city government.").

569. *E.g.*, *Millar*, 222 N.C. at 342 ("While the maintenance of public roads and highways is generally recognized as a governmental function, exception is made in respect to streets and sidewalks of a municipality."); Kirkpatrick v. Town of Nags Head, 213 N.C. App. 132, 140 (2011) ("[A] municipality has an obligation to protect individuals from injury resulting from defective street and roadway conditions without being allowed to avoid liability for negligently performing its street and road maintenance obligations by relying on a governmental immunity defense . . . ."); Sisk v. City of Greensboro, 183 N.C. App. 657, 659 (2007) (quoting *Millar*, 222 N.C. at 342) ("Maintenance of a public road and highway is generally considered a governmental function; however, 'exception is made in respect to streets and sidewalks of a municipality.' ").

570. *Millar*, 222 N.C. at 342 ("[T]he maintenance of streets and sidewalks is classed as a ministerial or proprietary function."); *Kirkpatrick*, 213 N.C. App. at 140 (same). *But see* City of Reidsville v. Burton, 269 N.C. 206, 210 (1967) ("The construction and maintenance of public streets and of bridges constituting a part thereof are governmental functions of a municipality . . . .").

571. Goodwin v. Town of Reidsville, 160 N.C. 411, 413 (1912) (internal quotation marks omitted) (citations omitted).

572. *Id.* at 414.

inadequate street maintenance.[573] In *Martin v. City of Greensboro*, the plaintiff alleged damage to his automobile resulting partly from the defendant city's negligent decision to locate sidewalk curbing too close to a streetcar track.[574] In ruling that governmental immunity foreclosed the plaintiff's negligence claim, the state supreme court remarked that, whereas street maintenance is a ministerial function, the adoption of a street plan involves the exercise of discretionary or legislative power for which a city is exempt from liability.[575]

The original plan doctrine may not be valid any longer. It has been decades since a city successfully raised it on appeal.[576] Moreover, the North Carolina Supreme Court may have overruled *Martin* in a later case *sub silentio*.[577] To the extent the doctrine still exists, it would probably apply only when the injury to the plaintiff was caused by a hazardous street design of which the plaintiff had adequate warning.[578]

- *Street Closure Decisions.* Governmental immunity covers a city's decision to close a road to vehicular traffic.[579] Accordingly, plaintiffs could not pursue negligence claims premised on a town's refusal to reconstruct a street washed away by the ocean.[580] Of course, if a city elects to allow traffic on a city street, it risks liability if it fails to keep the street in proper repair.
- *Street lighting.* By providing street lighting, a city performs a governmental function.[581] Thus, a city was not liable when a broken power line that was part of its street lighting system electrocuted a man.[582]

---

573. *See* Ferrell, *supra* note 564, at 161–67 (discussing cases applying or rejecting the original plan doctrine); Daye & Morris, *supra* note 1, § 19.40[2][c][vii][A], at 469–71 (same).

574. 193 N.C. 573, 574 (1927).

575. *Id.* at 575.

576. *See* Daye & Morris, *supra* note 1, § 19.40[2][c][vii][A], at 471 ("There have been no cases decided on the [the basis of the original plan doctrine] for many years."). The *Martin* decision was last cited by one of the state's appellate courts in *Hunt v. City of High Point*, 226 N.C. 74 (1946), a case the defendant city did not win.

577. Ferrell, *supra* note 564, at 165–67 (discussing *Hunt*).

578. *Id.* at 166–67.

579. Kirkpatrick v. Town of Nags Head, 213 N.C. App. 132, 142 (2011) ("[W]e hold that municipalities may exercise their discretion, while remaining subject to protection from liability by . . . governmental immunity, in deciding which roads to keep open for vehicular traffic and which roads should not continue to be open for travel.").

580. *Id.* at 142, 147.

581. Steelman v. City of New Bern, 279 N.C. 589, 591 (1971).

582. Baker v. City of Lumberton, 239 N.C. 401, 408 (1953).

- *Traffic Lights.* The installation, maintenance, and timing of traffic lights are governmental functions.[583] Accordingly, governmental immunity shielded a city from the negligence claim of a plaintiff who was injured in an automobile accident allegedly caused by the careless driving of a city employee on his way to repair a broken traffic light.[584]

Two other points about the street-maintenance exception warrant attention here.

1. A large body of case law concerns the kinds of street conditions that plaintiffs must prove to demonstrate that their negligence claims fall within the exception.[585] The cases in this group establish, for example, that cities are not liable for injuries caused by "trivial defects" in their sidewalks.[586]
2. While plaintiffs may seek damages for injuries to their persons or property caused by the failure of cities to keep their streets in proper repair, it appears that plaintiffs may not recover damages for mere economic loss.[587]

Interesting situations can arise when activities normally cloaked in governmental immunity create unsafe street conditions. In one case, the defendant city's fire department extinguished a fire in part of a building by pumping water from three pumps on it for more than an hour.[588] The next day, the plaintiff fell and hurt herself on the sidewalk in front of the building, allegedly because the fire department's action had left the sidewalk slippery. In ruling that the city was not liable for the plaintiff's injuries, the state supreme court reasoned that (1) "any damage done by the water was in the exercise of a gov-

---

583. Hamilton v. Town of Hamlet, 238 N.C. 741, 742 (1953); Hodges v. City of Charlotte, 214 N.C. 737, 739 (1939); Sisk v. City of Greensboro, 183 N.C. App. 657, 660 (2007); Rappe v. Carr, 4 N.C. App. 497, 499 (1969). The North Carolina Supreme Court has justified this position by asserting that a traffic light "is installed solely for the public benefit" and "is in effect the substituting of a signal for a policeman in regulating traffic[.]" *Hodges,* 214 N.C. at 740.

584. *Hodges,* 214 N.C. at 741–42.

585. *See generally* Ferrell, *supra* note 564, at 153–67 (reviewing case law on the standard of care in street maintenance cases).

586. Desmond v. City of Charlotte, 142 N.C. App. 590, 592 (2001). An example of a trivial defect would be a one-inch difference in elevation between two adjacent concrete sections in a sidewalk. Bagwell v. Town of Brevard, 256 N.C. 465, 466 (1962) (per curiam).

587. *See Kirkpatrick,* 213 N.C. App. at 140–41 (state's appellate courts have not applied the street maintenance exception to claims for purely economic injuries); Ferrell, *supra* note 560, at 167–68 (North Carolina Supreme Court "has uniformly held that decrease in the value of property due to change of street grade, cutting of trees, or the closing of streets is not compensable").

588. Klassette v. Ligget Drug Co., Inc., 227 N.C. 353, 355 (1947).

ernmental function" and (2) the city could not be expected to guard against wet sidewalks inasmuch as sidewalks are exposed to rain.[589] Arguably, by not clearly resolving the case solely on immunity grounds, the court left open the possibility of city liability for unsafe street conditions in cases where the performance of a governmental function created the particular condition at issue but the plaintiff can demonstrate that the city's failure to remedy the condition amounted to negligence.

9.2.2 Street Construction

Many of the same points made above about street maintenance apply to the construction of city streets. For one thing, although support exists for the view that street construction amounts to a governmental function, the state supreme court has held that governmental immunity will not defeat a claim for personal injury or property damage that stems from negligence in street construction.[590] If the claim is based on negligent design as opposed to negligence on the part of the workers in the actual construction of a street, the original plan may offer the city a defense, to the extent that the doctrine remains viable.[591]

9.3 Wrongful Death

Unlike negligence and most other torts claims, which are judicial creations, wrongful death lawsuits owe their existence entirely to legislative action, namely, the General Assembly's enactment of G.S. 28A-18-2.[592] Ordinarily, as noted in Section 1.8.1, *supra*, governmental immunity is not a defense to claims under federal or state statutes. Local government units have

---

589. *Id.* at 361.

590. Klingenberg v. City of Raleigh, 212 N.C. 549, 550–51 (1937) ("While the construction and maintenance of public roads and streets is a governmental function the courts have almost universally permitted recovery against a city or town where injury results from negligence in the construction of a street or from negligent failure to maintain the street in a reasonably safe condition."). *See also* Meares v. City of Wilmington, 31 N.C. 73, 78 (1848) (city was liable for the collapse of walls on the plaintiff's property caused by the city's negligence in lowering the grade of a nearby street).

591. *Klingenberg*, 212 N.C. at 551 (city was not liable for injuries plaintiff sustained when thrown from an automobile that struck a valley gutter at the intersection of two city streets because, in adopting the gutter as part of its street construction plan, the city had acted "in a legislative, quasi-judicial and discretionary capacity" rather than in a "ministerial" capacity). The court in *Klingenberg* further explained that the original plan doctrine "is not limited to cases where the plan was adopted and determined in advance"; rather, the doctrine "applies equally where [the plan] was ratified and adopted by the municipality after the actual work of construction." *Id.*

592. *See* DAYE & MORRIS, *supra* note 1, § 24.30[1], at 591 ("Since the common law did not recognize a cause of action for the death of a human being, the wrongful death action is entirely statutory.").

successfully invoked governmental immunity to defeat wrongful death actions, however.[593] The obvious explanation for the judiciary's willingness to apply governmental immunity to wrongful death claims is that, despite its origin in statute, the wrongful death action is fundamentally a tort claim. As one commentator has remarked, "[t]he basis for liability in a wrongful death action is that the defendant's act or omission is tortious."[594] By its own terms, the statute will sustain a wrongful death claim only when the death in question resulted from the defendant's "wrongful act, neglect or default . . . such as would, if the injured person had lived, have entitled the injured person to an action for damages."[595]

---

593. *E.g.*, Wright v. Gaston Cty., 205 N.C. App. 600, 607–08 (2010) (governmental immunity blocked plaintiffs' wrongful death and related tort claims arising from the alleged negligence of 911 operators).

594. DAYE & MORRIS, *supra* note 1, § 24.30[2][a], at 592.

595. G.S. 28A-18-2(a). *See generally* DAYE & MORRIS, *supra* note 1, § 24.30, at 591–610 (explaining fundamental aspects of wrongful death actions).

Chapter 10

Governmental Immunity Pleading Issues

This book has so far dealt mostly with the substantive law of governmental immunity, such as the distinction between governmental and proprietary functions. This chapter turns to some key procedural issues involving the doctrine. In particular, it examines (1) the pleading standards plaintiffs must satisfy to allege waivers of governmental immunity and (2) the steps local government units must take to raise immunity successfully as a defense in motions to dismiss or in their responses to lawsuits.[596]

10.1 Requirement to Plead Waiver of Governmental Immunity

As noted at the outset of Chapter 4, a unit may waive governmental immunity by undertaking a proprietary function, purchasing liability insurance, or entering into a valid contract. Yet even when there has been a waiver, the plaintiff cannot overcome a defense of governmental immunity unless the plaintiff has alleged waiver in the complaint.[597] If no allegation of waiver is present, "the complaint fails to state a cause of action."[598] In other words, if the complaint in a lawsuit against a unit fails to allege waiver, and the unit properly asserts governmental immunity in a motion to dismiss or other

---

596. This chapter incorporates material from Trey Allen, *Pleading Waiver of Governmental Immunity: What's Enough?*, COATES' CANONS: NC LOC. GOV'T L. blog (Nov. 14, 2017), https://canons.sog.unc.edu/pleading-waiver-of-governmental-immunity-whats-enough/; and Trey Allen, *Local Government Lawyers: Take Care in Asserting Governmental Immunity*, COATES' CANONS: NC LOC. GOV'T L. blog (Aug. 1, 2017), https://canons.sog.unc.edu/local-government-lawyers-take-care-in-asserting-governmental-immunity/.

597. *E.g.*, Fabrikant v. Currituck Cty., 174 N.C. App. 30, 38 (2005) ("[T]o overcome a defense of governmental immunity, the complaint must specifically allege a waiver of governmental immunity."); Phillips v. Gray, 163 N.C. App. 52, 56 (2004) ("The complaint must specifically allege a waiver of governmental immunity to overcome a defense of sovereign immunity."); Paquette v. Cty. of Durham, 155 N.C. App. 415, 418 (2002) ("In order to overcome a defense of governmental immunity, the complaint must specifically allege a waiver of governmental immunity.").

598. Wray v. City of Greensboro, 370 N.C. 41, 47 (2017) (citations omitted).

appropriate motion, the trial court must throw out any claims subject to the unit's immunity defense. Its ruling in favor of the unit will be upheld on appeal, even if evidence in the record shows that a waiver occurred.[599]

10.1.1 Adequate Waiver Allegations

How does the trial court go about determining whether a complaint sufficiently alleges a waiver of governmental immunity? It should not base its decision on whether the word "waiver" appears in the complaint. According to both the North Carolina Supreme Court and the North Carolina Court of Appeals, no particular language is necessary to allege a waiver of governmental immunity.[600] The proper test is whether the complaint alleges facts that, if true, demonstrate the existence of a waiver. Appellate cases discussing the different waiver mechanisms establish that this standard is not hard to meet.

10.1.1.1 Alleging Waiver by Proprietary Function

No *express* allegation of waiver is needed when the undertaking alleged to have caused the plaintiff's injury constitutes a proprietary function.[601] Why not? Because a claim based on a proprietary function necessarily concerns an incident for which the unit does not enjoy governmental immunity. In *Town of Sandy Creek v. East Coast Contracting, Inc.*, for example, the defendant city argued that governmental immunity shielded it from claims that its negligent supervision of a contractor had resulted in damage to a nearby town's streets. No explicit allegation of waiver was required because the city's handling of its business relationship with the contractor amounted to a proprietary function.[602]

---

599. Clark v. Burke Cty., 117 N.C. App. 85, 88–89 (1994) ("Plaintiff also argues that the absence of the allegations of waiver is not fatal as long as evidence of waiver is present in the record. This Court addressed and rejected this argument in *Gunter* [v. Anders, 115 N.C. App. 331 (1994)]."); *Gunter*, 115 N.C. App. at 337 (plaintiffs' failure to allege waiver of governmental immunity was fatal to their tort claims against defendant school board, regardless of whether the record contained evidence of liability insurance). *See also Fabrikant*, 174 N.C. App. at 39 ("Based on *Clark* and *Gunter*, we are limited to reviewing the complaint and its attachments to determine whether plaintiffs have alleged sufficient facts to establish a waiver by the State defendants of sovereign immunity.").

600. *Wray*, 370 N.C. at 48; Fullwood v. Barnes, ___ N.C. App. ___, ___, 792 S.E.2d 545, 550 (2016).

601. *See* Town of Sandy Creek v. E. Coast Contracting, Inc., 226 N.C. App. 576, 577 (2013) ("We held that waiver of governmental immunity need only be pled where a [city] is acting in a governmental capacity; and where a [city] is acting in a proprietary manner, waiver need not be pled.").

602. *Id.*

10.1.1.2 Alleging Waiver by Purchase of Insurance

A plaintiff can satisfy the waiver pleading requirement through a bare allegation that the defendant unit has liability coverage applicable to the plaintiff's claims. The allegation does not have to name the insurance provider or say anything about the policy limits. In one case, the complaint merely alleged: "Upon information and belief, [the town] maintain[s], and at all times relevant to this claim maintained, liability insurance affording coverage to this action."[603] Despite the omission of the word *waiver*, the court deemed the allegation sufficient to assert a waiver of immunity through the purchase of liability insurance, in part because the allegation afforded the town adequate notice of the basis for the plaintiffs' claim.

10.1.1.3 Alleging Waiver by Contract

Simply by alleging that a unit of local government has entered into a valid contract, a complaint effectively asserts that the unit has waived immunity as to actions on the contract.[604]

In *Wray v. City of Greensboro*, the plaintiff sued his former employer over costs he had incurred defending himself in several lawsuits arising from his tenure as chief of police. The complaint alleged that the unit was obligated to reimburse the plaintiff under a policy it had adopted concerning civil claims against the unit's officers and employees. Describing the plaintiff's claim as one "sounding in contract," the state supreme court held that the complaint "sufficiently allege[d] that the City ha[d] consented to be sued to the extent of any such contract."[605] Consequently, the complaint's allegations were "adequate to raise a waiver of governmental immunity[.]"[606]

The supreme court took pains to note that its ruling "express[ed] no opinion on the merits of the plaintiff's contract action."[607] The case was sent back to the trial court for it to determine whether the unit actually had a contractual obligation to reimburse the plaintiff.

10.1.2 Overcoming Waiver Allegations

The comment in *Wray* about the limited nature of the state high court's ruling brings up an important point relevant to all three categories of waiver allegations. Even if a plaintiff successfully pleads waiver, governmental immunity might ultimately defeat the plaintiff's claims. If, for instance, the plaintiff relies on the proprietary nature of the activity to establish a waiver, and the evidence leads the court to classify the undertaking as governmental—perhaps because

---

603. Anderson v. Town of Andrews, 127 N.C. App. 599, 600 (1997).
604. *Wray*, 370 N.C. at 48 ("[A] waiver of governmental immunity is implied, and effectively alleged, when the plaintiff pleads a contract claim.").
605. *Id.* at 51.
606. *Id.*
607. *Id.* at 50.

it did not generate significant revenue for the unit—the plaintiff may find his or her claims barred by governmental immunity. Similarly, an allegation that a unit has waived immunity through the purchase of liability insurance can be overcome by evidence that the unit lacks such insurance or that its policy does not cover the precise claims or amounts at issue. Finally, if an alleged contract turns out to have been invalid, the complaint's assertion of validity will not stop the unit from deploying governmental immunity to torpedo the plaintiff's contract claims.

10.1.3 Amending the Complaint to Allege Waiver

The North Carolina Rules of Civil Procedure allow a plaintiff to amend his or her complaint once without permission any time before a responsive pleading is served.[608] After the defendant serves its answer to the complaint, or if the complaint has been previously amended, the plaintiff may not amend the complaint without the trial court's permission or the opposing party's written consent.[609] Although the trial court should freely grant leave to amend when justice so requires, it has broad discretion to refuse to allow amendments.[610] The appellate courts will not disturb a denial of a motion to amend unless the ruling amounts to an abuse of discretion, that is, the ruling is so arbitrary that it cannot be the result of reasoned decisionmaking.[611]

Several appellate court decisions affirm trial court orders denying plaintiffs leave to amend to allege waivers of governmental immunity.[612] In one case, the defendant school board filed an answer that included a motion to dismiss the plaintiffs' tort claims arising from an automobile accident in a school driveway.[613] At the hearing on its motion, the board argued for dismissal based on the complaint's omission of any allegation that the board had waived governmental immunity through the purchase of liability insurance. The plaintiffs' attorney made an oral motion to amend the complaint to allege waiver, which the trial court denied. In upholding the denial, the court of appeals observed that the plaintiffs had learned of the board's purchase of liability insurance

---

608. N.C. R. Civ. P. 15(a).

609. *Id.*

610. Wilson, *supra* note 358, § 15-3, at 15-5 to 15-6.

611. Gunter v. Anders, 115 N.C. App. 331, 334 (1994).

612. *E.g.*, Pruett v. Bingham, 238 N.C. App. 78, 86 (2014), *aff'd*, 368 N.C. 709 (2016) (trial court did not abuse discretion by denying third-party plaintiffs' oral motion to amend the complaint to allege a waiver of governmental immunity by third-party defendant fire department); *Gunter*, 115 N.C. App. at 334 (no abuse of discretion when trial court denied plaintiffs' oral motion to amend the complaint to allege a waiver of governmental immunity by defendant school board); Brooks v. Martin, 235 N.C. App. 423 (2014) (unpublished) (trial court did not abuse discretion by denying plaintiff's written motion to amend complaint to allege a waiver of immunity by defendant county).

613. *Gunter*, 115 N.C. App. at 333.

nearly two and a half years prior to their last-minute attempt to amend their complaint.[614]

In another case, this one involving personal injuries allegedly sustained in an automobile accident negligently caused by a deputy sheriff, the appellate court affirmed the trial court's denial of the plaintiff's written motion to amend the complaint to allege waiver by the purchase of liability insurance.[615] The court pointed out that nearly three years had passed between the plaintiff's accident and the filing of her lawsuit against the defendant county, during which she had ample time "to investigate the factual and legal basis" for her lawsuit.[616] It further noted that the plaintiff had not taken advantage of the opportunity to amend her complaint as a matter of course prior to the county's filing of a responsive pleading.

10.2 Issues with Pleading Governmental Immunity

In litigation, cities and counties most often assert the defense of governmental immunity initially in their answers to complaints or in motions to dismiss (MTDs) filed pursuant to Rule 12(b) of the N.C. Rules of Civil Procedure. MTDs asserting governmental immunity typically seek dismissal on one or more of the following grounds.

- *Rule 12(b)(1) Lack of Subject Matter Jurisdiction.* By raising governmental immunity in the context of a 12(b)(1) motion, the unit essentially argues that dismissal is necessary because governmental immunity deprives the trial court of the power to adjudicate the claims alleged against the unit.
- *Rule 12(b)(2) Lack of Personal Jurisdiction.* By asserting governmental immunity under 12(b)(2), a unit maintains that dismissal is required inasmuch as governmental immunity prevents the trial court from exercising control over the unit in the case.
- *Rule 12(b)(6) Failure to State a Claim Upon Which Relief May Be Granted.* When a unit raises governmental immunity in a 12(b)(6) motion, it contends that dismissal is mandatory because, even if the plaintiff's factual allegations are accepted as true, governmental immunity bars the plaintiff's claims against the unit.

10.2.1 Adequately Pleading Governmental Immunity

Detailed allegations are not necessary for a unit to assert the defense of governmental immunity in an answer or in an MTD. In one case, the answer and MTD filed by a fire and rescue department merely asserted that the plaintiffs'

---

614. *Id.* at 334.
615. *Brooks*, 235 N.C. at 423.
616. *Id.*

negligence claims were "'barred by governmental or sovereign immunity.'"[517] On appeal from the trial court's order granting the MTD, the plaintiffs argued that the department had "failed to adequately plead or produce documents related to [its] claim of immunity."[618] The court of appeals rejected this argument and held that dismissal was proper given the total absence of any waiver allegation in the complaint. In the eyes of the appellate court, "there was sufficient information in the [department's] answer to give [the plaintiffs] adequate notice of the [department's] affirmative defense."[619]

What if a unit fails to assert governmental immunity in an MTD or in its answer? The N.C. Rules of Civil Procedure allow a defendant to amend its answer without permission any time within thirty days following service of the answer on the plaintiff.[620] After that, the defendant may not amend its answer without the court's leave or the plaintiff's written consent.[621] The court of appeals' opinion in *Mullis v. Sechrest* suggests that trial courts will usually be on solid legal footing if they permit units to amend their answers to raise governmental immunity.[622] The appellate court in *Mullis* held that the trial court had not abused its discretion by allowing the defendant school board to amend its answer to assert governmental immunity as an affirmative defense to tort claims stemming from the plaintiff student's injuries in a shop class.[623] The court of appeals reasoned that the plaintiffs (the student and his father) "knew or should have known that an action against a governmental entity and its officers and employees raises a question of [governmental] immunity."[624] This standard seems likely to apply to plaintiffs in most lawsuits against local governments.

The *Mullis* decision does highlight an important limitation on amendments alleging governmental immunity. Under the N.C. Rules of Civil Procedure, a defendant waives any objection to the trial court's personal jurisdiction if he or she fails to include the objection in the original answer or in an amendment to the answer as a matter of course within thirty days of

---

617. *Pruett*, 238 N.C. App. at 87 (Stroud, J., dissenting). Sections 3.2.2.1 and 3.2.2.2, *supra*, discuss the immunity protections available to nonprofit fire departments that contract with local government units to provide fire protection services or emergency medical services.

618. *Id*. at 85.

619. *Id*.

620. N.C. R. Civ. P. 15(a).

621. *Id*.

622. 126 N.C. App. 91 (1997), *rev'd on other grounds*, 347 N.C. 548 (1998).

623. *Id*. at 96.

624. *Id*. The court also noted that the trial court had allowed the plaintiffs to amend their complaint to add an allegation of waiver by insurance. *Id*. The amendment plainly demonstrated that the plaintiffs were aware of the board's potential immunity defense.

service of the original answer.[625] Thus, if the school board had characterized its immunity defense as a challenge to the trial court's personal jurisdiction over the board, the trial court would have been forced to deny the board's motion to amend.[626]

10.2.2 Pleading Governmental Immunity to Preserve Immediate Appeals

As a general rule, parties to a lawsuit may not immediately appeal a trial court's interlocutory orders. (An order is "interlocutory" if it does not dispose of all matters in dispute.) Two major exceptions to this rule are found in Chapter 1, Section 277 of the North Carolina General Statutes (hereinafter G.S.), which allows a party to appeal immediately from (1) a ruling on a legal issue that affects a "substantial right" or (2) an adverse ruling that concerns the trial court's jurisdiction over the defendant or the defendant's property. There is an enormous body of case law on what constitutes a substantial right under G.S. 1-277's first prong, but in broad terms, a substantial right is "one which will clearly be lost or irremediably adversely affected if the order is not reviewable before final judgment."[627] The second prong of G.S. 1-277 allows immediate appeals from orders rejecting challenges to the trial court's personal jurisdiction over the defendant in a case.[628]

A number of appellate court decisions flatly state that a unit may immediately appeal from an interlocutory order denying an MTD if the MTD asserts governmental immunity.[629] These broad statements have led some to believe that a unit always has a right to an immediate appeal when a trial court denies such an MTD. This belief is almost certainly wrong. In several cases involving governmental immunity, the court of appeals has conditioned the right of immediate appeal on whether the unit's MTD cited Rules 12(b)(1), 12(b)(2), or 12(b)(6) of the N.C. Rules of Civil Procedure. These three categories of dismissal motions will be examined in reverse order below, primarily

---

625. N.C. R. Civ. P. 12(h)(1), 15(a).

626. *See Mullis*, 126 N.C. App. at 95 (school board "amended [its] answer to plead [governmental] immunity as a defense 'pleaded in bar of any recovery by the plaintiffs,' not as a challenge to the [trial] court's personal jurisdiction over the [board]").

627. Darroch v. Lea, 150 N.C. App. 156, 159 (2002) (internal quotation marks omitted) (citations omitted).

628. More information on appeals from interlocutory orders can be found in the guide prepared by the Appellate Rules Committee of the North Carolina Bar Association and available here: https://www.ncbar.org/media/758546/ncba-appellate-rules-committee-guide-to-appealability-2017.pdf.

629. *E.g.*, Richmond Cty. Bd. of Educ. v. Cowell, 225 N.C. App. 583, 586 (2013) ("'This Court has consistently held that '[t]he denial of a motion to dismiss based upon the defense of sovereign immunity affects a substantial right and is thus immediately appealable.' ").

because the court's pronouncements regarding governmental immunity and Rule 12(b)(1) are the most complicated.

10.2.2.1 Immediate Appeals and Rule 12(b)(6) (Failure to State a Valid Claim)

According to the court of appeals, when governmental immunity is raised in a Rule 12(b)(6) motion, the denial of the motion creates a right to appeal immediately under G.S. 1-277's "substantial right" prong.[630] The substantial right affected is the unit's right under the doctrine of governmental immunity to be free not just from liability for the plaintiff's injuries but also from the burden of having to litigate the plaintiff's claims. The value of governmental immunity to local governments would be significantly diminished if a unit that unsuccessfully asserts the immunity in a 12(b)(6) motion could be forced to proceed to trial without appellate review.[631]

10.2.2.2 Immediate Appeals and Rule 12(b)(2) (Lack of Personal Jurisdiction)

The court of appeals has repeatedly opined that the defense of governmental immunity constitutes a challenge to the trial court's personal jurisdiction over the defendant local government.[632] For this reason, the appellate court has treated the denial of a Rule 12(b)(2) motion asserting governmental immunity as immediately appealable under the personal jurisdiction prong of G.S. 1-277.[633]

10.2.2.3 Immediate Appeals and Rule 12(b)(1) (Lack of Subject Matter Jurisdiction)

Because Rule 12(b)(1) concerns subject matter jurisdiction, not personal jurisdiction, the denial of a 12(b)(1) motion doesn't trigger a right to an immediate appeal under G.S. 1-277 unless a substantial right is affected. In *Teachy v. Coble Dairies*, the North Carolina Supreme Court appears to have concluded that the denial of a 12(b)(1) motion does not affect a substantial right.[634] Relying on *Teachy*, the court of appeals has held that there is no immediate appeal from a trial court's denial of a 12(b)(1) motion, even when governmental immunity is in play.[635]

---

630. *E.g.*, Davis v. DiBartolo, 176 N.C. App. 142, 144 (2006) ("The denial of a 12(b)(6) motion to dismiss for failure to state a claim is immediately appealable where the motion raises the defense of sovereign immunity.").

631. *See* Slade v. Vernon, 110 N.C. App. 422, 425 (1993) ("A valid claim of immunity is more than a defense in a lawsuit; it is in essence immunity from suit. Were the case to be erroneously permitted to proceed to trial, immunity would be effectively lost.").

632. Can Am S., LLC v. State, 234 N.C. App. 119, 123–24 (2014); Data Gen. Corp. v. Cty. of Durham, 143 N.C. App. 97, 100 (2001).

633. *Can Am S.*, 234 N.C. App. at 123–24; *Data Gen.*, 143 N.C. App. at 100.

634. 306 N.C. 324 (1982).

635. *Davis*, 176 N.C. App. at 144–45; *Data Gen.*, 143 N.C. App. at 100.

At first glance, the court of appeals' application of *Teachy* to immunity cases seems at odds with the court's treatment of Rule 12(b)(6) motions premised on governmental immunity. How can the denial of an immunity defense affect a substantial right if raised under 12(b)(6) but not 12(b)(1)?

The same decisions in which the court of appeals has held that governmental immunity calls a trial court's personal jurisdiction into question also declare that governmental immunity does not present a question of subject matter jurisdiction.[636] The decisions appear to imply that governmental immunity should not be viewed as affecting a substantial right when it is raised under Rule 12(b)(1) because a 12(b)(1) motion is the wrong vehicle for asserting that defense.

The court of appeals has not been entirely consistent in its approach to governmental immunity and 12(b)(1) motions. The court recently allowed an immediate appeal from the denial of a 12(b)(1) motion that raised the defense of governmental immunity, agreeing with the defendant that the trial court's ruling affected a substantial right.[637] The last word on whether governmental immunity may be used to challenge a trial court's subject matter jurisdiction belongs to the North Carolina Supreme Court, but so far it has resisted providing definitive guidance on the issue.[638]

In short, then, when governmental immunity is raised in a Rule 12(b)(2) or 12(b)(6) motion, the denial of the motion creates a right to an immediate appeal. On the other hand, if a unit unsuccessfully moves for dismissal on immunity grounds solely under Rule 12(b)(1), it may find itself unable to appeal immediately. The court of appeals' opinion in *Murray v. University of North Carolina at Chapel Hill* illustrates how these principles work in practice.[639] It also points to practical steps that a local government attorney should take to preserve the option for an immediate appeal from the denial of an MTD in which governmental immunity is asserted.

10.2.2.4 The Murray Decision

The plaintiff in *Murray* filed a grievance under the University's Title IX policy, alleging sexual misconduct on the part of a fellow student. She subsequently filed a lawsuit against the University, alleging it had unlawfully restricted her attorney's ability to participate in the grievance proceedings. The University

---

636. *E.g., Data Gen.*, 143 N.C. App. at 100 ("[A]n appeal of a[n] [MTD] based on sovereign immunity presents a question of personal jurisdiction rather than subject matter jurisdiction . . . .").

637. Sandhill Amusements, Inc. v. Sheriff of Onslow Cty., 236 N.C. App. 340, 347–48 (2014), *rev'd on other grounds and remanded*, 368 N.C. 91 (2015) (per curiam).

638. *See Teachy*, 306 N.C. at 328 (declining to resolve "whether sovereign immunity is a question of subject matter jurisdiction or whether the denial of a[n] [MTD] on grounds of sovereign immunity is immediately appealable").

639. ___ N.C. App. ___, 782 S.E.2d 531 (2016), *aff'd*, 369 N.C. 585 (2017) (per curiam).

filed an MTD under Rule 12(b)(1) for lack of subject matter jurisdiction and under Rule 12(b)(6) for failure to state a valid legal claim. The MTD did not cite Rule 12(b)(2), nor did it expressly mention sovereign immunity. At the hearing on the MTD, however, the University argued for dismissal under both 12(b)(1) and 12(b)(2) based on sovereign immunity. The trial court issued an order denying the MTD, and the University pursued an immediate appeal from that order.

The court of appeals held that the University was not entitled to an immediate appeal. As it has in other cases, the court opined that there is no right to an immediate appeal from the denial of a 12(b)(1) motion, even when sovereign immunity is at issue. It thus declined to review the trial court's denial of the University's 12(b)(1) motion.

Although the University argued for dismissal under Rule 12(b)(2) at the MTD hearing, and a trial court's denial of a 12(b)(2) motion may be appealed immediately, the court of appeals determined that the University had not taken the procedural steps necessary to preserve an appeal on 12(b)(2) grounds. Under the North Carolina Rules of Appellate Procedure, a party must obtain a ruling from the trial court in order to preserve an issue for appeal.[640] In *Murray*, the trial court's order referred to Rules 12(b)(1) and 12(b)(6) but omitted any reference to 12(b)(2), and the University didn't ask the trial court to supplement the order with a ruling on its oral 12(b)(2) motion.

The appellate court likewise rejected the University's argument that it could immediately appeal the denial of its 12(b)(6) motion. While the denial of a 12(b)(6) motion is subject to an immediate appeal if the motion asserts sovereign immunity, the University's MTD did not expressly assert that defense. Furthermore, although the University brought up sovereign immunity at the MTD hearing, it did so only with regard to Rules 12(b)(1) and 12(b)(2). Inasmuch as the University had not argued governmental immunity in connection with 12(b)(6), the court of appeals concluded that the University could not immediately appeal from the trial court's denial of its 12(b)(6) motion.

The court's opinion in *Murray* offers several practical takeaways for local government attorneys. To ensure that a unit may immediately appeal a trial court's denial of an MTD based on governmental immunity, the unit's attorney should

- cite Rules 12(b)(2) and 12(b)(6) in the MTD,
- clearly assert governmental immunity in the MTD under both 12(b)(2) and 12(b)(6),

---

640. N.C. R. App. P. 10(a)(1) ("In order to preserve an issue for appellate review . . . [i]t is also necessary for the complaining party to obtain a ruling upon the party's request, objection, or motion.").

- specifically argue governmental immunity under 12(b)(2) and 12(b)(6) at the hearing on the MTD, and
- obtain a ruling from the trial court that addresses both 12(b)(2) and 12(b)(6).

10.2.3 Immediate Appeal from Interlocutory Order Eliminating Claims Based on Governmental Immunity

The right to appeal immediately from interlocutory immunity rulings is not restricted to local governments. A plaintiff may immediately appeal a trial court's interlocutory order granting a unit's motion to throw out claims on immunity grounds.[641]

---

641. Greene v. Barrick, 198 N.C. App. 647, 650 (2009) (citations omitted) ("This Court has held that 'when the moving party claims sovereign, absolute or qualified immunity, the denial of a motion for summary judgment is immediately appealable.' Even though this case involves the grant, rather than the denial of sovereign immunity, we believe the same type of issues are called into question by the appeal, and therefore, plaintiff's appeal is properly before this Court."). *See also* Odom v. Lane, 161 N.C. App. 534, 535 (2003) (plaintiff could immediately appeal trial court's interlocutory order granting defendant hospital's summary judgment motion asserting governmental immunity).

The plaintiff's right to an interlocutory appeal can arise when, based on governmental immunity, the trial court throws out some but not all of the plaintiff's claims against a unit, or all of the claims against the unit but not the plaintiff's claims against other defendants.

Appendix A. Governmental Immunity Waiver Statutes

Note: All sections reproduced in this appendix are from the North Carolina General Statutes.

I. County Waiver Statute

§ 153A-435. Liability insurance; damage suits against a county involving governmental functions.

(a)   A county may contract to insure itself and any of its officers, agents, or employees against liability for wrongful death or negligent or intentional damage to person or property or against absolute liability for damage to person or property caused by an act or omission of the county or of any of its officers, agents, or employees when acting within the scope of their authority and the course of their employment. The board of commissioners shall determine what liabilities and what officers, agents, and employees shall be covered by any insurance purchased pursuant to this subsection.

    Purchase of insurance pursuant to this subsection waives the county's governmental immunity, to the extent of insurance coverage, for any act or omission occurring in the exercise of a governmental function. Participation in a local government risk pool pursuant to Article 23 of General Statute Chapter 58 shall be deemed to be the purchase of insurance for the purposes of this section. By entering into an insurance contract with the county, an insurer waives any defense based upon the governmental immunity of the county.

    If a county uses a funded reserve instead of purchasing insurance against liability for wrongful death, negligence, or intentional damage to personal property, or absolute liability for damage to person or property caused by an act or omission of the county or any of its officers, agents, or employees acting within the scope of their authority and the course of their employment, the county board of commissioners may adopt a resolution that deems the creation of a funded reserve to be the same as the purchase of insurance under this section. Adoption of such a resolution waives the county's governmental immunity only to the extent specified in the board's resolution, but in no event greater than funds available in the funded reserve for the payment of claims.

(b)   If a county has waived its governmental immunity pursuant to subsection (a) of this section, any person, or if he dies, his personal representative, sustaining damages as a result of an act or omission of the county or any of its officers, agents, or employees, occurring in the exercise of a governmental function, may sue the county for recovery of damages. To the extent of the coverage of insurance purchased pursuant to subsection (a) of this section, governmental immunity may not be a defense to the action. Otherwise, however, the county has all defenses available to private litigants in any action brought pursuant to this section without restriction, limitation, or other effect, whether the defense arises from common law or by virtue of a statute.

    Despite the purchase of insurance as authorized by subsection (a) of this section, the liability of a county for acts or omissions occurring in the exercise of governmental functions does not attach unless the plaintiff waives the right to have all issues of law or fact relating to insurance in the action determined by a jury. The judge shall hear and determine these issues without resort to a jury, and the jury shall be absent during any motion, argument, testimony, or announcement of findings of fact or conclusions of law relating to these issues unless the defendant requests a jury trial on them.

II. City Waiver Statutes

§ 160A-485. Waiver of immunity through insurance purchase.

(a)   Any city is authorized to waive its immunity from civil liability in tort by the act of purchasing liability insurance. Participation in a local government risk pool pursuant to Article 23 of General Statute Chapter 58 shall be deemed to be the purchase of insurance for the purposes of this section. Immunity shall be waived only to the extent that the city is indemnified by the insurance contract from tort liability. No formal action other than the purchase of liability insurance shall be required to waive tort immunity, and no city shall be deemed to have waived its tort immunity by any action other than the purchase of liability insurance. If a city uses a funded reserve instead of purchasing insurance against liability for wrongful death, negligence, or intentional damage to personal property, or absolute liability for damage to person or property caused by an act or omission of the city or any of its officers, agents, or employees acting within the scope of their authority and the course of their employment, the city council may adopt a resolution that deems the creation of a funded reserve to be the same as the purchase of insurance under this section. Adoption of such a resolution waives the city's governmental immunity only to the extent specified in the council's resolution, but in no event greater than funds available in the funded reserve for the payment of claims.

(b)   An insurance contract purchased pursuant to this section may cover such torts and such officials, employees, and agents of the city as the governing board may determine. The city may purchase one or more insurance contracts, each covering different torts or different officials, employees, or agents of the city. An insurer who issues a contract of insurance to a city pursuant to this section thereby waives any defense based upon the governmental immunity of the city, and any defense based upon lack of authority for the city to enter into the contract. Each city is authorized to pay the lawful premiums for insurance purchased pursuant to this section.

(c) Any plaintiff may maintain a tort claim against a city insured under this section in any court of competent jurisdiction. As to any such claim, to the extent that the city is insured against such claim pursuant to this section, governmental immunity shall be no defense. Except as expressly provided herein, nothing in this section shall be construed to deprive any city of any defense to any tort claim lodged against it, or to restrict, limit, or otherwise affect any defense that the city may have at common law or by virtue of any statute. Nothing in this section shall relieve a plaintiff from any duty to give notice of his claim to the city, or to commence his action within the applicable period of time limited by statute. No judgment may be entered against a city in excess of its insurance policy limits on any tort claim for which it would have been immune but for the purchase of liability insurance pursuant to this section. No judgment may be entered against a city on any tort claim for which it would have been immune but for the purchase of liability insurance pursuant to this section except a claim arising at a time when the city is insured under an insurance contract purchased and issued pursuant to this section. If, in the trial of any tort claim against a city for which it would have been immune but for the purchase of liability insurance pursuant to this section, a verdict is returned awarding damages to the plaintiff in excess of the insurance limits, the presiding judge shall reduce the award to the maximum policy limits before entering judgment.

(d) Except as otherwise provided in this section, tort claims against a city shall be governed by the North Carolina Rules of Civil Procedure. No document or exhibit which relates to or alleges facts as to the city's insurance against liability shall be read, exhibited, or mentioned in the presence of the trial jury in the trial of any claim brought pursuant to this section, nor shall the plaintiff, his counsel, or anyone testifying in his behalf directly or indirectly convey to the jury any inference that the city's potential liability is covered by insurance. No judgment may be entered against the city unless the plaintiff waives his right to a jury trial on all issues of law or fact relating to insurance coverage. All issues relating to insurance coverage shall be heard and determined by the judge without resort to a jury. The jury shall be absent during all motions, arguments, testimony, or announcement of findings of fact or conclusions of law with respect to insurance coverage. The city may waive its right to have issues concerning insurance coverage determined by the judge without a jury, and may request a jury trial on these issues.

(e) Nothing in this section shall apply to any claim in tort against a city for which the city is not immune from liability under the statutes or common law of this State.

§ 160A-485.5. Waiver of immunity for large cities through State Tort Claims Act.

(a) Any city with a population of 500,000 or more according to the most recent decennial federal census is authorized to waive its immunity from civil liability in tort by passage of a resolution expressing the intent of the city to waive its sovereign immunity pursuant to Article 31 of Chapter 143 of the General Statutes, as modified by subsection (b) of this section, and subject to the limitations set forth by subsection (c) of this section. Any resolution passed pursuant to this section shall apply to all claims arising on or after the passage of the resolution, until repealed.

(b) The following modifications of Article 31 of Chapter 143 of the General Statutes shall apply to the waiver of sovereign immunity described by subsection (a) of this section:

   (1) Jurisdiction for tort claims against the city shall be vested in the Superior Court Division of the General Court of Justice of the county where the city is principally located, and, except as otherwise provided in this section, tort claims against a city shall be governed by the North Carolina Rules of Civil Procedure. The city shall be solely responsible for the expenses of its legal representation in connection with claims asserted against it, and for payment of the amount for which it is found liable under this section. Therefore, G.S. 143-291, 143-291.1, 143-291.2, 143-291.3, 143-292, 143-293, 143-295, 143-295.1, 143-296, 143-297, 143-298, 143-299.4, and 143-300 shall not apply to claims under this section.

   (2) Appeals to the Court of Appeals from a decision of the Superior Court Division shall be treated in the same manner as an appeal from a decision of the Industrial Commission under G.S. 143-294.

   (3) The limitation on claims set forth in G.S. 143-299; the burden of proof and defense set forth in G.S. 143-299.1; notwithstanding G.S. 143-299.1A(c), the defense set forth in G.S. 143-299.1A; and the limitation on payments set forth in G.S. 143-299.2 shall apply to claims filed with the Superior Court Division under this section.

(c) If a city waives its immunity pursuant to subsection (a) of this section, G.S. 160A-485 shall not apply to that city. The city may purchase liability insurance or adopt a resolution creating a self-funded reserve to insure liability for negligence of any officer, employee, involuntary servant or agent of the city while acting within the scope of his office, employment, service, agency or authority, under circumstances where the city, if a private person, would be liable to the claimant in accordance with the laws of North Carolina.

(d) No document or exhibit that relates to or alleges facts as to the city's insurance against liability shall be read, exhibited, or mentioned in the presence of the trial jury in the trial of any claim brought pursuant to this section, nor shall the plaintiff, plaintiff's counsel, or anyone testifying on the plaintiff's behalf directly or indirectly convey to the jury any inference that the city's potential liability is covered by insurance. No judgment may be entered against the city unless the plaintiff waives the plaintiff's right to a jury trial on all issues of law or fact relating to insurance coverage. All issues relating to insurance coverage shall be heard and determined by the judge without resort to a jury. The jury shall be absent during all motions, arguments, testimony, or announcement of findings of fact or conclusions of law with respect to insurance coverage. The city may waive its right to have issues concerning insurance coverage determined by the judge without a jury and may request a jury trial on these issues.

III. Additional Waiver Statutes

A. School Board Waiver Statute

§ 115C-42. Liability insurance and immunity.

Any local board of education, by securing liability insurance as hereinafter provided, is hereby authorized and empowered to waive its governmental immunity from liability for damage by reason of death or injury to person or property caused by the negligence or tort of any agent or employee of such board of education when acting within the scope of his authority or within the course of his employment. Such immunity shall be deemed to have been waived by the act of obtaining such insurance, but such immunity is waived only to the extent that said board of education is indemnified by insurance for such negligence or tort.

Any contract of insurance purchased pursuant to this section shall be issued by a company or corporation duly licensed and authorized to execute insurance contracts in this State or by a qualified insurer as determined by the Department of Insurance and shall by its terms adequately insure the local board of education against liability for damages by reason of death or injury to person or property proximately caused by the negligent act or torts of the agents and employees of said board of education or the agents and employees of a particular school in a local administrative unit when acting within the scope of their authority. The local board of education shall determine what liabilities and what officers, agents and employees shall be covered by any insurance purchased pursuant to this section. Any company or corporation which enters into a contract of insurance as above described with a local board of education, by such act waives any defense based upon the governmental immunity of such local board of education.

Every local board of education in this State is authorized and empowered to pay as a necessary expense the lawful premiums for such insurance.

Any person sustaining damages, or in case of death, his personal representative may sue a local board of education insured under this section for the recovery of such damages in any court of competent jurisdiction in this State, but only in the county of such board of education; and it shall be no defense to any such action that the negligence or tort complained of was in pursuance of governmental, municipal or discretionary function of such local board of education if, and to the extent, such local board of education has insurance coverage as provided by this section.

Except as hereinbefore expressly provided, nothing in this section shall be construed to deprive any local board of education of any defense whatsoever to any such action for damages or to restrict, limit, or otherwise affect any such defense which said board of education may have at common law or by virtue of any statute; and nothing in this section shall be construed to relieve any person sustaining damages or any personal representative of any decedent from any duty to give notice of such claim to said local board of education or to commence any civil action for the recovery of damages within the applicable period of time prescribed or limited by statute.

A local board of education may incur liability pursuant to this section only with respect to a claim arising after such board of education has procured liability insurance pursuant to this section and during the time when such insurance is in force.

No part of the pleadings which relate to or allege facts as to a defendant's insurance against liability shall be read or mentioned in the presence of the trial jury in any action brought pursuant to this section. Such liability shall not attach unless the plaintiff shall waive the right to have all issues of law or fact relating to insurance in such an action determined by a jury and such issues shall be heard and determined by the judge without resort to a jury and the jury shall be absent during any motions, arguments, testimony or announcement of findings of fact or conclusions of law with respect thereto unless the defendant shall request a jury trial thereon: Provided, that this section shall not apply to claims for damages caused by the negligent acts or torts of public school bus, or school transportation service vehicle drivers, while driving school buses and school transportation service vehicles when the operation of such school buses and service vehicles is paid from the State Public School Fund.

B. Charter School Waiver Statute

§ 115C-218.20. Civil liability and insurance requirements.

(a)   The board of directors of a charter school may sue and be sued. The State Board of Education shall adopt rules to establish reasonable amounts and types of liability insurance that the board of directors shall be required by the charter to obtain. The board of directors shall obtain at least the amount of and types of insurance required by these rules to be included in the charter. Any sovereign immunity of the charter school, of the organization that operates the charter school, or its members, officers, or directors, or of the employees of the charter school or the organization that operates the charter school, is waived to the extent of indemnification by insurance.

(b) No civil liability shall attach to the State Board of Education, the Superintendent of Public Instruction, or to any of their members or employees, individually or collectively, for any acts or omissions of the charter school.

C. Area Authority Waiver Statute

§ 122C-152. Liability insurance and waiver of immunity as to torts of agents, employees, and board members.

(a) An area authority, by securing liability insurance as provided in this section, may waive its governmental immunity from liability for damage by reason of death or injury to person or property caused by the negligence or tort of any agent, employee, or board member of the area authority when acting within the scope of his authority or within the course of his duties or employment. Governmental immunity is waived by the act of obtaining this insurance, but it is waived by only to the extent that the area authority is indemnified by insurance for the negligence or tort.

(b) Any contract of insurance purchased pursuant to this section shall be issued by a company or corporation licensed and authorized to execute insurance contracts in this State and shall by its terms adequately insure the area authority against any and all liability for any damages by reason of death or injury to a person or property proximately caused by the negligent acts or torts of the agents, employees, and board members of the area authority when acting within the course of their duties or employment. The area board shall determine the extent of the liability and what agents, employees by class, and board members are covered by any insurance purchased pursuant to this subsection. Any company or corporation that enters into a contract of insurance as described in this section with the authority, by this act waives any defense based upon the governmental immunity of the area authority.

(c) Any persons sustaining damages, or, in the case of death, his personal representative, may sue an area authority insured under this section for the recovery of damages in any court of competent jurisdiction in this State, but only in a county located within the geographic limits of the authority. It is no defense to any action that the negligence or tort complained of was in pursuance of a governmental or discretionary function of the area authority if, and to the extent that, the authority has insurance coverage as provided by this section.

(d) Except as expressly provided by subsection (c) of this section, nothing in this section deprives any area authority of any defense whatsoever to any action for damages or to restrict, limit, or otherwise affect any defense which the area authority may have at common law or by virtue of any statute. Nothing in this section relieves any person sustaining damages nor any personal representative of any decedent from any duty to give notice of a claim to the area authority or to commence any civil action for the recovery of damages within the applicable period of time prescribed or limited by statute.

(e) The area authority may incur liability pursuant to this section only with respect to a claim arising after the authority has procured liability insurance pursuant to this section and during the time when the insurance is in force.

(f) No part of the pleadings that relate to or allege facts as to a defendant's insurance against liability may be read or mentioned in the presence of the trial jury in any action brought pursuant to this section. This liability does not attach unless the plaintiff waives the right to have all issues of law or fact relating to insurance in the action determined by a jury. These issues shall be heard and determined by the judge, and the jury shall be absent during any motions, arguments, testimony, or announcement of findings of fact or conclusions of law with respect to insurance.

D. District Board of Health Waiver Statute

§ 130A-37. District board of health.

(a) A district board of health shall be the policy-making, rule-making and adjudicatory body for a district health department and shall be composed of 15 members; provided, a district board of health may be increased up to a maximum number of 18 members by agreement of the boards of county commissioners in all counties that comprise the district. The agreement shall be evidenced by concurrent resolutions adopted by the affected boards of county commissioners.

(b) The county board of commissioners of each county in the district shall appoint one county commissioner to the district board of health. The county commissioner members of the district board of health shall appoint the other members of the board, including at least one physician licensed to practice medicine in this State, one licensed dentist, one licensed optometrist, one licensed veterinarian, one registered nurse, one licensed pharmacist, and one professional engineer. The composition of the board shall reasonably reflect the population makeup of the entire district and provide equitable district-wide representation. All members shall be residents of the district. If there is not a licensed physician, a licensed dentist, a licensed optometrist, a licensed veterinarian, a registered nurse, a licensed pharmacist, or a professional engineer available for appointment, an additional representative of the general public shall be appointed. If however, one of the designated professions has only one person residing in the district, the county commissioner members shall have the option of appointing that person or a member of the general public.

(c) Except as provided in this subsection, members of a district board of health shall serve terms of three years. Two of the original members shall serve terms of one year and two of the original members shall serve terms of two years. No member shall serve more than three consecutive three-year terms unless the member is the only person residing in the district who represents one of the professions designated in subsection (b) of this section. County commissioner members shall serve only as long as the member is a county commissioner. When a representative of the general public is appointed due to the unavailability of a licensed physician, a licensed dentist, a licensed optometrist, a licensed veterinarian, a registered nurse, a licensed pharmacist, or a professional engineer that member shall serve only until a licensed physician, a licensed dentist, a licensed optometrist, a licensed veterinarian, a registered nurse, a licensed pharmacist, or a professional engineer becomes available for appointment. The county commissioner members may appoint a member for less than a three-year term to achieve a staggered term structure.

(d) Whenever a county shall join or withdraw from an existing district health department, the district board of health shall be dissolved and a new board shall be appointed as provided in subsection (c).

(e) Vacancies shall be filled for any unexpired portion of a term.

(f) A chairperson shall be elected annually by a district board of health. The local health director shall serve as secretary to the board.

(g) A majority of the members shall constitute a quorum.

(h) A member may be removed from office by the district board of health for:

    (1) Commission of a felony or other crime involving moral turpitude;

    (2) Violation of a State law governing conflict of interest;

    (3) Violation of a written policy adopted by the county board of commissioners of each county in the district;

    (4) Habitual failure to attend meetings;

    (5) Conduct that tends to bring the office into disrepute; or

    (6) Failure to maintain qualifications for appointment required under subsection (b) of this section.

    A board member may be removed only after the member has been given written notice of the basis for removal and has had the opportunity to respond.

(i) A member may receive a per diem in an amount established by the county commissioner members of the district board of health. Reimbursement for subsistence and travel shall be in accordance with a policy set by the county commissioner members of the district board of health.

(j) The board shall meet at least quarterly. The chairperson or three of the members may call a special meeting.

(k) A district board of health is authorized to provide liability insurance for the members of the board and the employees of the district health department. A district board of health is also authorized to contract for the services of an attorney to represent the board, the district health department and its employees, as appropriate. The purchase of liability insurance pursuant to this subsection waives both the district board of health's and the district health department's governmental immunity, to the extent of insurance coverage, for any act or omission occurring in the exercise of a governmental function. By entering into a liability insurance contract with the district board of health, an insurer waives any defense based upon the governmental immunity of the district board of health or the district health department.

E. Transportation Authority Waiver Statute

§ 160A-627. Civil liability.

Except as provided in G.S. 160A-626, the Authority shall be deemed a city for purposes of civil liability pursuant to G.S. 160A-485. Governmental immunity of the Authority is waived to a minimum of twenty million dollars ($20,000,000) per single accident or incident. The Authority shall maintain a minimum of twenty million dollars ($20,000,000) per single accident or incident of liability insurance. Participation in a local government risk pool pursuant to Article 23 of Chapter 58 of the General Statutes shall be deemed to be the purchase of insurance for the purpose of this section.

Appendix B. The Governmental/ Proprietary Distinction in Public School Cases

I. Cases Recognizing Governmental Functions

A. **Benton v. Board of Education of Cumberland County, 201 N.C. 653 (1931)** (not paginated on Westlaw) (holding that school board's transportation of students to and from school was a governmental function and thus "[n] o action can . . . be maintained against a county board of education to recover damages for a tort alleged to have been committed by the board in the transportation of pupils to and from the school which they are required to attend or which they do attend").

B. **Smith v. Hefner, 235 N.C. 1 (1952)** (holding that construction of grandstand on school athletic field was governmental activity and that school district did not waive governmental immunity by leasing field to a baseball club when primary use of field was reserved for students and their sports activities).

C. **Turner v. Gastonia City Board of Education, 250 N.C. 456 (1959)** (holding that governmental immunity barred plaintiff's claims against defendant board over injuries plaintiff suffered when a school maintenance worker ran over a steel cable with a lawnmower, thereby causing the cable to strike plaintiff on the ankle). (NOTE: The distinction between governmental and proprietary functions is not expressly discussed in *Turner*.)

D. **Fields v. Durham City Board of Education, 251 N.C. 699 (1960)** (holding that immunity barred plaintiff's claims for injuries that occurred when plaintiff stepped through an iron grate that was part of a drainage system on school grounds). (NOTE: The distinction between governmental and proprietary functions is not expressly discussed in *Fields*.)

E. **Overcash v. Statesville City Board of Education, 83 N.C. App. 21 (1986)** (holding that governmental immunity was a "complete defense" to claims arising from injuries a student sustained when he fell during a school baseball game because of a metal spike embedded in the ball field). (NOTE: The distinction between governmental and proprietary functions is not expressly discussed in *Overcash*.)

F. **Beatty v. Charlotte-Mecklenburg Board of Education, 99 N.C. App. 753 (1990)** (holding that governmental immunity barred claims that defendant board's negligent location of a bus stop resulted in serious and permanent injuries to plaintiff when he was struck by an automobile as he attempted to cross the four-lane road separating him from the bus stop). (NOTE: The distinction between governmental and proprietary functions is not expressly discussed in *Beatty*.)

G. **Rowan County Board of Education v. United States Gypsum Co., 332 N.C. 1 (1992)** (characterizing the construction and maintenance of public schools as a governmental function for purposes of the doctrine of *nullum tempus occurrit regi* (no time runs against the king)).

H. **Vester v. Nash/Rocky Mount Board of Education, 124 N.C. App. 400 (1996)** (holding that governmental immunity barred plaintiff's lawsuit seeking damages for an assault on a school bus that ruptured plaintiff's spleen). (NOTE: The distinction between governmental and proprietary functions is not expressly discussed in *Vester*.)

I. **Schmidt v. Breeden, 134 N.C. App. 248 (1999)** (holding that school district's operation of a voluntary after-school enrichment program for a fee of $35.00 per week had to be viewed as a "traditional governmental function[]" in light of *Kiddie Corner v. Board of Education*, 55 N.C. App. 134 (1981)). (NOTE: The court deemed the after-school program to be a governmental function in part because no evidence in the record "reveal[ed] the profit, if any derived by the Board from the weekly fees collected from participants in the program." *Schmidt*, 134 N.C. App. at 255.)

J. **Herring *ex rel*. Marshall v. Winston-Salem/Forsyth County Board of Education, 137 N.C. App. 680 (2000)** (holding that an assistant principal performed governmental functions when he disciplined students who assaulted plaintiff on a school bus and reassigned plaintiff to a new bus stop). (NOTE: *Herring* holds as a matter of first impression that the doctrine of governmental immunity applies to negligent supervision claims; it further declares that claims for constructive fraud are likewise subject to the doctrine.)

K. **Lucas v. Swain County Board of Education, 154 N.C. App. 357 (2002)** (holding that governmental immunity barred plaintiff from recovering damages from defendant board in negligence for injuries plaintiff sustained in a fall at a school football stadium, except to the extent those injuries were covered by the board's excess liability insurance). (NOTE: The distinction between governmental and proprietary functions is not expressly discussed in *Lucas*.)

L. **Bass v. New Hanover County Board of Education, 158 N.C. App. 312 (2003) (unpublished)** (holding that governmental immunity barred plaintiff teacher's negligence and defamation claims arising from (1) the principal's decision to have a sheriff's deputy escort plaintiff and her son from the school after a student of another race physically and verbally assaulted plaintiff and then accused plaintiff of slapping her and (2) the public information officer's incorrect reporting to various media sources that plaintiff had been suspended for fighting with a student).

(NOTE: The distinction between governmental and proprietary functions is not expressly discussed in *Bass*.)

M. **Willett v. Chatham County Board of Education, 176 N.C. App. 268 (2006)** (holding that charging admission to school basketball games did not render defendant board's competitive basketball program a proprietary function when G.S. 115C-47(4) grants school boards "exclusive authority to control the interscholastic athletic program for the county's public schools"). (NOTE: *Willett* also holds that the duty imposed by G.S. 115C-524 on school boards to maintain school property in proper condition does not create a private right of action.)

N. **Webb *ex rel.* Bumgarner v. Nicholson, 178 N.C. App. 362, 365 (2006)** (declaring that "supervision of [a] school dance [is] a governmental function" because G.S. 115C-47(4) grants school boards the "responsibility for supervision and oversight of extracurricular activities, such [as] a school dance to raise yearbook funds").

O. **Magana v. Charlotte-Mecklenburg Board of Education, 183 N.C. App. 146 (2007)**(holding that defendant board had not waived its governmental immunity against claims by a student with Asperger's Disorder who alleged that a behavior management technician had injured him by grabbing and twisting his arm). (NOTE: The distinction between governmental and proprietary functions is not expressly discussed in *Magana*.)

P. **Craig *ex rel.* Craig v. New Hanover County Board of Education, 363 N.C. 334 (2009)** (observing that governmental immunity was an "absolute bar" to mentally disabled student's claim that school personnel negligently failed to protect him from sexual assault by another student). (NOTE: The distinction between governmental and proprietary functions is not expressly discussed in *Craig*.)

Q. **Johnson v. Avery County Board of Education, 221 N.C. App. 669 (2012)** (unpublished) (holding that governmental immunity barred plaintiff's negligence claims against defendant board arising from alleged sexual abuse of plaintiff by a school resource officer). (NOTE: The distinction between governmental and proprietary functions is not expressly discussed in *Johnson*.)

R. **Irving v. Charlotte-Mecklenburg Board of Education, No. 13-34, 2013 WL 5508370 (N.C. Ct. App. Oct. 1, 2013)** (unpublished) (holding that governmental immunity barred plaintiff from recovering from defendant board in negligence for injuries allegedly caused when a school employee drove an activity bus into the rear end of the plaintiff's vehicle while plaintiff was stopped at a traffic light). (NOTE: The distinction between governmental and proprietary functions is not expressly discussed in *Irving*.)

S. **Bellows v. Asheville City Board of Education, 243 N.C. App. 229 (2015)** (holding that governmental immunity foreclosed plaintiff's claims for injuries suffered in a fall on school grounds because G.S. 115C-40 and 115C-521 designate the ownership, maintenance, and repair of school property as governmental functions).

II. Cases Recognizing Proprietary Functions

A. North Carolina Cases

1. It appears that there are no appellate court decisions in North Carolina classifying any public school activity as a proprietary function.

B. Other Jurisdictions

1. **Lupke v. School District No. 1 of Multnomah County, 275 P. 686 (Or. 1929)** (holding that painting of a school flag pole by plaintiff hired for that purpose was not a governmental function).

2. **Sawaya v. Tucson High School District No. 1 of Pima County, 281 P.2d 105 (Ariz. 1955)** (holding that a school district undertook a proprietary function when it leased, for a sum of $300, a stadium to another school district for the purposes of hosting a football game).

3. **Allen v. Salina Broadcasting, Inc., 630 S.W.2d 225, 228 (Mo. Ct. App. 1982)** (concluding that, because defendant district's radio station, which allegedly broadcast defamatory statements, was used for both educational and non-educational purposes, "[t]he particular use of the radio station at the time of the [alleged defamation] [was] determinative" as to whether the broadcast occurred as part of a governmental or a proprietary function).

III. Statutory Claims

A. **Craig v. Asheville City Board of Education, 142 N.C. App. 518 (2001)** (holding that governmental immunity did not bar a probationary teacher's lawsuit alleging that defendant board had arbitrarily and capriciously failed to renew her employment because the teacher alleged a violation of statute rather than a tort claim).

Appendix C. Selected Statutory Immunities for Local Government Activities

Part I: City and County Undertakings

A. Alcoholic Beverage Control

§ 18B-700. Appointment and organization of local ABC boards.

. . .

(j)   Limited Liability. – A person serving as a member of a local ABC board shall be immune individually from civil liability for monetary damages, except to the extent covered by insurance, for any act or failure to act arising out of this service, except where the person:

   (1)   Was not acting within the scope of his official duties;
   (2)   Was not acting in good faith;
   (3)   Committed gross negligence or willful or wanton misconduct that resulted in the damage or injury;
   (4)   Derived an improper personal financial benefit from the transaction; or
   (5)   Incurred the liability from the operation of a motor vehicle.

   The immunity in this subsection is personal to the members of local ABC boards, and does not immunize the local ABC board for liability for the acts or omissions of the members of the local ABC board. . . .

B. Construction Contracts

§ 160A 413.5. Alternate inspection method for component or element.

(a)   Notwithstanding the requirements of this Article, a city shall accept, without further responsibility to inspect, a design or other proposal for a component or element in the construction of buildings from a licensed architect or licensed engineer provided all of the following apply:

   (1)   The design or other proposal is completed under valid seal of the licensed architect or licensed engineer.
   (2)   Field inspection of the installation or completion of the component or element of the building is performed by a licensed architect or licensed engineer or a person under the direct supervisory control of the licensed architect or licensed engineer.

(3) The licensed architect or licensed engineer provides the city with a signed written document stating the component or element of the building so inspected under subdivision (2) of this subsection is in compliance with the North Carolina State Building Code or the North Carolina Residential Code for One and Two Family Dwellings. The inspection certification required under this subdivision shall be provided by electronic or physical delivery and its receipt shall be promptly acknowledged by the city through reciprocal means.

(b) Upon the receipt of a signed written document as required under subsection (a) of this section, notwithstanding the issuance of a certificate of occupancy, the city, its inspection department, and the inspectors shall be discharged and released from any liabilities, duties and responsibilities imposed by this Article or in common law from any claim arising out of or attributed to the component or element in the construction of the building for which the signed written document was submitted. . . .

C. Emergency Management

§ 166A-19.60. Immunity and exemption.

(a) Generally. – All functions hereunder and all other activities relating to emergency management as provided for in this Chapter or elsewhere in the General Statutes are hereby declared to be governmental functions. Neither the State nor any political subdivision thereof, nor, except in cases of willful misconduct, gross negligence, or bad faith, any emergency management worker, firm, partnership, association, or corporation complying with or reasonably attempting to comply with this Article or any order, rule, or regulation promulgated pursuant to the provisions of this Article or pursuant to any ordinance relating to any emergency management measures enacted by any political subdivision of the State, shall be liable for the death of or injury to persons, or for damage to property as a result of any such activity.

(b) Immunity. – The immunity provided to firms, partnerships, associations, or corporations, under subsection (a) of this section, is subject to all of the following conditions:

(1) The immunity applies only when the firm, partnership, association, or corporation is acting without compensation or with compensation limited to no more than actual expenses and one of the following applies:

a. Emergency management services are provided at any place in this State during a state of emergency declared by the Governor or General Assembly pursuant to this Article, and the services are provided under the direction and control of the Secretary pursuant to G.S. 166A-19.10, 166A-19.11, 166A-19.12, 166A-19.20, 166A-19.30, and 143B-602, or the Governor.

b. Emergency management services are provided during a state of emergency declared pursuant to G.S. 166A-19.22, and the services are provided under the direction and control of the governing body of a municipality or county under G.S. 166A-19.31, or the chair of a board of county commissioners under G.S. 166A-19.22(b)(3).

    c.   The firm, partnership, association, or corporation is engaged in planning, preparation, training, or exercises with the Division, the Division of Public Health, or the governing body of each county or municipality under G.S. 166A-19.15 related to the performance of emergency management services or measures.

(2)   The immunity shall not apply to any firm, partnership, association, or corporation, or to any employee or agent thereof, whose act or omission caused in whole or in part the actual or imminent emergency or whose act or omission necessitated emergency management measures.

(3)   To the extent that any firm, partnership, association, or corporation has liability insurance, that firm, partnership, association, or corporation shall be deemed to have waived the immunity to the extent of the indemnification by insurance for its negligence. An insurer shall not under a contract of insurance exclude from liability coverage the acts or omissions of a firm, partnership, association, or corporation for which the firm, partnership, association, or corporation would only be liable to the extent indemnified by insurance as provided by this subdivision.

(c)   No Effect on Benefits. – The rights of any person to receive benefits to which the person would otherwise be entitled under this Article or under the Workers' Compensation Law or under any pension law and the right of any such person to receive any benefits or compensation under any act of Congress shall not be affected by performance of emergency management functions.

(d)   License Requirements Suspended. – Any requirement for a license to practice any professional, mechanical, or other skill shall not apply to any authorized emergency management worker who shall, in the course of performing the worker's duties as such, practice such professional, mechanical, or other skill during a state of emergency.

(e)   Definition of Emergency Management Worker. – As used in this section, the term "emergency management worker" shall include any full or part-time paid, volunteer, or auxiliary employee of this State or other states, territories, possessions, or the District of Columbia, of the federal government or any neighboring country or of any political subdivision thereof, or of any agency or organization performing emergency management services at any place in this State, subject to the order or control of or pursuant to a request of the State government or any political subdivision thereof. The term "emergency management worker" under this section shall also include any health care worker performing health care services as a member of a hospital-based or county-based State Medical Assistance Team designated by the North Carolina Office of Emergency

Medical Services and any person performing emergency health care services under G.S. 90-12.2.

(f) Powers of Individuals Operating Pursuant to Mutual Aid Agreements. – Any emergency management worker, as defined in this section, performing emergency management services at any place in this State pursuant to agreements, compacts, or arrangements for mutual aid and assistance to which the State or a political subdivision thereof is a party, shall possess the same powers, duties, immunities, and privileges the person would ordinarily possess if performing duties in the State, or political subdivision thereof, in which normally employed or rendering services.

D. Enemy Attacks

§ 147-33.4. Immunity.

Neither the State nor any political subdivision thereof, nor the agents or representatives of the State or any political subdivision thereof, under any circumstances, nor any individual, firm, partnership, corporation or other entity, or any agent thereof, in good faith complying with or attempting to comply with any order, rule or regulation made pursuant to this Article, shall be liable for the death or any injury to persons or for any damage to property as the result of any air raid, invasion, act of sabotage, or other form of enemy action, or of any action taken under this Article or such order, rule or regulation. This section shall not be construed to impair or affect the right of any person to receive any benefits or compensation to which he may otherwise be entitled under Workers' Compensation Law, any pension law, or any other law, or any act of Congress, or any contract of insurance or indemnification.

E. Firefighting Services

§ 58-82-5. Liability limited.

(a) For the purpose of this section, a "rural fire department" means a bona fide fire department incorporated as a nonprofit corporation which under schedules filed with or approved by the Commissioner of Insurance, is classified as not less than Class "9" in accordance with rating methods, schedules, classifications, underwriting rules, bylaws, or regulations effective or applied with respect to the establishment of rates or premiums used or charged pursuant to Article 36 or Article 40 of this Chapter and which operates fire apparatus of the value of five thousand dollars ($5,000) or more.

(b) A rural fire department or a fireman who belongs to the department shall not be liable for damages to persons or property alleged to have been sustained and alleged to have occurred by reason of an act or omission, either of the rural fire department or of the fireman at the scene of a reported fire, when that act or omission relates to the suppression of the reported fire or to the direction of traffic or enforcement of traffic laws or ordinances at the scene of or in connection with a fire, accident, or other hazard by the department or the fireman unless it is established that the damage occurred because of gross negligence, wanton conduct or intentional wrongdoing of the rural fire department or the fireman.

(c) Any member of a volunteer fire department or rescue squad who receives no compensation for his services as a fire fighter or emergency medical care provider, who renders first aid or emergency health care treatment at the scene of a fire to a person who is unconscious, ill, or injured as a result of the fire shall not be liable in civil damages for any acts or omissions relating to such services rendered, unless such acts or omissions amount to gross negligence, wanton conduct or intentional wrongdoing.

§ 58-80-45. Rights and privileges of firemen; liability of municipality.

When responding to a call and while working at a fire or other emergency outside the limits of the municipality by which they are regularly employed or in volunteer fire service, all members of the State Volunteer Fire Department shall have the same authority, rights, privileges and immunities which are afforded them while responding to calls within their home municipality. In permitting its fire department or equipment to attend an emergency or answer a call beyond the municipal limits, whether under the terms of this Article or otherwise, a municipality shall be deemed in exercise of a governmental function, and shall hold the privileges and immunities attendant upon the exercise of such functions within its corporate limits.

§ 69-25.8. Authority, rights, privileges and immunities of counties, etc., performing services under Article.

Any county, municipal corporation or fire protection district performing any of the services authorized by this Article shall be subject to the same authority and immunities as a county would enjoy in the operation of a county fire department within the county, or a municipal corporation would enjoy in the operation of a fire department within its corporate limits.

No liability shall be incurred by any municipal corporation on account of the absence from the city or town of any or all of its fire-fighting equipment or of members of its fire department by reason of performing services authorized by this Article.

Members of any county, municipal or fire protection district fire department shall have all of the immunities, privileges and rights, including coverage by workers' compensation insurance, when performing any of the functions authorized by this Article, as members of a county fire department would have in performing their duties in and for a county, or as members of a municipal fire department would have in performing their duties for and within the corporate limits of the municipal corporation.

§ 160A-293. Fire protection outside city limits; immunity; injury to firemen.

. . .

(b)   No city or any officer or employee thereof shall be held to answer in any civil action or proceeding for failure or delay in answering calls for fire protection outside the corporate limits, nor shall any city be held to answer in any civil action or proceeding for the acts or omissions of its officers or employees in rendering fire protection services outside its corporate limits.

(c)   Any employee of a city fire department, while engaged in any duty or activity outside the corporate limits of the city pursuant to orders of the fire chief or council, shall have all of the jurisdiction, authority, rights, privileges, and immunities, including coverage under the workers' compensation laws, which they have within the corporate limits of the city.

F. Fiscal Management

§ 159-31. Selection of depository; deposits to be secured.

. . .

(b)   . . . When deposits are secured in accordance with this subsection, no public officer or employee may be held liable for any losses sustained by a local government or public authority because of the default or insolvency of the depository. . . .

G. Law Enforcement

§ 153A-222. Inspections of local confinement facilities.

Department personnel shall visit and inspect each local confinement facility at least semiannually. The purpose of the inspections is to investigate the conditions of confinement, the treatment of prisoners, the maintenance of entry level employment standards for jailers and supervisory and administrative personnel of local confinement facilities as provided for in G.S. 153A-216(4), and to determine whether the facilities meet the minimum standards published pursuant to G.S. 153A-221. The inspector shall make a written report of each inspection and submit it within 30 days after the day the inspection is completed to the governing body and other local officials responsible for the facility. The report shall specify each way in which the facility does not meet the minimum standards. The governing body shall consider the report at its first regular meeting after receipt of the report and shall promptly initiate any action necessary to bring the facility into conformity with the standards. Notwithstanding the provisions of G.S. 8-53 or any other provision of law relating to the confidentiality of communications between physician and patient, the representatives of the Department of Health and Human Services who make these inspections may review any writing or other record in any recording medium which pertains to the admission, discharge, medication, treatment, medical condition, or history of persons who are or have been inmates of the facility being inspected. Physicians, psychologists, psychiatrists, nurses, and anyone else involved in giving treatment at or through a facility who may be interviewed by representatives of the Department may disclose to these representatives information related to an inquiry, notwithstanding the existence of the physician-patient privilege in G.S. 8-53 or any other rule of law; provided the patient, resident or client has not made written objection to such disclosure. The facility, its employees, and any person interviewed during these inspections shall be immune from liability for damages resulting from the disclosure of any information to the Department. Any confidential or privileged information received from review of records or interviews shall be kept confidential by the Department and not disclosed without written authorization of the inmate or legal representative, or unless disclosure is ordered by a court of competent jurisdiction. The Department shall institute appropriate policies and procedures to ensure that this information shall not be disclosed without authorization or court order. The Department shall not disclose the name of anyone who has furnished information concerning a facility without the consent of that person. Neither the names of persons furnishing information nor any confidential or privileged information obtained from records or interviews shall be considered "public records" within the meaning of G.S. 132-1. Prior to releasing any information or allowing any inspections referred to in this section the patient, resident or client must be advised in writing that he has the right to object in writing to such release of information or review of his records and that by an objection in writing he may prohibit the inspection or release of his records.

§ 132-1.4A. Law enforcement agency recordings.

. . .

(k) No civil liability shall arise from compliance with the provisions of this section, provided that the acts or omissions are made in good faith and do not constitute gross negligence, willful or wanton misconduct, or intentional wrongdoing. . . .

H. Public Enterprise Services

§ 153A-283. Nonliability for failure to furnish water or sewer services.

In no case may a county be held liable for damages for failure to furnish water or sewer services.

§ 160A-312. Authority to operate public enterprises

(a) A city shall have authority to acquire, construct, establish, enlarge, improve, maintain, own, operate, and contract for the operation of any or all of the public enterprises as defined in this Article to furnish services to the city and its citizens. Subject to Part 2 of this Article, a city may acquire, construct, establish, enlarge, improve, maintain, own, and operate any public enterprise outside its corporate limits, within reasonable limitations, but in no case shall a city be held liable for damages to those outside the corporate limits for failure to furnish any public enterprise service. . . .

I. Public Health Services

§ 130A-37. District board of health.

. . .

(k)   A district board of health is authorized to provide liability insurance for the members of the board and the employees of the district health department. A district board of health is also authorized to contract for the services of an attorney to represent the board, the district health department and its employees, as appropriate. The purchase of liability insurance pursuant to this subsection waives both the district board of health's and the district health department's governmental immunity, to the extent of insurance coverage, for any act or omission occurring in the exercise of a governmental function. By entering into a liability insurance contract with the district board of health, an insurer waives any defense based upon the governmental immunity of the district board of health or the district health department.

J. Public Hospitals

§ 131E-47.1. Limited Liability.

(a)   A person serving as a director, trustee, or officer of a public hospital as defined in G.S. 159-39, or as a commissioner, member, or officer of a hospital authority established under Part 1 or 2 of this Article, or as a director, trustee, or officer of North Carolina Memorial Hospital, shall be immune individually from civil liability for monetary damages, except to the extent covered by insurance, for any act or failure to act arising out of this service, except where the person:

(1)   Is compensated for his services beyond reimbursement for expenses,

(2)   Was not acting within the scope of his official duties,

(3)   Was not acting in good faith,

(4)   Committed gross negligence or willful or wanton misconduct that resulted in the damage or injury,

(5)   Derived an improper personal financial benefit from the transaction,

(6)   Incurred the liability from the operation of a motor vehicle, or

(7)   Is defendant in an action brought under G.S. 55A-28.1 or 55A-28.2.

(b)   The immunity in subsection (a) is personal to the directors, trustees, officers, commissioners, and members, and does not immunize the hospital or hospital authority for liability for the acts or omissions of the directors, trustees, or officers.

K. Public Housing

§ 157-14. Types of bonds authority may issue. (housing authorities and projects)

. . . Neither the commissioners of an authority nor any person executing the bonds shall be liable personally on the bonds by reason of the issuance thereof. The bonds and other obligations of an authority (and such bonds and obligations shall so state in their face) shall not be a debt of any city or municipality and neither the State nor any such city or municipality shall be liable thereon, nor in any event shall such bonds or obligations be payable out of any funds or properties other than those of said authority. The bonds shall not constitute an indebtedness within the meaning of any constitutional or statutory debt limitation of the laws of the State ... Bonds may be issued under this Article notwithstanding any debt or other limitation prescribed in any statute. ...

L. Public Parks (Hazardous Recreation Parks)

§ 99E-25. Liability of governmental entities.

(a) This section does not grant authority or permission for a person to engage in hazardous recreational activities on property owned or controlled by a governmental entity unless such governmental entity has specifically designated such area for these activities.

(b) No governmental entity or public employee who has complied with G.S. 99E-23 shall be liable to any person who voluntarily participates in hazardous recreation activities for any damage or injury to property or persons that arises out of a person's participation in the activity and that takes place in an area designated for the activity.

(c) This section does not limit liability that would otherwise exist for any of the following:

   (1) The failure of the governmental entity or public employee to guard against or warn of a dangerous condition of which a participant does not have and cannot reasonably be expected to have had notice.

   (2) An act of gross negligence by the governmental entity or public employee that is the proximate cause of the injury.

(d) Nothing in this section creates a duty of care or basis of liability for death, personal injury, or damage to personal property. Nothing in this section shall be deemed to be a waiver of sovereign immunity under any circumstances.

(e) Nothing in this section limits the liability of an independent concessionaire or any person or organization other than a governmental entity or public employee, whether or not the person or organization has a contractual relationship with a governmental entity to use the public property, for injuries or damages suffered in any case as a result of the operation of equipment for hazardous recreational activities on public property by the concessionaire, person, or organization.

(f) The fact that a governmental entity carries insurance that covers any activity subject to this Article does not constitute a waiver of the liability limits under this section, regardless of the existence or limits of the coverage.

M. Public Street Maintenance

§ 160A-297. Streets under authority of Board of Transportation.

(a) A city shall not be responsible for maintaining streets or bridges under the authority and control of the Board of Transportation, and shall not be liable for injuries to persons or property resulting from any failure to do so. . . .

Part II: Public Education

A. Local School Administrative Units

§ 115C-332. School personnel criminal history checks.

. . .

(g) There shall be no liability for negligence on the part of a local board of education, or its employees, or the State Board of Education, the Superintendent of Public Instruction, or any of their members or employees, individually or collectively, arising from any act taken or omission by any of them in carrying out the provisions of this section. The immunity established by this subsection shall not extend to gross negligence, wanton conduct, or intentional wrongdoing that would otherwise be actionable. The immunity established by this subsection shall be deemed to have been waived to the extent of indemnification by insurance, indemnification under Articles 31A and 31B of Chapter 143 of the General Statutes, and to the extent sovereign immunity is waived under the Tort Claims Act, as set forth in Chapter 31 of Chapter 143 of the General Statutes. . . .

§ 115C-333. Evaluation of licensed employees including certain superintendents; mandatory improvement plans; State Board notification upon dismissal of employees.

. . .

(e) Civil Immunity. – There shall be no liability for negligence on the part of the State Board of Education, the Superintendent of Public Instruction, or a local board of education, or their members or employees, individually or collectively, arising from any action taken or omission by any of them in carrying out the provisions of this section. The immunity established by this subsection shall not extend to gross negligence, wanton conduct, or intentional wrongdoing that would otherwise be actionable. The immunity established by this subsection shall be deemed to have been waived to the extent of indemnification by insurance, indemnification under Articles 31A and 31B of Chapter 143 of the General Statutes, and to the extent sovereign immunity is waived under the Tort Claims Act, as set forth in Article 31 of Chapter 143 of the General Statutes. . . .

§ 115C-333.1. Evaluation of teachers in schools not identified as low-performing; mandatory improvement plans; State Board notification upon dismissal of teachers.

. . .

(g) Civil Immunity. – There shall be no liability for negligence on the part of the State Board of Education, the Superintendent of Public Instruction, or a local board of education, or their members or employees, individually or collectively, arising from any action taken or omission by any of them in carrying out the provisions of this section. The immunity established by this subsection shall not extend to gross negligence, wanton conduct, or intentional wrongdoing that would otherwise be actionable. The immunity established by this subsection shall be deemed to have been waived to the extent of indemnification by insurance, indemnification under Articles 31A and 31B of Chapter 143 of the General Statutes, and to the extent sovereign immunity is waived under the Tort Claims Act, as set forth in Article 31 of Chapter 143 of the General Statutes.

§ 115C-333.1. Evaluations of teachers in schools not identified as low-performing.

There shall be no liability for negligence on the part of the board of directors, or its employees, or the State Board of Education, the Superintendent of Public Instruction, or any of their members or employees, individually or collectively, arising from any act taken or omission by any of them in carrying out the provisions of this section. The immunity established by this subsection shall not extend to gross negligence, wanton conduct, or intentional wrongdoing that would otherwise be actionable. The immunity established by this subsection shall be deemed to have been waived to the extent of indemnification by insurance, indemnification under Articles 31A and 31B of Chapter 143 of the General Statutes, and to the extent sovereign immunity is waived under the Tort Claims Act, as set forth in Article 31 of Chapter 143 of the General Statutes.

§ 115C-390.3. Reasonable force.

(c) Notwithstanding any other law, no officer, member, or employee of the State Board of Education, the Superintendent of Public Instruction, or of a local board of education, individually or collectively, shall be civilly liable for using reasonable force in conformity with State law, State or local rules, or State or local policies regarding the control, discipline, suspension, and expulsion of students. Furthermore, the burden of proof is on the claimant to show that the amount of force used was not reasonable. . . .

§ 115C-524. Repair of school property; use of buildings for other than school purposes.

(a) Repair of school buildings is subject to the provisions of G.S. 115C-521(c) and (d).

(a1) Local boards of education may employ personnel who are licensed to perform maintenance and repairs on school property for plumbing, heating, and fire sprinklers pursuant to Article 2 of Chapter 87 of the General Statutes.

(b) It shall be the duty of local boards of education and tax-levying authorities, in order to safeguard the investment made in public schools, to keep all school buildings in good repair to the end that all public school property shall be taken care of and be at all times in proper condition for use. It shall be the duty of all principals, teachers, and janitors to report to their respective boards of education immediately any unsanitary condition, damage to school property, or needed repair. All principals, teachers, and janitors shall be held responsible for the safekeeping of the buildings during the school session and all breakage and damage shall be repaired by those responsible for same, and where any principal or teacher shall permit damage to the public school buildings by lack of proper discipline of pupils, such principal or teacher shall be held responsible for such damage: Provided, principals and teachers shall not be held responsible for damage that they could not have prevented by reasonable supervision in the performance of their duties.

(c) Notwithstanding the provisions of G.S. 115C-263 and 115C-264, local boards of education may adopt rules and regulations under which they may enter into agreements permitting non-school groups to use school real and personal property, except for school buses, for other than school purposes so long as such use is consistent with the proper preservation and care of the public school property. No liability shall attach to any board of education or to any individual board member for personal injury suffered by reason of the use of such school property pursuant to such agreements.

(d) Local boards of education may make outdoor school property available to the public for recreational purposes, subject to any terms and conditions each board deems appropriate, (i) when not otherwise being used for school purposes and (ii) so long as such use is consistent with the proper preservation and care of the outdoor school property. No liability shall attach to any board of education or to any individual board member for personal injury suffered by reason of the use of such school property.

B. Charter Schools

§ 115C-218.20. Civil liability and insurance requirements.

(a) The board of directors of a charter school may sue and be sued. The State Board of Education shall adopt rules to establish reasonable amounts and types of liability insurance that the board of directors shall be required by the charter to obtain. The board of directors shall obtain at least the amount of and types of insurance required by these rules to be included in the charter. Any sovereign immunity of the charter school, of the organization that operates the charter school, or its members, officers, or directors, or of the employees of the charter school or the organization that operates the charter school, is waived to the extent of indemnification by insurance.

(b) No civil liability shall attach to the State Board of Education, the Superintendent of Public Instruction, or to any of their members or employees, individually or collectively, for any acts or omissions of the charter school.

§ 115C-218.90. Employment requirements.

(b) Criminal History Checks. –

(2) There shall be no liability for negligence on the part of the State Board of Education or the board of directors of the charter school, or their employees, arising from any act taken or omission by any of them in carrying out the provisions of this subsection. The immunity established by this subsection shall not extend to gross negligence, wanton conduct, or intentional wrongdoing that would otherwise be actionable. The immunity established by this subsection shall be deemed to have been waived to the extent of indemnification by insurance, indemnification under Articles 31A and 31B of Chapter 143 of the General Statutes, and to the extent sovereign immunity is waived under the Tort Claims Act, as set forth in Article 31 of Chapter 143 of the General Statutes.

Case Index

North Carolina cases, United States Supreme Court cases, and federal appeals court cases are listed in alphabetical order by case name. Federal district court cases are listed in alphabetical order by district.

Table of Statutes and Rules

Subject Index

L

M